JOHN ROMERIL began his writing career while a Monash University undergraduate with *I Don't Know Who to Feel Sorry For* (1969) and *Chicago, Chicago* (1969–70). A founding member of the Australian Performing Group, his other plays from that period include *Mrs Thally F*, *Bastardy*, *The Floating World*, *The Golden Holden*, *Mickey's Moomba* and *Carboni*. He co-wrote APG successes like *Marvellous Melbourne*, *The Hills Family Show*, *Dudders* and *Waltzing Matilda*; and collaborated on most of the APG's outdoor, factory and touring shows.

In 1974 Romeril wrote the screenplay for *The Great McCarthy*, and his other film and television credits include *Six of the Best* (1982) and, with Rachel Perkins, *One Night the Moon* (2000).

Romeril's produced plays during the 1980s include *Samizdat*, *Definitely the Last*, *Jonah*, *The Kelly Dance*, *Legends*, *Lost Weekend*, *Top End* and *Koori Radio*, and he helped shape *Manning Clark's History of Australia: The Musical*. Produced plays from the 1990s include *Black Cargo*, *Bring Down the House*, *Reading Boy*, *Doing the Block*, *Expo: The Human Factor*, *Acronetic*, *Kate'n'Shiner*, *Love Suicides* and *Hanoi-Melbourne*.

In 2001 *Miss Tanaka* premiered at Playbox. Since then he has concentrated on dramaturgical work, often with young writers, and on research-driven community projects such as *Landmines*, *The Dukes of Windsor* and *Dancing the Line*, which await production. He was Honorary Chair of Strange Fruit, a Melbourne-based, largely outdoor, physical performance group whose work on sway poles has toured the world.

He has been Playwright-in-Residence with certain theatre companies and tertiary institutions thanks to support from the Literature Board of the Australia Council, and educational, civic and sometimes philanthropic entities. Prizes include the Canada-Australia Literary Award (1976) and the Patrick White Award (2008).

damage

A COLLECTION OF PLAYS BY
JOHN ROMERIL

CURRENCY PRESS
SYDNEY

CURRENCY PLAYS

First published in 2010 by
Currency Press Pty Ltd,
PO Box 2287, Strawberry Hills, NSW, 2012, Australia
enquiries@currency.com.au; www.currency.com.au

The Floating World first published in 1975 by Currency Methuen Drama Pty Ltd.

Music for *Jonah* available through HLA Management, PO Box 1536,
Strawberry Hills NSW 2012; email hla@hlamgt.com.au

National Library of Australia CIP data
    Author: Romeril, John, 1945–.
    Title: Damage: a collection of plays; The floating world;
                          Jonah; Top end; Lost weekend / by John Romeril.
    ISBN: 9780868198767 (pbk.)
    Subjects: Australian drama–21st century.
    Dewey Number: A822.3

Typeset by Dean Nottle for Currency Press.
Printed by Hyde Park Press, Richmond, SA
Cover image and design by Emma Vine for Currency Press.

Contents

Introduction: Well Again

For more than forty years John Romeril has been one of Australia's most important and prolific playwrights. Despite this, none of his plays, other than *The Floating World*, have ever become part of the acknowledged repertoire. That repertoire is, of course, appallingly limited—a few David Williamson plays, a few hoary old school texts such as *Summer of the Seventeenth Doll*, and the odd one-off that some director or producer has seized on for idiosyncratic reasons of their own.

The only great Australian playwright who is regularly revived is Patrick White. No-one ever revives Dorothy Hewett, or Alma de Groen, or Jack Hibberd; or even more recent (!) playwrights such as Louis Nowra or Stephen Sewell. Plays on school lists, many of them lesser works, are regularly revived, because there is a clearly identifiable student audience for them. Aside from this, nobody seems to know what is waiting to be rediscovered. Most of our theatres now pay lip-service to the past but their actual record of reviving great plays is shameful. We need more classics—plays that directors and actors want to test themselves on, to revisit, remake and re-appropriate.

In the case of Romeril there is perhaps some excuse because many of his major plays have never been published. This is partly because he has always been a writer who has worked at the coalface, writing for occasions, for communities, around contemporary issues, working with companies and groups to produce the words and shape the shows dramaturgically in a self-effacing way, using his skills to allow people to tell their stories and to allow actors to play them.

During the 1970s, when he was the principal writer for the legendary Australian Performing Group at the Pram Factory in Melbourne, he called himself a 'public servant of the pen', an enabler, a facilitator, whatever you want to call a writer who in the most collaborative of arts always put himself at the service of his colleagues. Years later he said in an interview, perhaps regretting a little his earlier enthusiasm for collective creation, 'Unless you're careful you become a kind of bureaucratised pen'.

This volume welcomes Romeril's work into the canon. Whatever you might think of the idea of a canon—with its ideological implications of stamping works with an imprimatur—there is no doubt that if you don't publish the texts of great plays and revive them in innovative ways in real theatres they get forgotten. In the theatre we forget our past at great peril, for without a history new writers have to keep reinventing the wheel.

In this volume Currency Press is republishing Romeril's only widely-known play, *The Floating World*, along with three plays that should have been classics years ago: his wonderfully theatrical musical reinvention of Louis Stone's novel *Jonah*; his powerful play *Top End*, set in Darwin during the Indonesian invasion of East Timor; and *Lost Weekend*, a great play that reinterprets the role of the old bush/city dichotomy in constructing 'Australianness' in terms of class, a category that was once supposed not to exist in Australia but which Romeril reveals to be real and urgent. These plays deserve to be in the repertoire. In each of them Romeril tells, with a theatrical vividness that should spur new directors, stories of individuals struggling within and against the social, historical and political circumstances in which they are trapped.

In the style of the familiar curse, 'may you live in interesting times', Romeril's plays tell strong human stories of characters living through their own 'interesting times'. His characters face great social and political movements and events as they struggle to find, like Brecht's great characters, ways of reconciling their desire for a better world with their own personal desire for a better life.

Romeril includes polemic and political argument, and sometimes a lot of current affairs detail, but always in the mouths of idiosyncratic characters who have problems and faults of their own. You only have to look at *Top End* to see the complexity of his dramaturgy. The play is set in Darwin in 1975 eleven months after its devastation by Cyclone Tracy, and during the Australian election battle between the sacked Prime Minister Gough Whitlam and the Opposition Leader Malcolm Fraser. Fraser had forced the election by controversially blocking the money supply bills in the Senate which left the Government without funds to meet its day-to-day costs. On top of this, a month previously a group of Australian journalists (the 'Balibo Five') had been killed in East Timor during the Indonesian incursions that were a prelude to their invasion in early December. It is hard to think of a more highly charged and 'interesting' time in which to set a play that is also about interpersonal conflicts, yearnings and alliances. Thirty-five years later, this period remains highly controversial for many reasons, most of which Romeril foreshadows in this play.

There is a lot of political commentary in *Top End*, some of it, perhaps, things the writer wanted to say, but it is delivered by a collection of characters, huddled together in the far north, who have personal problems to solve. The old union battler Dolly, the humanitarian nurse Rosa, and the idealistic young journalist Jill are all in some way traumatised by the events around them, but they also have intimate needs of their own. And they meet up with the old digger Dight and his rabidly right-wing but passionately loving wife Norma in a series of encounters which establish this as a community in a war zone full of people who, for all their differences, are not themselves at war with each other.

The play gives a mad portrait of Darwin as a city of exiles, trapped in a no-man's-land between postcolonial Australia and its dangerous near-north, in a splendid series of scenes set in pubs, private digs and social spaces (including Dolly's wonderful bathing set-up and Norma and Dight's boat). The characters meet, form couples, bond and then, as often as not, go their separate ways into the difficult and dangerous world.

A similar drama, if more classically constrained, is played out in *Lost Weekend* which brings together two couples for a weekend at Xanadu, the fading but luxurious homestead and property that Margie, like a generation of matriarchs before her, struggles to maintain. Alongside them is the wonderfully sensible Theresa, a young but highly capable and independent representative of the old servant/slave class on which rural Australia once built its economic power.

The conflict here—between Charles and Margie on the one hand and Eric and Zelda on the other—is partly class-based. The old squattocracy (the Australian equivalent of the English rural landed gentry) comes up hard against the new industrial world represented by Eric's long battle as a trade union activist.

But they are all getting old and the struggle is hard to sustain. In this play, compared with *Top End*, the interpersonal problems between the couples take over from the political struggle. Eric is recovering from a debilitating stroke and Charles is clearly not recovering from his post-traumatic stress disorder as a result of his experiences as a prisoner-of-war in Korea. The characters express their political conflict in their individual rhetorical styles, but this threatens to be overwhelmed by their present needs: Eric's for his new love, Zelda's for stability after her dreadful marriage, Margie's for financial and matriarchal salvation, and Charles's for redemption from his feelings of personal guilt and failure. As the long weekend becomes a lost one, only Theresa, increasingly baffled, survives.

The abrupt sacking of 600 workers by GMH looms behind the action in a series of interrupted phone calls and dimly understood traumas for the victims. In each case, the past keeps rising up to thwart present hopes and plans: Eric's bush-child poverty and alienation from his roots, Charles's war experiences, Zelda's loss of her home and children and Margie's nostalgic dreams of her glorious past, played out in the endless succession of beautiful meals that she prepares during the long day and night of the action. It is a very fine and complex play—an elegy for lost dreams, personal and political.

Jonah, with music by Alan John, is Romeril's Brechtian adaptation of Louis Stone's 1911 novel about Sydney's larrikin Push at the turn of the nineteenth century. Stone was writing, in ignorance of what was to come, about the transition of the street-based, poverty-stricken but solid communities into the new age of twentieth-century hard-nosed retail capitalism. Jonah Jones, the Leader of the inner-city Push, uses the boots-and-all techniques he learnt fighting on the streets, to become a wealthy shoe-shop magnate. He expands first towards the city, because that's where his dreams lie, and then out into the suburbs, creating a prototype of Westfields.

Romeril's version tells Stone's original story but adds layers, especially with the exploitative manufacturer Packer, whom Jonah eventually buys out. More importantly this version of the story takes it forward to the First World War, making Jonah a war profiteer and setting his company firmly on the path towards twentieth-century corporate success.

The stories of the women he meets on his way—Ada, the teenage mother of his beloved son; Clara, the woman he loves but rejects when she turns out to be criminally mercenary; and Miss Giltinan, the dull but business-like woman in the store, for whom he finally settles—are told with much less sentimentality than in Stone's novel. Once again they show Romeril's ability to bring together the public and private lives of its characters.

Which brings us to the classic, *The Floating World*, the first script in this volume, and the earliest in writing. In 1974 Les Harding has been dragged, by his comically complacent suburban wife Irene, into going on a *Women's Weekly* Cherry Blossom Cruise to Japan. Much of the on-board ship action feels like a parody of the 'burbs worthy of Barry Humphries or Romeril's contemporaries from the early New Wave, such as Alex Buzo, Jack Hibberd or the early David Williamson. But Les—a prisoner-of-war survivor who was once tortured by the Japanese on the notorious Burma-Thailand railroad—is taken deeper and deeper into his heart of darkness; and as the theatrical style of the play moves from comic satire into something much blacker and more expressionistic, Les goes quietly mad. We watch his descent with increasingly horrified fascination. The play has a notoriously long, harrowing speech at the end in which Les finally gets to tell the story of his hellish experience during the war, and a magnificently ironic ending, in which he suddenly finds himself, in his straightjacket, bound for another institution, more up-to-date than Changi, for the rest of his life. 'I was well again!', he says, as they cart him off.

This is what Romeril does so well in all his plays. Here is a story that has a simple human dimension in which the everyday seems at first to be the most important thing. But then the history of the twentieth century, in all its horror, keeps suddenly erupting in our lives threatening to damage us all.

John McCallum
Sydney, 2010

John McCallum lectures in theatre at the University of New South Wales, is Sydney theatre critic for the Australian, *and the author of* Belonging: Australian Playwriting in the 20th Century.

The Floating World

Frederick Parslow as Les in the 1982 Melbourne Theatre Company
production of *The Floating World*. (Photo: David Parker)

The Floating World was first produced by the Australian Performing Group at the Pram Factory, Melbourne, on 6 August 1974 with the following cast:

LES HARDING	Bruce Spence
IRENE HARDING	Jane Clifton
HERBERT ROBINSON	Robert Meldrum
COMIC	Peter Cummins
HARRY	Eddie van Roosendael
McLEOD	Wilfred Last
WAITER	Carol Porter

Director, Lindzee Smith
Setting Designer, Peter Corrigan

CHARACTERS

LES HARDING, a former prisoner of war held by the Japanese during the Second World War.

IRENE HARDING, his wife

HERBERT ROBINSON, Royal Navy, retired

COMIC, Entertainment Officer on board

HARRY, narrator, straight man and band

McLEOD, a figment from Les's past

WAITER, a Malay

SHIP'S OFFICER

Several of the characters take on additional identities: the Comic becomes an Australian Army Officer in Les's fantasy; McLeod is a passenger called Mr Williams to everyone except Les; the Waiter becomes a Japanese soldier in Les's fantasy, the Captain of the Dippy Birds and a bald professor who is a passenger.

SETTING

The events depicted occur on board a liner bound for Japan on a Cherry Blossom Cruise.

PART ONE

SCENE ONE: DRUM POEM ONE

The stage is in darkness. A loudspeaker asks all visitors to leave the ship. Light comes up slowly on HARRY *on a bandstand as he speaks the following, patterning it with percussive sequences, et cetera, in the basic style of a jazz poetry reading. Other cast members might join in.*

HARRY: One day—sulphurous sky maniac traffic—a Japanese business-man drives his company car to the airport—is driven—a briefcase and a swathe of silk shirts—travelling light—the JAL 747 banks into the yellow sky—Tokyo is a carpet below him—he orders raw fish and green tea—eats drinks considers having it off with a hostess farts doesn't want any magazines—adjusts his reading glasses does his homework—three seats so he can spread himself out—maps business cards figures layouts a briefcase full of blueprints a genius with the slide rule.

From Mascot he transfers to a private jet—Sydney is a carpet below him—no hostesses—an ex-Qantas steward mixing vermouths for twelve Australian boardroom cowboys in white shirts pink shorts blue ties—everyone sweats—the interpreter crawls up the aisle like a worm on his honourable belly—to and fro like a worm on his up-front—name of Sid—ex-crop duster on a sweet cop—passes low over twelve thousand acres of virgin rainforest—flat like a carpet below him the steward with the Benson and Hedges smile caught in the crossfire of champagne bottles—corks and boardroom cowboys.

The twelve Judases point out the lagoon the coral reef the white sand the blue non-sulphurous sky—imagine an eighty-three storey hotel straddling the mangrove swamp—see figures leap into view on imaginary cash registers.

Jabber jabber—the two Nips argue the precise location of the golf course.

The seats drip with champagne—the glasses are sticky—the Jap hands over a Samurai sword—Judas number one parts with a koala bear—a nice gesture at two thousand feet—the rainforest like a carpet.

And back to Amberley to re-fuel—chicken-in-the-basket restaurant—the flash of photographers on the tarmac—the press has
got wind of something in the air—smiles but no answers—white-
fanged evasions—everyone shakes hands—everyone bows—a nice
reciprocal gesture—the tarmac a tarmac below them.

Meanwhile in the Coral Sea the Australian invasion of Nippon
is underway traffic going the other way—the 1974 *Women's Weekly*
Cherry Blossom Cruise.

He starts to sing it.

The 1974 *Women's Weekly* Cherry Blossom Cruise.
The 1974 *Women's Weekly* Cherry Blossom Cruise.
The 1974 *Women's Weekly* Cherry Blossom Cruise.
The 1974 *Women's Weekly*...

*He is getting a rhythm going. Perhaps from among the group on
the bandstand, perhaps from elsewhere,* LES *staggers forward,
grips the handrail, and vomits. Blackout.*

SCENE TWO: A LONG YAWN

The lights come up to reveal LES *still gripping the rail. Perhaps there is
sea noise from somewhere (a water machine, the cast?).* ROBINSON, *in
shorts and Hawaiian shirt, comes down a staircase.*

ROBINSON: What, not got your sea legs yet?

LES *looks at him.*

Thing is to try and hold it down.

LES: Yeah, gimme some four-inch nail, I'm a yogi.

ROBINSON: Fortunately it doesn't worry me. I'm used to it.

LES: In your element, are you?

ROBINSON: Robinson. Royal Navy. Vice-Admiral. Retired.

LES: Not exactly— [*he vomits again*] wearing your uniform, are you,
sport?

ROBINSON: Ha! Holiday gear, don't you know.

LES: Les Harding. Ex-AIF. Private. I'd shake your hand but I don't want
to let go the railing. Vice-Admiral?

ROBINSON: Yes. Spent most of my time in the Mediterranean. Malta and
whatnot. Lieutenant then.

LES: Didn't get to rise— [*he retches again*] through the ranks myself.

ROBINSON: Sometimes happens…

LES: Didn't get a chance to…

ROBINSON: Good men…

LES: Singapore.

ROBINSON: Oh.

LES: Yeah. Oh.

He retches—a false alarm.

ROBINSON: Saw a bit of you Digger chaps in the Mediterranean.

LES: That so?

ROBINSON: Excellent types.

LES: We Digger chaps didn't see much of you British Navy chaps in the Straits of Johore.

ROBINSON: No, we—

LES: Sold up the river again—just like in the first one.

ROBINSON: Couldn't be everywhere at once, old man.

LES: Churchill. First, Gallipoli—then Singapore.

ROBINSON: Still, he did pull us through—in the end.

LES: His pud, that's what he pulled, in between brandies. A great lump of— [*he retches*] shit with a cigar in one end.

ROBINSON: I say.

LES: What do you say?

ROBINSON: No need to swear.

LES: Sorry.

ROBINSON: Ladies in earshot.

LES: Forgot I was talking to a Pommy bastard.

ROBINSON: I say.

LES: I say I say. Look, cut out the Mo stuff with me, Captain, and give us the good oil. You're a Navy man.

ROBINSON: The good oil?

LES: On the vessel. Are we gonna make it or aren't we?

ROBINSON: Should do. Bit slow, of course.

LES: Long in the tooth, isn't it?

ROBINSON: Isn't she. Converted troopship, I'd say.

LES: Troopship, eh?

ROBINSON: Lot of 'em still about. Turned into cruisers and whatnot. Should have been scrapped but—

He looks on, pained, as LES *vomits.*

LES: And what vices were you admirable in, old son?

ROBINSON: Well, there was a little Arab piece in Cairo—You alright?

LES: Just green.

ROBINSON: Taken anything for it?

LES: Everything. What about her?

ROBINSON: You ever in Cairo?

LES: Never.

ROBINSON: Well, this Arab belly dancer—she said I was amongst the best she'd ever had.

LES: Said you were amongst the best she'd ever had.

ROBINSON: Yes.

LES: That's it, is it? Straight from the dirty memoirs of a well-endowed Vice-Admiral. Hang on a bit— [*He retches over the rail.*] Well, I tell you, after I'd done my bit for the Burma railroad—after MacArthur and me had watched the yellowies sign on the dotted—I slipped a geisha what was left of my length and she said shagging me was like making love to a birdcage. [*He stands straight and breathes deeply.*] Can I buy you a drink?

ROBINSON: Of course. Never say no. Though I'd watch it, if I were you.

LES: Bullshit. The bloody meal they give me. Meat must have been off.

ROBINSON: Even the best of us sometimes—

They start walking off. They mime the impact of a giant swell. In unison they turn to the rail and vomit.

LES: That why you wear the shirt, is it? Camouflage?

LES laughs. They exit. Blackout.

SCENE THREE: FIRST-RATE JAPANESE PRODUCT FOR INTERNATIONAL MARKET

A WAITER *enters, dressed as a Japanese Army officer (Captain of the Dippy Birds). Throughout the play, four of these insane objects (dippy birds) will be set into motion. They may be set up on a mobile tray, in niches on the walls or whatever is thought suitable. The following is taken straight from an actual instructions slip.*

WAITER: One, firstly, set down Bird's head completely into the water for get wet. Two, balance Bird's by inserting the crosspiece in the two slots provided in the stand. The crosspiece does not be adjusted or bent. Three, water in glass filled every time. Body of the Bird's is a precision instrument so please carry on carefully. Four, Bird's is move more smoothly put the place of warm and well ventilation but do not set it near signs of fire. The contents is Not-Inflammable but if the high heat is touched then the pressure of contents are going up so please take care of above caution.

The bird is in place, in working order. He grins broadly. Blackout.

LOUDSPEAKER: The following things have been handed in: a pair of binoculars, a purple and tan bikini, and a child's spade. Thank you. That's a pair of binoculars, a purple and tan bikini, and one child's spade.

SCENE FOUR: A LETTER HOME

Lights up on a deck tableau. ROBINSON *is sunning himself,* McLEOD *(Mr Williams) is taking a stroll,* LES *is listening to* IRENE *read a letter. Early in the scene the lunch chimes are heard.*

IRENE: '… I still can't get over it. And coming from the two of them like that, out of the blue. I knew Marge had her head screwed on right when she married Stan. Sensible, like her mum. And the suitcases, what a lovely thought.'

LES: Lovely thought. They'll get knocked off. I'll betcha they'll get knocked off.

IRENE: Do you want to hear it or not?

LES *demurs.*

'The ship is very modern. Les thinks he's in paradise—a bar every few yards. He's even starting to enjoy himself!'

LES: He's even starting to enjoy himself.

He mocks the idea.

IRENE: Well, you are. 'He was a bit reluctant to go at first, but like he says, it is the chance of a lifetime and we'd be fools not to take it. I've been reading all about Japan in the brochures so I'll know what to see and where to go. It's so exciting. I wish you were with me 'cause I do miss having someone to talk to.'

LES: What's that you do to me?

IRENE: There's a difference, Les, between talking to someone who's listening and talking to someone whose mind's elsewhere.

LES: My mind's elsewhere, is it?

IRENE: Either that or non-existent.

LES: Eh?

IRENE: Can I finish?

LES: Yeah. Get it over with.

IRENE: 'Give my love to Jack and tell him Les misses him too—he reckons the ship's full of foreigners and ignoramuses. Regards to all at the bowling club. Yours, love to all, Rene. PS: I know it's a bit much to ask, Vi, but if it hots up could you do the lawns for us? Thanks.' [*She stands.*] Well, I'm going to get ready for lunch.

LES: I couldn't face it.

IRENE: After last night I don't wonder.

LES: Might write a letter myself.

IRENE: Good for you. How about to Stan and Marge, thanking 'em for the trip?

LES: Come off it.

IRENE: Why not? And the suitcases.

LES: Think I'll write to the blokes at work.

IRENE: Well, don't bother reading it to me, thanks. I know what that'll be like.

She exits. Lights begin to fade.

LES: Dear Mates, Mongrels and Assorted Filth of My Acquaintance. Here I am on the good ship *Venus*... dot dot dot...
    The cabin boy's named Jimmy Wong,
    He has a most enormous dong,
    Twice round the deck, once round his neck,
    And on his foot for a thong.

SCENE FIVE: HALF A MO

Lights up on the bandstand. A few potted palm fronds. HARRY *is at the drums; when music is required he works either a tape deck or an old phonograph. There could be a cut-out combo backing him up. The* COMIC *walks into his spotlight.*

COMIC: I've got a memo [*pronounced 'meemo'*] here from the Captain— [*He flourishes a piece of paper.*] Actually the Captain doesn't send me mos—he knows I've already got one. [*He tears off his cardboard moustache.*] Ar, you've gotta have a laugh, eh, right right, eh? You've gotta have a laugh. It's true, though—the Captain—all he does is have a good blow—and if anyone here thinks that's into a handkerchief they've never been to sea before. Or have they? Okay. Substance of the Captain's latest blow is this: Tell 'em Smile Week is coming. During Smile Week, every hour on the hour we— [*He grins a large grin.*] People who don't— [*grinning*] won't get breakfast—and if this morning was any indication that'll make 'em— [*He grins.*] Because they're— [*grinning*] they'll be allowed to take breakfast, which'll make 'em— [*He sets his mouth in a portrait of disgust.*] They'll get had up for not smiling and told breakfast is off for them, news which'll bring a— [*grinning*] to their chops, whereupon they'll be told—It's all a plot, of course. There's no way you can win, you poor... [*the word eluding him*] you poor... you poor—Whatcha call those people who never knew who their parents were?

HARRY *answers with a crash of drums.*

Yeah. Thanks, Harry, you poor—

Crash of drums.

Before we go any further, I want you to meet Harry. Stand up and take a bow, son.

With a flourish of drums, HARRY *stands and slowly bows. Suddenly he groans and pitches forward. There is an arrow stuck in his back.*

I said a bow, Harry—not an arrow. Actually we were lucky to get Harry. [*He removes the arrow and disposes of it.*] He was drunk when he took the job. Staggered up the gangway—didn't know if he was Harry or Hairy. Not so the other drummers. They had their wits about 'em. Took one look at the ship, noticed the rivets were wearing lifebelts and shot through. I want you all to give Harry a nice big hand.

The COMIC *produces a stuffed glove and hurls it at* HARRY.

And here's one from me, you dirty little philanderer. [*To the audience*] That's right, put your hands together no—in prayer, in prayer—Harry's just become the father of a nine-pound baby, but there's been complications. For one thing, he hasn't told his wife yet.

Drum rim.

Here, by the way, is my card. [*Attached to his belt is a roll of toilet paper. He starts to tear off sheets and distribute them.*] I'm the Entertainment Officer on board. What's that mean? Well, for a start, whenever you see me you've got to salute. That should be pretty entertaining.

Drum rim.

I was talking before about breakfast. The trouble with this ship isn't the food. It's not the food, it's the way it's served—with tennis racquets!

Drum rim.

People have been coming up to me and saying, this's our first time out, is there anything you have to know? Only one thing. Four bells. Keep your ears peeled for that. It means four o'clock and time everyone went back to their right cabins.

Drum rim.

But they are, aren't they—people are very ignorant about the sea. That poem—for the men who go down to the sea in ships—I mean that poem is the height of ignorance. I dunno how you got here, but me, I took a taxi down to the wharf. For the men who go down to the sea in ships! We did not pass one boat on the road.

Drum rim.

'Course you'll all love shipboard life. Anyone chasing a gay time can always find it—that's what we have deck quoits for. While we're on the subject, the purser by the way'll try and put a sign up in your cabins: 'Home Sweet Homo'. Don't mind him. He just likes his little pokes.

Drum rim.

Speaking of cabins, you oughta see mine. Inlaid white tiles, twelve handbasins, four showers. Only trouble is all sorts of ratbags keep coming in and using my towel.

Drum rim.

That's not the last of my complaints either. It's so small, my cabin, I'm turning into a wowser. All I can drink in there's condensed milk.

Drum rim.

Ar, you've gotta have a laugh, don't you? You've gotta have a laugh. Still, it's not too bad. I mean they do change the sheets every day—

from one cabin to another. That's why no-one eavesdrops on this ship. No peeping toms. Nothing. No need. If you want to know what's been happening next door, just go to bed and look at your sheets.

Drum rim.

'Course the news is always a day late, but like they say, stale news is better than none. It's designed to keep you healthy, this ship. No matter where you are you're always half a mile from the nearest toilet. My advice to anyone who's desperate is just follow your nose. That'll bring you to the kitchen and the cook'll tell you where to go—will he ever!

Drum rim.

Actually it's very modern, the kitchen, very modern. We'd be the only ship in the world that employs a draughtsman to do blueprints of the sandwiches. We've got everything—dish-washing machines. Nice feller, Bob Dish. Spends most of the time wrapped in thought. That's why we call him the Nudist. You reckon I'm kidding? If you gave him a penny for his thoughts you'd have change coming.

Drum rim.

I told you about my cabin—how small it is. [*He hunches up small.*] Small—if I wanted to grow a beard I'd have to shift out. Well, last night I turned on the reading lamp— [*He is suddenly blinded.*] Instantly I was back where I belong—the interrogation room at D24—alright, alright, I did it, I did it! What'd I do? After finding my sunglasses I started leafing through my contract. I'm not joking—leafing through—it was drawn up last autumn. An interesting document, my contract. For the first time ever I read the fine print. That's the bit that's fine for them. In the event of the ship sinking and my being able to wring a laugh from you lot at the time, I get paid double. I get paid, by the way, in transistors—That cabin on Thursday nights when I bring home my pay! If—if out there in the lifeboat I crack the odd gag, you know the sort of thing, knife in one hand, fork in the other—Okay, okay, who's next?—You know the sort of thing—knife in one hand, fork in the other—Okay, okay, women and children first—You know the sort of thing—If I can manage that, I get paid triple. Triple. Think of it. The king of bloody transistors.

He and HARRY *drum up a vision.*

My only regret is I didn't read the fine print sooner. Could have got paid in Black and Deckers and started boring a few holes. Speaking of boring, I'd like to introduce the next act: Sarah Touchbottom. Careful, careful—back, you dogs.

He mimes treading on fingers at the edge of the bandstand.

It's not an open invitation. It's a stage name. Her real name's Grabarse. You've got to hand it to them, don't you—managers they're an inventive breed. Of louse. Anyway—I don't have one, by the way—a manager—I'm content to handle myself.

HARRY *boos.*

Anyway, Sarah. Sarah's going to sing. [*He tears off a sheet of toilet paper and reads.*] 'Yalousy'. Sorry, it's this German dunny paper. That should read 'Jealousy'. She's gonna sing... You'll be hearing a lot of Sarah. Tomorrow morning, for instance. She'll be coming through the intercom. We have to do it. So'll you, I tell you, if you leave the knob down—or up—I can't remember which. No, we do. It's the only way we can get everyone up on deck for lifeboat drill.

Drum rim.

But first I want to answer the question of who killed vaudeville. Not only will I answer the question, I'll re-enact the crime. My impression—right—my impression of a tube of toothpaste. [*He places his hands on his ribs and slowly squeezes. Just as slowly his tongue pokes out.*] Which reminds me of the time I was on top of Raquel Welch's brush—

Blackout. As the light goes he slurps.

SCENE SIX: LATER ON

Lights up on IRENE *sitting alone at a table, sipping a long drink. There are two empty chairs at the table. In staggers* LES, *holding a can of beer, half drunk. He drags* ROBINSON *with him. They bump into* McLEOD *(Mr Williams) on his way out. Pause.*

LES: Want you to meet the little woman, Robinson. Irene. Robinson.

She nods hello.

ROBINSON: Good evening.

LES: [*sung*] Good evening, Irene, good evening, Irene.

IRENE: Sit down, Les.

LES: I had no intention of standing, woman, not in my state of condition.

He collapses into a chair. ROBINSON *also sits.*

IRENE: What a dirty man.

LES: Go and wash, Robinson.

IRENE: No, no—the Entertainment Officer.

LES: I thought he was alright, eh, Robinson, al-bloody-right.

ROBINSON: He was a little on the blue side.

IRENE: Blue. He needs his mouth washed out with Velvet, that's what he needs.

LES: Yeah, Raquel Welch's national velvet.

IRENE: I dunno who's worser, Les, you or him. I must apologise for my husband, Mr Robinson, he's not usually this bad.

ROBINSON: I'm afraid I'm a little under the weather myself, Mrs—

IRENE: Irene, Mr Robinson, please.

ROBINSON: Very well, Mrs Harding—Irene.

LES: Robinson's retired.

IRENE: Are you? That must be nice. Les is just on his long service leave, aren't you, Les?

LES *grunts.*

And Mrs Robinson, Mr Robinson? Is she—?

ROBINSON: Deceased, alas.

IRENE: Oh, I am sorry to hear that. My condolences.

LES: He met her in Cairo.

ROBINSON: Fair's fair, Les.

IRENE: Yes, Leslie, sit up and behave.

LES: This piss—

IRENE: Les!

LES: —is so cheap, it's so cheap a man oughta live permanently outside the twelve-mile limit.

IRENE: You didn't say that last night, if I remember right.

ROBINSON: No, he didn't, did he?

IRENE: Looked like death warmed up.

LES: Me! Never!

IRENE: Talk about seasick.

LES: I've got seafaring in my blood, I'll have you know.

ROBINSON: He was a bit of a mess.

LES: My bloody uncle—I'll have you know my bloody uncle was none other than Captain Cook's— [*he belches*] cook.

IRENE: And I'm the queen of Moonee Ponds.

LES: Irene, you are my queen.

IRENE: My husband, Mr Robinson, in case you haven't noticed, is a pathochronic liar.

LES: All I lie in, Robinson, is my bed.

IRENE: And your vomit. It's his livid imagination.

ROBINSON: I had begun to think that perhaps he was a little prone to exaggerate.

LES: A little what? What'd you call me?

IRENE: Sit down, Les. He said you were a little prone to exaggerate.

LES: Exaggerate. Humph. [*He slips back into his chair.*] The best invention since beer, Robinson, what is it?

ROBINSON: Radar.

LES: Radar. Ha ha! What a bloody card, eh? Bloody radar. Bullshit—

He leans forward suddenly, putting a hand on ROBINSON's *arm.*

The best invention, cock, since beer, cock, is beer in tins.

IRENE: I really think, Les, you oughta turn in.

LES: What'd I do with me tickets?

He falls to searching his pockets.

IRENE: They've got a good system, don't you think, Mr Robinson? These tickets. You know just how much you're spending.

ROBINSON: It goes just as fast though, doesn't it?

IRENE: That's true.

LES: Lost the bastards.

IRENE: I suppose it's to stop the staff from stealing.

LES: Eh?

ROBINSON: That's probably it.

LES: Stolen? Some cow's—

IRENE: That Entertainment Officer, he looks the criminal type. Probably arranges offshore abortions.

LES: Your tickets or your life.

IRENE: Sit down, Les, you're making a debacle of yourself.

LES: Can I prevail upon you, old cock, for a blue ticket and a red ticket—or two blues and a yellow—or four yellows—four little Nips—four little Nips. We'll stand 'em to attention and make 'em salute the fried egg and then the barman'll give us a can each to drown our tomorrows.

IRENE: What are you talking about?

ROBINSON: [*handing* LES *some tickets*] A blue and a red.

LES: Thank you, old cock.

ROBINSON: I think he means the rising sun.

LES: There's a pub called the Rising Sun in Sydney Road, right? Right. But no bugger worth his salt'd drink there, right? Right. A course I'm right.

He staggers away.

ROBINSON: It's the Japanese flag. They used to call it the fried egg.

IRENE: Oh.

A crossfade begins.

ROBINSON: That was in the War. God knows what they call it now.

Light on LES, *who addresses the audience as though talking to a crowded bar room. During his speech, the* WAITER, *dressed as Captain of the Dippy Birds, sets up the second bird.*

LES: Are you saying I haven't? 'Cause I have. Have I what! This bloody trip isn't news to me, mate. I've been there and back. In '41. Late '41. Me and Bubbles Elliot. And Nobby. He never washed, that bastard. Nobby never washed. Says it was the secret of his success. It was a troopship then. This ship was a troopship then, as my mate Robinson will testify before God and grand juries of Australia, being a sailor himself, Robinson will. In '41. In late '41 in our stink-pit of a cabin we had a bloke you might have heard of. A Jew you might have heard of. Rosenberg? Harold Rosenberg? Whose chief claim to fame was his ability to shave in a matter of seconds. He'd shave—and this is ridge, boy—he'd shave, cut-throat razor and all, no mirror, lying down, rain, hail or bloody typhoon. [*He mimes shaving in two swipes.*] Voom voom. In five, in three seconds flat—rain, hail or hurricane lamp. Ridge. An' no bloody mirror. Rain'd be a joke though, eh—out here? Same then. Hot. You call this hot? This is bloody winter. January '42—no, December '41—hot as a Herbert Adams plonked on a gibber in the Simp-bloody-son Desert. Well, I dunno about you blokes, says Snow White, but I'm parking the carcass on the bloody deck and no mug's saying otherwise. In no time at all—faster in fact than Rosenberg shaved scruff off his face—we were up the rungs to a bloody man. Clip bloody clop clop

clop. 'This Deck Out Of Bounds To Other Ranks', says the sign. Over-fucking-board it went. Sp-lash. The only spot a bloke could get a bit of breeze—officers only. Sp-lash to that, eh? And rightly so. Am I right, eh, am I right? And rightly so to that. Half an hour and there's not one bugger left sweating it out below. We're all up top airing our anuses. Then some mug officer sticks his bib in. Did he go off his brain! Can't you men read, he bawls. There's a sign, you know, he says. Not now, there ain't, says half a hundred voices. Piss off, says another half a hundred. Take those men's names, Sergeant, he yells, and, God al-fucking-mighty, what's this officer do? Pitch black it is, there's a war on, no cunt's game to so much as light a fag—and this prick flicks his torch out and flashes it round. Douse that light, says half a thousand voices. Sp-lash. Over it goes. And Snow White's heard saying nice and slow: And you'll follow it, poon, if you don't piss off. Which was the last we saw of him, by Jesus. And rightly so, eh, am I right, am I right? And rightly bloody so.

The light on LES *blacks out. The* WAITER *finishes setting up his bird in a pin spotlight.*

WAITER: The contents is Not-Inflammable but if the high heat is touched then the pressure of the contents are going up so please take care of above caution.

Blackout.

SCENE SEVEN: BREAKFAST. LATITUDE 12° LONGITUDE 153°

Breakfast chimes are heard, then some low groaning from LES. *A table and two chairs are being set up for breakfast.*

IRENE: Never again, never again. Oh yes, I'll bet.

The light reveals LES *and* IRENE *sitting down for breakfast.*

I won't say I told you so, but I did, didn't I? If I'd have known—

She starts to drink an orange juice. LES *looks at her, horrified at the thought of drinking anything.*

—the minute we got out to sea you'd start drinking like a fish, I'd have thought twice about this trip, I can tell you. [*The juice finished, she begins to inspect the menu.*] Fancy breakfasts they give us, eh? Fruit juice and porridge, then your choice of Spanish omelette or sausages and egg or bacon and egg or lamb's fry and egg or rissoles and—rissoles.

LES *wants to know none of this.* IRENE *starts into her porridge. She stops.*

Aren't you going to touch your porridge? They'll put a cross on that and give it to you tomorrow.

He groans. She tucks in. He groans again.

Serve yourself right—all that beer. You can't drink and avoid the reconcussions, you know. You think you'd have learnt that by now, but oh no, mad as a snake. I mean you must be. Only an idiot'd drink thirty-three tickets worth in one sitting, and don't try telling me it wasn't that much, if anything it was more.

LES *silently tells her to shut her trap, but she carries on eating and talking.*

This, by the way, is how you like it, a little bit runny. Considering they're all Chinese in the kitchen— [*she finishes, pushes the plate from her and straightens up*] it's not too bad. Especially that cook— he's really Chinese.

The WAITER *approaches.*

Not going to give it a try?

LES *looks nauseous.*

WAITER: Has madam made up her mind?
IRENE: Madam has. I think I'll have the Chinese-Spanish omelette.
WAITER: [*taking her plate*] I'll take that for madam. And you, sir?

LES *moans and shakes his head.*

IRENE: He'll have the lamb's fry.
WAITER: Very good, madam.

He takes LES*'s porridge and goes.* LES *says nothing.* IRENE *looks around at the other guests.*

IRENE: I must say they're very polite though, aren't they? They're very polite, the Asians. Yes, madam, no, madam, has madam made up her mind? It's like the Saveloy Plaza, almost. One thing they're not good at, though, and that's toast. You can't beat the toast you make yourself. [*She scrapes butter audibly onto her toast.*] Hard as your old boots. If they buttered it while it was hot—but then they probably think some people have just a little and others have none, have it dry, and some have so much their arteries'll clog before they're twenty-seven according to medical science. They don't presume, you see, do they, to butter it for you. Not that I'd mind. I wouldn't. But there are some who'd find that the depths of presumption and throw it back at them. Mrs Proudfoot would, for one. I was at a restaurant once with her and she sent her spoon back 'cause it had a grease spot. Myself, I'd have wiped it with a serviette. [*She munches some toast.*] Too posh by half, if you ask me. There's an activity— [*eating*] sheet up on the board this morning, you know. Saw it on my way back from the loo. Talk about keeping us busy!

> *The* WAITER *returns with the next course.*

Bingo and whist.

WAITER: Madam.

> *He serves* IRENE.

IRENE: Thank you. Ping-pong.

WAITER: Sir.

> *He serves* LES.

IRENE: The Miss Cruise contest.

WAITER: Coffee or—

IRENE: Tea. We always have tea, don't we, Les, first up?

> *The* WAITER *nods, bows and exits.*

Talent night, umpteen tournaments—chess, billiards—you should go in for the billiards, Les. Coffee. The library's open from two on, too. I dunno how some people can stand to have coffee this early, do you? Turns my stomach, the thought of it— [*She hoes into the omelette.*] Alright, don't answer. [*She eats, stops and looks at him.*] Good God, look at you. Old Smiler. Wonder somebody doesn't ask you when's the funeral. [*She eats. Pause.*] Spanish omelette. If this is Spanish omelette I'm Nefrettiti—whoever she was.

LES: Eggs saved lives.

IRENE: Eh?

LES: Nothing.

IRENE: There's a stripper, too, I'm told. Part of the floor show. What with him and his foul mouth and her doing dirty dances it'll get so I daren't be seen in the bar.

LES: You'll be sadly missed.

IRENE: And just what do you mean by that?

He stands unsteadily.

LES: I'm going to lie down.

IRENE: You just got up.

LES: Well, I'm going back, alright? [*He stands there, rocking gently. Pause.*] Biyoke.

IRENE: [*looking up*] What'd you say?

LES: Uh?

He seems not to understand and starts to walk away.

IRENE: You keep away from that bar.

LES: [*on his way out, mumbling*] A rice diet. Plain bloody rice. They paid us five cents a day and we bought eggs with it. If it wasn't for those eggs, only officers would have got back alive.

IRENE *reaches over, grabs his plate and scrapes it onto hers. She eats.*

IRENE: Lamb's fry! I wouldn't be surprised to learn this lot came over with MacArthur.

Blackout.

SCENE EIGHT: KHAKI AND GREEN

McLEOD *is heard whistling 'She'll Be Coming Round the Mountain'. The whistling goes on for some time. Green lights fade up to reveal a four-berth cabin, represented by a set of double bunks, or perhaps two sets, either wheeled in during the blackout or built into the set.* LES *is asleep on his bunk.* McLEOD, *on an upper bunk, continues whistling.* LES *twists in his sleep, then sits bolt upright, sweating and staring. The whistling stops. He sees no-one.* McLEOD *leans over to look at him. During this scene atmospherics might be used to heighten a sense of the internal.*

McLEOD: Like the old days, isn't it?

LES: Eh?

McLEOD: In with the blokes again—four bunks to a room.

LES: Aw well, they have to have segregation, don't they? [*He seems disoriented.*] We were too late, Irene and me, to get a twin. It's only the twins that sleep—

McLEOD: Just like the old days.

LES: —together—What days?

He rubs his eyes. Something is wrong, as if he is sick or not seeing too well.

McLEOD: All of us in those Nissen huts, row after—

LES: Row.

McLEOD: You were in the Second Sixty-Fifth.

LES: How'd you—

McLEOD: Artillery.

LES: —know?

McLEOD: You told me.

LES: Did I?

Pause. LES *walks about unsteadily.*

McLEOD: What's a bloke like you doing going to Japan?

LES: Eh?

McLEOD: You're a bit of a smash-and-grab, aren't you, doing that?

LES: What do you mean?

McLEOD: Who'd have thought Les Harding'd scab on his mates?

LES: Scab?

McLEOD: When I saw your name on the passenger list—

LES: Look—

McLEOD: —I couldn't believe it.

LES: —I dunno what you're doing here, but the War's over.

McLEOD: So I'm told.

LES: Finished.

McLEOD: Yeah.

LES: This is my cabin, this is. I'm here with a young fella called Tom Doughty, a fella called Fletcher—that's his bunk you're on—and a bloke called Fred Daley who I haven't spoken to yet. And that's the four of us, so how come—?

McLEOD: Wonder if it's really over, ever over?

LES: What?

McLEOD: The War. If you die in it—like Noel Gillespie or Terry Ryan— I wonder if it ever finishes?

LES: You knew Terry Ryan?

McLEOD: Maybe it just stops there and you live the last bit over and over. [*Pause.*] Laurie Peasley. Big Laurie. All hands and feet. Remember Laurie?

LES *is splashing water on his face. He stops.*

LES: How am I scabbing, eh? Tell me. I never yet split on a mate.

McLEOD: Hundreds, weren't there, with one leg or one arm? First the tropical ulcers. Then the gangrene. Weary was doing twenty-five— thirty amputations some days.

LES: You knew Weary?

McLEOD: Who didn't know Weary?

LES: He was a bloody hero, that bloke.

McLEOD: Was he what!

LES: You don't get doctors like that these days.

> LES *sits on the edge of his bunk.* McLEOD *perhaps whistles for a bit or there is a silence.*

McLEOD: Gordon McGrath's still alive and kicking, though kicking's hardly the sort of word you oughta use, is it, about a bloke on stumps. So's Harry.

LES: Harry?

McLEOD: Sniper. Now there's a hard luck story. [*He whistles.*] Everyone with tropical ulcers got the spoon treatment—remember the spoon treatment?

LES: I had a few. Small ones. Round me ankles.

McLEOD: Every day the MOs'd scoop out the rotten flesh with spoons, sterilised spoons. Bloody hurt.

LES: Never worked either. Nothing worked.

McLEOD: Except iodoform.

LES: Yeah, but you could never get it.

McLEOD: That's right. Not that there wasn't any. Just that the Japs wouldn't issue any. [*Pause.*] You had to laugh about Harry.

> LES *stands, blinking.*

LES: My eyes must be up the shit.

McLEOD: After, I mean.

LES: It was bloody cruel, what happened to Harry.

McLEOD: Lying there, abusing shit out of the MOs.

LES: I oughta be up top.

McLEOD: Hack the bastard off, he'd yell. Get rid of it, get rid of it!

LES: You couldn't laugh about Harry.

McLEOD: So they cut it off for him—obliged the poor bastard.

LES: Not even after.

McLEOD: Put him out of his misery.

LES: He asked to see it.

McLEOD: That's right. You'd volunteered for orderly duties, hadn't you?

LES: Held it in his hands. That's the last bit of trouble you'll give me, you cunt of a thing, he said.

McLEOD: Changed his tune, though, two days after, didn't he? He got gangrene in the other leg and off it came as well.

LES: Would have killed lesser men, what happened to him.

McLEOD: Here.

> *He dangles a bottle of Scotch over the side.* LES *takes it and sits down to drink.*

They were lesser men, were they—Jack Mahoney, Frank Wade— the ones that died—Red Dudley, Craigee, Cliff McRae. Hellfire Pass, that was. Five hundred and eighty yards of hell. You ever look up the figures, Les?

LES: No.

McLEOD: Three hundred and fifty men hath that cutting. Dead. Three hundred and fifty. [*He drinks.*] Sixty-eight of the three hundred and fifty were beaten to death. Kicked. Clubbed. Smashed. Pushed over the side. The Maggot—remember the Maggot? Brutal as all buggery. And Battlegong. Remember one day someone wondered what he'd been in civilian life and Vic Charlesworth said: A butcher. And you said: That'd be right, fits him like a French letter. [*He laughs briefly.*] Bandy legs and a flat face.

LES: The Maggot once thumped a bloke on the ear. Clenched fist. Broke his eardrum.

McLEOD: Saw that, did you?

LES: Thought all his Christmases had come at once.

McLEOD: You and me, you or me, we'd have taken stock of ourselves after that. But not the Maggot. He was overjoyed, wasn't he? Became his special party trick. From then on he went round trying to repeat the act. [*Pause.*] Suppose you'll look him up, will you?

LES: Who?

McLEOD: Chat over old times. Must be a lot of 'em still about. Blood and Slime, the Undertaker, the Silent Basher. You could track 'em all down—knock back a few *sakes*.

LES: I—I oughta be up top—the wife…

McLEOD: Wonder what Ernie King'd think, eh, and Tommy Cahill and all the others.

LES: It's the son-in-law's idea, this trip. I didn't—

McLEOD: Think? Wonder what they'd think? Hundreds of people getting round in Toyotas, eh, and other mugs selling the country to old Nippon, and transistors—the Japs have cornered the market, haven't they, you get down the beach and every second radio—

LES, *discomforted, stands up.*

LES: It's over.

McLEOD: They'd wonder what it had all been for, wouldn't they?

LES: It's dead and buried, all that. I mean, it's a different world we live in today.

McLEOD: Jimmy Coussens who was always smiling.

LES: You can't stand still. Life goes on.

McLEOD: For some of the boys it does. Even Harry. Harry. Gordon McGrath. Both on the TPI. There's a sign about standing up for 'em in trains but no-one bothers much anymore. It's getting work, though, that's their trouble. That gets to 'em. Not being able to get work. Hendo would have been the same.

LES: Hendo? Who was at Gemas?

McLEOD: Last I saw, he was running through the rubber when a gun ripped four fingers off his hand. He just looked at his mitt. They'd been his livelihood, his hands. A plumber, that's what he'd been. He just looked and you could see him thinking: Christ, how's a man gonna make out!

LES: He was just down the line from me.

McLEOD: Didn't have to wait long for the answer.

LES: Stood there—like he'd stopped.

McLEOD: Another blast ripped shit out of him. One of the few who actually fell in battle was Hendo.

LES: How do you—?

McLEOD: Know? How do I know? I was there, mate. All the way to Chungkai.[*He looks at* LES.] McLeod. Gavin McLeod.

LES: McLeod?

McLEOD: You were getting over your beri-beri at Chungkai, and helping out as an orderly.

LES: I know, I know, I'm just trying to place you.

McLEOD: You closed my eyes for me.

LES: Eh?

McLEOD: Orderly, the boat! Too late, mate, bring the shovel. Dysentery. I was a bad dysentery.

LES: McLeod? McLeod?

McLEOD: Just wasted away. You tidied me up a bit. Had to use the rag trick on my eyelids.

LES: A rag, dipped in cold water.

McLEOD: We were going out like lights, weren't we?

LES: I don't even remember a McLeod.

McLEOD: You will, Les. It all comes back, son, it all comes back.

The lights fade down to black with a siren beginning a crescendo, wailing in the dark.

Like for Wadee and Craigee, Cliff McRae—those last few moments— over and over again, never ending.

The noise becomes very loud and chaotic.

SCENE NINE: ALL HANDS

The siren wails on and on. Lights come up to reveal a row of people in life jackets being addressed by a SHIP'S OFFICER: LES, IRENE, ROBINSON *and others.*

OFFICER: … and before you hit the water give this cord a bit of a pull, alright, just a bit of a pull. Now on the string here you'll find your whistle. Everyone find their whistle?

He demonstrates blowing the whistle. They all blow their whistles.

Good. That's to help people make contact with each other in the water. [*He mimes swimming a few strokes, whistling.*] Good. Whistles away. Now a word about panic. Don't. When the call comes to abandon ship—

The siren sounds again.

—the whole thing will go much smoother, and fewer people will lose their lives, if you don't panic. Panic must be fought, squashed, sat upon, banished. *You must keep calm*, alright? Don't *panic*, don't. That's my word about panic: don't. When the call comes to abandon ship—

The siren sounds.

—perhaps you'll be down in your cabin, perhaps you'll be having a meal, or a drink, or—

PASSENGER: Perhaps you'll be in the toilet, yuk yuk!

The OFFICER *smiles a pained smile, and proceeds.*

OFFICER: Whatever, you should proceed quickly and quietly to this point here and form up in your group. Because we want to abandon ship in an orderly sequential fashion with very little *panic* or no *panic* whatsoever, it'll help if we all have a number, so starting with you, madam, from the right.

LES *comes to attention. The light goes green. People number off.*

FIRST PASSENGER: *Ichi.*

SECOND PASSENGER: *Ni.*

THIRD PASSENGER: *San.*

FOURTH PASSENGER: *Chi.*

FIFTH PASSENGER: *Go.*

LES: *Rokos.*

LES *snaps his heels. They all look at him. The green light goes out.*

Ha! What'd you all number off in Japanese for, eh? Ha?

IRENE: No-one else did, Les, except you. You're the one speaking in tongues.

LES: You're trying to get at me, aren't you? You're all—

OFFICER: Now if you try and remember those few points—

Blackout.

SCENE TEN: TALENT NIGHT

A loudspeaker announcement is heard.

LOUDSPEAKER: 'I'll be seeing you in all the old familiar places, all the old'—Would entrants in tonight's talent quest please put their names on a slip of paper and slip their slips of paper under the Entertainment Officer's door. That's entrants in tonight's—

The sound of a ukulele terminates the announcement. A spotlight reveals LES *on the bandstand, wearing a straw boater. He sings to the accompaniment of an inexpertly played ukulele, no more than a vague strum.*

LES: [*sung*]

> My old man's liver, my old man's liver,
> He keeps on drinking till he gets stinking,
> But my old man's liver, it keeps on floating along.
>
> He drinks cheap whisky, he drinks cheap brandy,
> He'll drink any liquid that happens to be handy,
> Still my old man's liver, it keeps on floating along.
>
> You and me, we'll drink what's right,
> And try our best not to get too tight,
> But he don't care, he just gets plastered,
> That's how he is, the no-good—

He shrugs.

> We all keep trying to curb his buying,
> And he looks fine but all his friends are dying,
> My old man's liver, it just keeps floating along.

The spotlight widens as the COMIC *approaches.* LES *has finished.*

COMIC: How about that, eh? Les Harding, ladies and gentlemen, getting up and having a go. Would you accept a token of my esteem, Les?

He has a hand behind his back. LES *nods.*

It's a little something for your throat. Here! [*He whips out a butcher's cleaver.*] No, I'm only joking, Les. What a voice. You're like a frog with a man in his—Ar, you've got to have a laugh. Okay, ladies and gentlemen, what'll you give Les Harding of 47C? Six out of ten? [*He scans the audience for a response.*] Alright, seven because he's such a nice fella. And he is, too. Not like some of you.

He shows LES *the way out.*

Some of you I can't stand the sight of already. Like the bald-headed professor—where is he?— [*he peers out*] who came up to me and said: Man is supposed to have evolved from the monkey—what happened in your case? What happened in my case? What happened in his? 'Course you have to feel sorry for these intellectuals. They go on a picnic, and all day kids are running up wanting to borrow their heads for the egg and spoon race. Alright, don't laugh—throw money. [*Suddenly he half chokes and puts a hand to his mouth.*] Make that paper money. This stuff— [*a few coins fall from his hand*] can do damage. Okay, the next act. Time to answer the question, how corny can you get? A few upstarts from 53G.

HARRY: They've been.

COMIC: You mean they've done their thing?

HARRY: They've finished.

COMIC: I could have told them that before they started. Not that we haven't discovered a few acts at our talent nights. It may not be the greatest show on earth, but we're at sea, aren't we, so you can't compare. So 53G's been and gone—like one bloke we discovered made his start diving off the bar into a thimble of water. That leaves— [*He consults a clipboard.*] Pretty soon—and this is when we put him on the payroll—he was diving from the top of the radio mast into a teacup. Then into a damp rag. Somebody and his magic camel—

HARRY: King Fuckroot.

COMIC: That's what I said—we run a clean ship—Somebody and his magic camel. He's still be doing it—diving from the mast—except some ratbag wrung out the rag, but now... [*in a high-pitched Arabian whine*] King Fuckroot... [*drums joining in*] and his magic camel.

> KING FUCKROOT *rides in on* ABDULLAH THE CAMEL. *The* WAITER, *wearing a towel for a turban, plays the* KING *and the* CAMEL'*s front end.* McLEOD, *covered by a sheet, is the back end. The* CAMEL *stops.*

That's it, is it? Alright, one out of ten.

WAITER: No, no. This is a magic camel, sahib white pig.

COMIC: A magic camel! Well, if it's so bloody magic why doesn't it try looking more like a camel and less like a couple of blokes out of 59H under a sheet? Haw haw!

> *He lifts the sheet and mucks them about.*

WAITER: Two and two, Abdullah?

> *The* CAMEL *brings its foot down four times. The* COMIC *whistles in mock admiration.*

COMIC: Alright then, you're a hard camel—four out of ten.

WAITER: Two minus two, Abdullah?

> *The* CAMEL *does nothing.*

COMIC: Aw, yes. It's very good, isn't it? Two minus two and it does nothing, which, by the by, is the way politicians earn their money. Six out of ten!

WAITER: Please to be lying down.

COMIC: Eh?

WAITER: Please to be lying down.

> *Reluctantly, the* COMIC *lies down on the bandstand.*

Watching now, ladies and gentlemen and assorted white scum of the Occident, as Abdullah walks over second-rate comedian without touching.

> *The* CAMEL *passes slowly over the* COMIC.

Good Abdullah, ridgey-didge, [*ad lib*] Ali Baba...

> *The* CAMEL *turns around to repeat the act. The* WAITER *spiels on.*

Once more, ship of the Sahara will tread carefully over—

> *A hand shoots out from under the camel sheet to snatch the water-bag the* WAITER *wears around his neck.*

—infidel albino without touching. Hi hi ridgey-didge Ali Baba ho ho Bagdad Damascus Beirut.

> *The* CAMEL *gets halfway over the* COMIC, *stops, raises a leg and pisses. It runs off, revealing a sodden* COMIC *whose rage knows no bounds.*

COMIC: None! None out of ten.

WAITER: King Fuckroot immensely sorry. Here. Dry face and hands.

> *He unwinds his towel revealing a bald head.*

COMIC: Argh! It's that bloody smart-arse professor.

WAITER: 59H not finished yet. Back half of camel will now do impressions.

COMIC: Yeah, well pardon me while I do an impression of a man leaving the stage.

> *He exits. The* CAMEL*'s back half (*McLEOD*) appears.*

McLEOD: Back half of camel will now do most famous impression of vegetarian eating one lettuce leaf too many.

> *He mimes eating a mammoth number of lettuce leaves, chewing for a long time. A spotlight narrows around him. The* WAITER *hovers in the background.* LES *can be seen in the dimness.*

LES: One of the camp institutions was this Dutchman.

COMIC: [*starting back on*] Now for my impression of a man returning to the stage to do an impression of a man with a soda syphon behind his back.

LES: Permanently sick, he was. Relieved of all duties. All he did was eat. Rice. His three bowls of rice a day, one grain at a time. He timed each meal so he finished one bowl as the next one was being dished out. Just sat there.

> McLEOD *has chewed on. Suddenly—one leaf too many—the spotlight on him turns green.*

McLeod! Of course. McLeod, you were with the concert party at Changi.

McLEOD: Thank you, thank you!

> *The* COMIC *has begun to spray the* WAITER.

LES: You remember me, don't you? Les Harding. The bloke who knew 'Eskimo Nell' backwards?

COMIC: Truce, truce! Let's hear it for them, ladies and gents. The professor and Mr Williams here.

> *He pats* McLEOD.

Put your hands together.

> *No-one notices* LES.

LES: Gavin McLeod. Yes. Bugger me. Of course it is. Gavin bloody McLeod. Long time no—

> *They all freeze. General light returns.* IRENE *steps forward.*

IRENE: God knows what got into Les. Just got up and wandered out there. Babbling away. Was my face red! I didn't know which way to look.

SCENE ELEVEN: OH, WHAT A LOVELY WAR

What follows is essentially an internal scene, revealing LES*'s memories and turning time present into time past. Light and sound could usefully heighten this effect. The* WAITER *carries a Japanese sword.*

LES: Did I tell you about Rosenberg? Late '41. In our stink-pit of a cabin? I did, eh? Eh, mate— [*he turns to* McLEOD] you were in the War, weren't you, you were—

> ROBINSON *starts singing.*

ROBINSON: [*sung*]
> What do you want with eggs and ham
> When you've got plum and apple jam?

Form fours, right turn,
What do you want with the money you earn?
Oh oh oh, what a lovely,
Oh oh oh, what a lovely,
Oh oh oh, what a lovely—

IRENE: I met Les at the Trocadero in 1949. The War was over then.

WAITER: Beer, sir?

McLEOD: Not me, mate, you've got the wrong bloke. My name's Williams,
59H, Williams, 59H—

COMIC: [*into a microphone*] This is a message from the Entertainment
Officer. The following games equipment has not been returned: two
ping-pong bats (the Japanese have started to overrun the peninsula),
the hookey board (half of Malaya has been systematically
abandoned), three decks of cards, one red draught and seven darts.
That's the Argylls, Leicesters and Ghurkhas who fought so valiantly
on the Siam frontier have been withdrawn, together with three decks
of cards, one red draught and seven darts.

ROBINSON: Seven darts.

LES: The Argylls.

ROBINSON: A bad business.

McLEOD: Williams, mate, Williams.

IRENE: Rationing had finished. I remember rationing. Couldn't get rubber.

LES: You were an officer, weren't you?

IRENE: There were kids who didn't know what a balloon was.

WAITER: Beer, sir?

IRENE: When I met Les the War was over.

COMIC: Alright, you men, and I call you men because I can hardly call
you soldiers.

McLEOD: Homo Officerus—a cut above your ordinary human being.

COMIC: I shall not comment on your appearance except to say that beards
aren't reggie.

McLEOD: Eighteen months ago these men were issued with their last
razor blades.

LES: Some days you'd wonder who the enemy was…

COMIC: This morning two tin cans were not returned to the cookhouse.
That's why the midday drink was withheld from the work party.

McLEOD: Fifteen hours a day on sharp rock in unbelievable heat with no
midday drink.

COMIC: The two men caught smoking after the five-minute warning parade have had their Jap pay stopped for a week.

McLEOD: Five cents a day. From the Japs.

LES: Eggs saved lives.

McLEOD: With it the men buy eggs.

LES: No egg money—

He mimes cutting his throat.

McLEOD: Translated, Homo Officerus means—

McLEOD & LES: [*together*] The White Nip.

COMIC: Morale. Is morale a forgotten word? Have we just lost it?

McLEOD: Like the two tin cans from the cookhouse.

LES: Like our lives.

The WAITER *begins to sing. Everyone else is quiet.*

WAITER: [*sung*]
> *Kuni o deta kara ito tsuki zo*
> *Tomo ni shinu de kono uma to*
> *Semete susuna yama ya kawa*
> *Tota susuna ni chi ka yo-o.*

LES: [*desperate*] I tell you, Robinson, I thought the whole thing was insane.

WAITER: Beer, sir?

ROBINSON: Couldn't be everywhere at once, old man.

LES: Beer—yeah, beer.

COMIC: You men are becoming crap-happy.

McLEOD: Down with dysentery—men dragged themselves to the latrine a hundred times a day.

COMIC: Men are reading in the latrines! Soon you'll want smoker stands. Soon it'll be an exclusive club.

WAITER: All men, whenever egg is fried, the yolk broken to prevent any funny ha ha the flag of Nippon, okay?

IRENE: You'll get sick again, Les.

McLEOD: These men are sick with dysentery.

IRENE: You'll drink yourself stupid.

WAITER: Dysentery *nei*!

McLEOD: *Biyoke*, you lump of lard. No can work today.

COMIC: Your dartboard? See it gets back to me, won't you?

WAITER: Me are not believe these men *biyoke*. Australian soldier no goodera. Very bad worker. Steal all the time from Nippon. *Benjo*

benjo all the time. Speak bad words all the time. Jiggy-jig, fucka and cunta. These men dysentery?

McLEOD: That's right, you tin of pus.

COMIC: And you call yourselves soldiers.

McLEOD: These men dysentery!

IRENE: I dunno what got into Les. Just got up there. In the middle of it, and started babbling. Was my face red.

LES: The Nips were morons, Robbo.

ROBINSON: We have no reason to believe the Japanese will enter the War.

WAITER: Nippon number one!

LES: But we weren't much better.

ROBINSON: For one thing the Japanese are a very small and myopic race, thus totally unsuited to jungle warfare.

LES: We had no idea…

IRENE: You oughta look after yourself, Les.

WAITER: Imperial Japanese Army number one!

LES: You know how we knew the War had started?

WAITER: You lookee you readee Japanese newspaper.

McLEOD: What's this, Tojo—more shit paper?

ROBINSON: Their aeroplanes are made from kettles and old kitchen utensils.

WAITER: Great Japanese hero in Zero—

McLEOD: Aw, yes.

WAITER: —attacks British battleship by himself.

ROBINSON: As for their guns—

LES: You know how we knew it had started?

ROBINSON: —their guns—

LES: This'll get you, Robbo.

ROBINSON: —their guns are of a sort last used by civilised peoples in films! Films about the Red Indians! Ha ha ha!

LES: Hang on, I haven't even told you yet.

WAITER: Finally gun empty.

ROBINSON: What's more, they're frightened of the dark! Ha ha!

LES: We knew it had started—

WAITER: Mighty hero in Zero—

LES: —we knew because we all got issued with five rounds of ammunition.

WAITER: —takes out sword. Flies low upside down over battleship—

LES: Before that, the only ammo you ever saw was when you went on guard duty. The bloke on guard'd take it out of his gun and you'd put it in yours! Ha ha ha!

WAITER: —and cuts off dishonourable head of British Captain, complete with binoculars now in museum at Okinawa—*hei hei*! Beer, sir?

LES: Eh?

ROBINSON: Morning, Les.

McLEOD: Not me, mate. Williams, 59H, Williams is the name.

LES: You're having me on, aren't you?

IRENE: I'm worried about him. Doesn't seem himself. Probably just the—

WAITER: Beer, sir?

> *They are all halted by the* COMIC *at the microphone, who delivers the following as if it were a comic routine.*

COMIC: Men, in our few brief moments together I'd like to put you in the picture. The following intelligence report has been prepared for your benefit: After the slaughter—I mean skirmishes—on the Slim River, half of Malaya has been systematically abandoned.

> *Everyone laughs as at a joke.*

That's one red draught and seven darts. The dredges in the tin mines have had their distributor caps removed, the rubber stores erased.

ALL: Ha ha—the rubber stores erased—ha ha!

COMIC: The acid used to coagulate latex—

ALL: Coagulate latex!

COMIC: —carried round the corner and our bridges burnt behind us.

ALL: Ha ha—burnt behind—ha ha!

COMIC: That's two ping-pong bats and a hookey board. The calamitous loss in short of a million pounds worth of machinery, tin, rubber and installations need not concern you, so I shall refer to it no further.

ALL: The calamitous loss of a million pounds worth of hookey boards, ha ha!

COMIC: As to Jap landings at places other than Kota Bahru (that's fancy dress this coming Sunday, fancy dress this coming Sunday), the Japs have landed at Kota Bahru and Kota Bahru only, and if you don't believe me why don't you go there and ask them, ha ha ha!

> *No-one laughs at this one. He carries on.*

Mrs Hicks will make costumes available, but if you've bought your own so much the better, so much the enemy—the enemy—I don't think you need to know that the enemy has been able to advance faster than we've been able to retreat—the news that you face an enemy not just to the north but to your southern rear may disturb you, so— [*He screws up a piece of paper.*] That's all then. An up-to-date ship's bulletin. Fancy dress Sunday, and notice that if games equipment continues to be mislaid in this fashion the future of such activities will be jeopardised. Thank you. [*He starts to go, then sees* McLEOD.] Second Sixty-Fifth?

McLEOD: Yes, sir.

COMIC: Mersing?

McLEOD: Yes, sir.

COMIC: Dug in, have you?

McLEOD: Yes, sir—cleared fire lanes, built ammo dumps, got rid of the natives. Take the Japs a month to get us out of here.

COMIC: High Command wants it done sooner. They're ordering a retreat. See to it.

> *He goes.* ROBINSON *and* IRENE *start to go.*

ROBINSON: [*sung*]
> Form fours, right turn,
> What do you want with the money you earn?
> Oh oh oh, what a lovely war.

IRENE: The Trocadero. In 1949. The War was over then. The Trocadero, 1949. The War was over then. The Trocadero… [*et cetera*]

> LES *and* McLEOD *begin to leave. The* WAITER *runs at* LES *and brings him down.*

WAITER: Nippon guard slap, *hei hei*!

> McLEOD *helps* LES *up.*

McLEOD: He says they slap us about a bit.

WAITER: But Nippon guard get slapped.

McLEOD: But he gets slapped as well.

WAITER: If I makee mistake—send off wrong message—

> *He mimes getting hit.*

McLEOD: His own officers beat him black and blue and yellow.

WAITER: This is the law—all country soldier *sama sama*.

McLEOD and LES *laugh.*

LES: *Sama sama.*

The WAITER *whistles them to a halt.*

WAITER: Psst. Rockhampton, boom boom boom!

McLEOD: Go on! You've bombed Rockhampton!

WAITER: *Hei hei!*

LES: And Sydney. Sydney, boom boom boom?

WAITER: *Hei hei!* Sydney, boom boom boom.

McLEOD: And Melbourne?

LES: Yeah, what about Melbourne?

WAITER: *Hei!* Melbourne, boom boom boom.

LES: Not Wagga?

McLEOD: Wagga, boom boom boom?

WAITER: *Hei hei!* Wagga, boom boom boom.

McLEOD: And Tokyo?

WAITER: *Hei!* Tokyo, boom boom—Tokyo *nei!*

He runs at them with drawn sword. LES *drops. Pause.*

Beer, sir?

LES *looks up.*

McLEOD: No, mate. Never heard of him. Williams. 59H, Williams.

WAITER: Beer, sir?

A fading exit begins.

Beer...

McLEOD: 59H. Williams. Second Sixty-Fifth! 59H.

LES: Eh, Robbo, Robbo—did I tell you about—?

He realises ROBINSON *is not there.*

WAITER: Nippon number one.

McLEOD: Williams.

WAITER: War over in one month.

McLEOD: Second Sixty-Fifth.

LES: I thought it was insane, you know that? Insane!

McLEOD: 59H.

LOUDSPEAKER: All passengers please note that coffee, tea and biscuits are now being served on D Deck. That's coffee, tea and biscuits on D Deck.

END OF PART ONE

PART TWO

SCENE ONE: CROSSING THE EQUATOR

After interval we find two deckchairs in place, LES *in one,* IRENE *in the other. She wears sunglasses and a bit of paper covers her nose. She is in bathers,* LES *is bare-chested, wearing shorts and a sunhat. On the ground between them lies his discarded shirt.*

IRENE: What'd the doctor say?

LES: Nothing.

IRENE: He said nothing was wrong?

LES: Yeah.

IRENE: That's all he said?

LES: He told me to cut back my drinking.

IRENE: I could have told you that.

LES: Jesus! What's a man supposed to do round here? Go bloody fishing?

> *Pause.*

IRENE: Funny, isn't it?

LES: Yeah, hilarious.

IRENE: Real cosmopolitan, isn't it?

LES: Yeah. What?

IRENE: The ship. They're Filipinos that do the cabin.

LES: They'd work for sixpence, those jokers.

IRENE: Chinese cooks, and Malays and Gherkins.

LES: Ghurkhas.

IRENE: And that doctor, what's he?

LES: A Paki.

IRENE: As in Pakistani?

LES: Well, it wouldn't be Paki as in Welshman, would it?

IRENE: He'd be a Muslin, then.

LES: If he wanted to be one he'd be one and a man'd be a dope to stand in his way.

IRENE: I read an article about Muslin doctors. They don't touch women.

LES: All the more for me.

IRENE: Hope he's not like the ones in the article. I mean, what happens if I get sick?

LES: If you get sick you go to the bloody doctor like I did.

IRENE: What's the point if he doesn't touch women? [*Pause.*] It's all to do with it being against their religion. [*Pause.*] 'Course, maybe he touches western women and not the others.

LES: They're the ones causing all the trouble in England.

IRENE: Who are?

LES: Taking all the jobs.

IRENE: Who?

LES: The Pakistanleys.

IRENE: Well, it's a bit of a turn-up having one for a doctor, especially with their well-known idiotsyncrasies. In this article, when a woman falls sick he doesn't visit her, he visits the husband.

LES: Who does?

IRENE: The doctor does.

LES: Yeah, well east is east and west is west.

IRENE: She's in the other room and the doctor, because he's not allowed to see her, what he does is asks the husband questions, then the husband goes in and asks the wife the questions, then he comes out and tells the doctor: No, it doesn't hurt there, and, yes it does, and so the doctor sets about building up a picture in his mind's eye of what's wrong with her and gives her some pills or something. [*Pause.*] Not that all of 'em take pills—some of 'em won't. Only ointments. Like in New Guinea they won't take pills. Injections—in fact they seem to like having injections, I guess because they're used to having bones in their noses. But they won't have pills.

LES: That's got a lot to do with the price of beer in Bourke, hasn't it?

IRENE: What has?

LES: Carry on like a pork chop about Paki Doctor Stan and end up talking about New Guinea.

IRENE: His name's Mr Walker-Taylor, MD.

LES: What do you mean: Mister. Is he a quack or isn't he?

IRENE: When you're a doctor but a bit better than a doctor they call you a mister.

LES: Mister! Jesus, the bloody apprentices call me mister.

IRENE: He's probably a first-class surgeon or something.

LES: If he's so shit-hot what's he doing here? He oughta be in Collins Street or somewhere.

IRENE: Probably wanted the rest.

LES: He doesn't need a tan, I'll tell you that.

IRENE: That's probably why, then. His colour. He couldn't get into Collins Street, I suppose, because of his colour.

LES: Don't you believe it. They're all over the joint. On the bloody trams to Ascot Vale. And not just giving you your ticket either—some of 'em are driving the bastards—and when you get inside the showgrounds they're ahead of you in the queue at the tote splashing their dough.

IRENE: The TAB and the pub. If you're not in one you're in the other.

> LES *grunts.*

After hay, you're God's gift to the horses.

LES: Comes of having a nag for a wife.

IRENE: Funnee. [*Reaching for the shirt*] Is the pong on this gonna kill me, or what?

LES: Wish it would. The perfect crime.

IRENE: Don't want my nose getting burnt.

LES: Why not? Go to the fancy dress ball as Rudolph.

IRENE: Christmas. Seems such a long way away. And Marge. And the kids.

LES: Don't talk about Christmas.

IRENE: Something about having the family sit down to dinner.

LES: Old Harris from up the road coming in at nine o'clock with three of beer and one of Pimms, which reminds me.

IRENE: What?

> *She puts the shirt over her head.*

LES: I've got a thirst.

IRENE: You heard the doctor.

LES: I know, I know.

> *He looks around. In the distance he spies the* WAITER. *He glances at* IRENE, *then whistles furtively.*

IRENE: What are you whistling for?

LES: I'm happy. Hey!

IRENE: Shouting.

LES: Haven't you heard of anyone shouting for joy?

IRENE: Wish I was happy.

LES: You wanted to go on this flaming trip, didn't you?

> *The* WAITER *enters.* LES *signals him to be quiet. He orders, miming and mouthing, a can of beer. The* WAITER *exits.*

IRENE: Could be a bit more romantic, couldn't it? Tropical nights, moonlight on the waves, dinner suits, a trio from Hawaii. Hasn't been much of that, has there?

LES: There's a big deal tonight, what's wrong with yer?

IRENE: It's more boring than you'd have thought, going on the brochures.

LES: So?

IRENE: And we're crossing the equator. It's supposed to be a time of fun and frolic. King Neptune's supposed to duck us and all that.

LES: It doesn't just come to you.

IRENE: What doesn't?

> *The* WAITER *appears with an orange juice.* LES *groans.* IRENE *takes off the shirt.*

What doesn't just come to you? [*She sees the* WAITER *and smiles.*] Oh, heh, hello.

LES: Thanks, pal. [*He takes the juice, wincing.*] Fun and bloody frolic doesn't!

WAITER: Will that be all, sir?

LES: Eh?

IRENE: He wants to know will that be all.

LES: I dunno, will it?

IRENE: Well, I don't want a drink and you seem to have one—against orders, I might add.

LES: A bloody orange juice!

IRENE: That's all it is?

LES: What's it look like—radish wine?

IRENE: Yes, I think that'll be all, thank you.

> *The* WAITER *bows.* IRENE *dons the shirt again.* LES *goes after the* WAITER*, miming and gesturing: Orange juice, no; beer, yes; okay? The* WAITER *exits.*

Is that what he put you on, orange juice?

LES: Yeah—does wonders for the nerves.

IRENE: You wouldn't think we were on a ship, would you?

LES: No, no. I won't believe it till a swordfish lands in me lap.

IRENE: We could be anywhere, couldn't we?

LES: Or a seagull shits on me shoulder.

IRENE: I feel like I'm in the beer garden of the Queenscliff Hotel, Queenscliff.

LES: Half your luck.

IRENE: Remember the Queenscliff Hotel, Queenscliff?

LES: Yeah. Like a bad dinner.

IRENE: We got there by ferry from Sorrento.

LES: And chundered going both ways.

IRENE: That's right. I made you go up the other end of the boat.

LES: Prawn cutlets.

IRENE: What about them?

LES: That's what we had for lunch.

IRENE: Your memory isn't as bad as you always make out, then, is it?

LES: The gulls grabbed most of it before it hit the wake we were making. The Sorrento to Queenscliff seasick shift. They follow the ferry—Oh, Jesus!

The WAITER *returns, this time with a can of baked beans.*

IRENE: What now?

LES: Eh? Oh. Just a fly in me eye.

He goes through the motions again.

IRENE: That year we were camping on the foreshore with your brother Ernie, remember? We've come up in the world.

LES: [*whispering*] No, no—beer. B for Betty.

IRENE: You and he fished off the jetty.

LES: E for Eric.

IRENE: Who was Eric?

LES: E for Eric again.

IRENE: Oh. Eric Egan. I'd forgotten about him.

LES: R. As in you *are* a prick.

IRENE: Marge was just so high.

LES: When?

IRENE: When we camped on the foreshore at Dromana.

LES: Aw, then.

IRENE: The mozzies were bad. She was all over lumps.

LES: And some thieving cow knocked off the Porta Gas container when we took her to the aquarium.

IRENE: The Harrises went the year after and said they'd drained the swamp. If we'd gone with the Harrises we'd have missed the mozzies.

LES: Yeah. Well, I know who I'd choose out of the Harrises and the mozzies.

IRENE: She loved the snake pit.

LES: Who did?

IRENE: Marge did. Couldn't drag her away. [*Pause. She takes off the shirt and stands.*] Why doesn't something happen? [*She crosses to the railing and gestures.*] That could be the equator right there.

LES: Couldn't be. They'd have double lines like down the middle of Droop Street.

IRENE: I could be in the northern hemisphere for the first time in my life and I don't feel a thing.

LES: What do you expect, a jab in the quoit?

IRENE: Here's that nice waiter again.

LES: Eh? Oh! So it is, what do you know?

> *The* WAITER *appears with a can of beer on his tray.* LES *refuses to look.*

IRENE: He's carrying a can of beer. Bet that makes your mouth water.

LES: Eh? Oh, not particularly—take it or leave it.

IRENE: Hello.

> *She and the* WAITER *smile at each other. The* WAITER *stops near* LES *with the tray.*

He's offering it to you.

LES: [*still not looking*] He's not, is he?

WAITER: Beer, sir?

LES: Beer! I didn't order any beer.

IRENE: No, you see, my husband's off it till six.

LES: Bloody ning-nongs, these waiters.

WAITER: Ning-nong yourself.

LES: Eh?

IRENE: Now, Les, watch your language.

WAITER: Do you want it or don't you?

LES: [*shouting*] No, I don't.

WAITER: Well, nor do I!

The WAITER *hurls the tray and can to the deck and storms off.*

IRENE: Now you've put him in a huff.

LES: Who are you throwing trays at, mug?!

IRENE: You've gone and upset him.

LES: Upset him. I'd give him one on the ear except it'd be like hitting granite.

IRENE: Well, someone must have ordered it.

LES: Yeah.

IRENE: Poor little chap must have got mixed up. It's quite a job.

She picks up the tray and can.

LES: What are you doing?

IRENE: No point in wasting it, is there?

LES: My sentiments exactly.

IRENE: And since you can't drink it, I might as well.

LES *groans and throws himself back into the deckchair.*

LES: Give us me shirt.

She throws it to him. He drapes it over his face.

At least I don't have to watch.

IRENE: Well, that's an improvement.

LES *mumbles curses.*

Means I won't be blinded by your sunny disposition.

LES: Will you shut your trap.

IRENE: My lips are sealed— [*she drinks*] round the ice-cold rim of a can of Fosters. [*She drinks and sits.*] Export quality. [*Pause.*] Are you missing me?

LES: I've just got a shirt over me face, you dag—I haven't gone to Antarctica.

IRENE: No, I mean at night.

LES *grunts.*

Stan was ready to pay the extra.

LES: So he reckons.

IRENE: We were top of the list in case of cancellations, but it's a very popular cruise, the Cherry Blossom. No-one with a two-berth cabin cancelled. [*Pause.*] I don't mind it, I suppose, I mean I get on alright with the other women—all except Myra.

LES: Who's Myra?

IRENE: I told you. She's the one who leaves her teeth in the basin. [*Pause.*] It would have been better though—sleeping in the same cabin—you and me.

LES: Business as usual.

IRENE: They reckon a change is as good as a holiday but this is a change and a holiday.

LES: Change is right. Some mugs can't touch a drop till six.

IRENE: I dunno if I like it.

> *The* WAITER *appears leading the* COMIC *and* HARRY, *dressed as Neptune and his apprentice. He points towards* LES. *The* COMIC *and* HARRY *nod and start to creep up on their quarry.*

First time in God knows how many years. 'Course we'll be unrecognisable when we get back.

LES: Why?

IRENE: Brown as berries. All this sun—Oh!

> *They grab* LES *and haul him off, complaining.*

LES: What the fuck!

> *The* WAITER *appears at* IRENE'*s elbow. She too has been taken by surprise.*

WAITER: It's alright, madam.

IRENE: Oh. I got such a fright.

WAITER: Just Neptune, madam. We're crossing the equator.

IRENE: Yes, of course. Ha! Poor Les.

WAITER: A drink, madam?

> *He carries a drink on his tray.*

IRENE: Yes, thank you. And poor me. What a scare. I felt like I had my heart in my mouth.

WAITER: What does it mean, this—had my heart in my mouth?

IRENE: Eh? Oh. Ha! It's just a saying. It means a person's so scared that their heart leaps from—from—

> *She wonders how to explain. He uses her body to demonstrate. It is the beginning of a seductive pass.*

WAITER: [*touching her breast*] From here… [*touching her cheek*] to here.

IRENE: Yes, ha, hum!

WAITER: But the heart—surely it cannot do this?

IRENE: Oh, no—it's just a—

WAITER: Unless it is in love, eh? Then—don't you say this in English—the heart does strange things.

> *She gives a little laugh, faintly flattered. He sits down. There is a giant splash offstage. They both look towards the pool.*

IRENE: Poor Les.

WAITER: Les we forget, eh?

IRENE: Why not? He can swim.

WAITER: Better we talk about you?

IRENE: [*sipping*] Oh me, ha! What's there to say?

WAITER: You are English, dear lady?

IRENE: Heavens, no. Australian.

WAITER: Ar… [*shifting his deckchair closer*] you are from down under.

IRENE: Well, um— [*disquieted, shifting her deckchair*] it depends what you mean by the term.

> *He shifts closer again, and she away. The duel of the deckchairs.*

WAITER: I like Australian women, such nice bodies, so—

IRENE: [*helpfully*] Brown?

WAITER: Sexy.

IRENE: Oh, I don't kn—

WAITER: Yes. This is so. The English, bah! Only a very young English lady would wear a swimsuit like this. But all Australian ladies—whoo!

IRENE: I—you're—you're not a Muslin, are you, Mr um…?

WAITER: Not mister, dear lady, not to you. To you I am Puteh, at your service, dear lady.

IRENE: And do you come from a Muslin country, Puteh?

WAITER: Oh indeed, indeed dear lady, very much so, I am happy to report.

IRENE: Then you don't touch women, do you?

WAITER: Touch women?

IRENE: In public.

WAITER: Oh, dear lady, if only you knew. In my country it is so strict that if I held a lady's hand [*taking hers*] like so, then— [*He makes a cutthroat sign.*] And if I were to touch a lady's stomach [*touching hers*] or even—

> *His hand moves to her breast.*

And to kiss!

He kisses her. They part gently.

Such terrible consequences.

IRENE: [*smiling*] But surely people aren't killed for a kiss?

WAITER: Mine is a very backward country, dear lady, and only slowly coming forward.

The COMIC *and* HARRY *begin to creep back.*

In my lifetime, I do not expect to see—and yet this is something I am witness to the young white people doing on the deck after dark—in my lifetime, I do not expect to be able to stroke a lady's thighs so. [*Starting to stroke hers*] Alas. I will be dead well and truly before I ever do this harmless little thing.

IRENE: Poor Puteh.

She sinks back, contemplating the injustice of it all. He avidly strokes her thighs. Suddenly, with a roar, the COMIC *pounces.* IRENE *is swept from her deckchair and dragged towards the pool.*

Help! Help!

WAITER: [*suddenly losing his accent*] Not her, you silly bastards—I was just about to—

He stops. A sodden LES *appears as they carry* IRENE *past. He does nothing. His vengeful eye falls on the* WAITER.

LES: Hey, you've forgotten someone, Captain.

As LES *comes slowly forward, the* WAITER *backs slowly away. He laughs placatingly.* LES *laughs back, briefly. Finally the* WAITER *turns tail and* LES *gives chase. Blackout.*

LOUDSPEAKER: Mrs Hicks, calling Mrs Hicks, Mrs Hicks wanted on C Deck. Anyone lacking fancy dress for tonight should see Mrs Hicks when she's available.

SCENE TWO: FANCY DRESS

The COMIC, *still in Neptune garb, appears on the bandstand. He says nothing for a time, then slowly opens his mouth into a big cheesy grin. A few teeth have been blacked out. He points to his mouth.*

COMIC: See that! It's started. Smile Week is upon us.

Drum rim. The weight of it drives him, as it were, a few feet into the ground.

'Course, the Australian contingent isn't going to like it. An Australian'd prefer to shoot himself in the foot, half bleed to death, save himself by cutting it off with a rusty razor blade, and go the way of all flesh from blood poisoning than smile. Fair dinkum, without doubt, they'd be the biggest bunch of whingeing, no-good, down-mouthed bludgers that ever drew breath, and to illustrate my point—

Drum rim. HARRY *stands with a picture of a penis.*

Oooh, he's quick. To illustrate my point, Harry will not stand—

He thumps him down amid a clatter of cymbals.

—with a picture of Yours Truly taken during the slacker months of the year, no. Instead I'll tell you a little allegory. Allegory? That's like an allergy but you don't itch it. A little allegory that happened to me when I was selling seafood out the back of Bourke, travelling by shanks' pony from station to station with my putrid wares on my back, hence the disguise. I'm not done up like this just because it's fancy dress night, I tell you. I'm done up like this to illustrate my point.

A rather phallic part of his Neptune garb starts to do the Indian rope trick. A drum rim sends it back where it came from.

There I was—and like all good fishermen I'd learned the only way to sell week-old seafood was to set up shop somewhere that smelt worse than the article itself—so there I was, flicking off the redbacks, spreading my wares on the toilet seat and singing: I've got 'em, come and get 'em—crabs! crabs!—when in he walks.

Drum rim.

He was your typical Australian—long as a lamppost and mean as a Glasgow Jew, nose on him like a turd inspector. How'd you be, Dig? I asks him. I'd seen him at work through a chink in the dunny door knocking a fleece off a four-year-old wether. How'd I be, he says, and spits a stream of what looks like molten lead the length of a cricket pitch, decapitating a passing kookaburra. How'd I be! And he turns two black, hate-filled eyes in my direction. How would you flaming well expect me to be? Get a load of me, will yer? Burrs on every square inch of me flaming hide, dags in me moleskins, swallowing dirt with every breath I take, shearing sheep that should have been dog's meat years ago, working for the lousiest nigger-driver in Australia and too frightened to leave because me old woman's got a maintenance order out against me. I haven't tasted a beer for weeks and the last glass I had was knocked out of me hand by some clumsy cow before I'd half finished it. How would I be? How do you reckon I'd be?

He spits. Drum tok.

The next time I saw him was during the War. He was sitting on an upturned ammo box halfway up the Kokoda Trail, a tin helmet over one eye and a cigarette butt hanging from his mouth. He had a rifle alright. It was leaning against his knee and he was trying to clean his nails with the tip of his bayonet. Like a bloody fool, I goes up to him and enquires: How would you be—Dig?

Drum support.

He fixes me with a mad look, swallows the butt, kicks the rifle half a mile and thumps a crease in the tin helmet like it was a porkpie hat gone out of shape. How'd I be? How would you flaming well expect me to be? Six months in this joint being shot at by every Nip in New Guinea, maggots in me meat, ticks in me prick if not halfway to me brain, flies in me eyes and more leeches than hairs on me legs. I'm too scared to sleep a wink, I'm wearing in a new pair of boots on account of the last pair walked down the throat of history's biggest crocodile, I've written me last will and testament five times this morning, that's how often I've looked death in the eye and it wouldn't even be nine o'clock. How'd I be? How do you flaming well reckon I'd be? [*With a spit he moves on to chapter three.*] The last time I saw him was in heaven. I should have known, but overcome by the brotherhood of man in the eyes of God I goes up to him and says: How'd you be, Dig? How'd I be? he snarls. Just slap your bo-peeps on the nightshirt, will yer. It's so long a man trips over it fifty times a day. It takes ten minutes to hoist every time a man wants a— [*He mimes rolling it up to have a splash.*] Righto, righto. But have a gander at the wings they give me. Feathers missing everywhere—a man must be flaming well moulting—and the halo, only me blasted ears to keep it from falling off. As for the harp. Look at it. Five ruddy strings missing and there's a band practice in ten minutes. How'd I be? How do you reckon I'd— [*he looks around and mouths a string of silent obscenities*] be! Shortly after that, every Australian in heaven got transferred to the other place for knocking off the altar wine. Dig, by the way, 's in the boiler room stoking this tub's eternal fire and I'm here with strict orders to— [*he smiles*] every few seconds. Talk about— [*he smiles every few seconds*] hell. How'd I be? How do you reckon I'd be? And to top it all off I'm supposed to judge which of you mugs is turned out the best. Jesus! Give 'em a number, Harry, and slip me a sherbet.

> HARRY *sets the phonograph going, and drums to it. The* COMIC *locates a can of beer and steps down to wander around inspecting the audience, who are the ship's passengers done up for fancy dress night.*

Aw, will you look at her. Give her a hand, ladies and gentlemen. Came along as the bull in the china shop and brought her husband disguised as a piece of bullsh— [*He finds someone else.*] Sheba and Solomon— very nice, very nice. And who's this, Harry?

HARRY: Caesar.

> *The* COMIC *goes to grab someone.*

As in, I have come to bury Caesar not to praise him.

COMIC: Oh—oh—as in: Give unto Caesar what is Caesar's. Okay, okay, would the smart alec who took it give the gentleman back his toga. How's he expected to conquer the world in a pair of underpants? [*Passing on*] Very modern they were, the Romans. Not only did they have underpants, they had brassieres—and they burnt them. It's bloody true. Virgil wrote all his poems by the light of a burning brassiere. Hello, sailor!

> *He has spied* ROBINSON, *who is dressed as Lord Nelson. The* COMIC *goes into a provocative bum-wiggling routine. Meanwhile* LES *and* IRENE *appear on the periphery,* LES *in AIF gear,* IRENE *as Cleopatra.*

LES: If he says anything to me, I'll clock the bastard.
IRENE: Les!
LES: Why'd you get me this garbage for?
IRENE: It was all they had left.
LES: Have a look at the strides.
IRENE: Sssh!
COMIC: Let me look into your eyes, sailor—

He smooches up to ROBINSON, *then he double-takes.*

Strike me lucky! Just a passenger. I thought he was the Captain and I was a choirboy. I sing like one, you know— [*He sings a falsetto note.*] It's because when I was young I ate my nuts. It's true. My old ma always said: Eat your almonds if you want to sing your amens on Sunday, there's a good—Hello, hello! [*He has spied* LES.] I spy with my little eye something beginning with G.

HARRY: Jesus of Nazareth.

COMIC: No.

HARRY: I give in.

COMIC: And not that Chinese gentleman either. None other than General Blameless himself. [*To* LES] Attention!

> LES *comes to attention.*

Eyes right.

> LES *obliges.*

Eyes left.

> LES *obliges.*

Eyes closed.

> LES *closes them. The* COMIC *seizes his opportunity and starts to kiss* IRENE. *He finishes.*

And how'd you be, Dig?

LES: [*straightening*] How would I be? How do you flaming well reckon I'd be? The missus goes down to get us some clobber for the fancy dress ball and comes back with this lot. Have a look at me hat—size nine-and-a-half and I take a six-and-a-quarter—strides as big as a giant in a hurry—you could fit a ready-mix truck down the bastards and there'd still be room for me and half the Collingwood Football Club. Get onto the shirt. I have to chain myself down or else get blown away. And the boots. A man's feet are like a coupla fleas in a top hat. And you ask me how I'd be! How do you flaming well reckon I'd be!

> *During this he grabs the* COMIC *and frogmarches him towards the bandstand. He shoves him the last few yards and stands there staring up. He spits. A drum tok as it lands, and/or a portrait of the Queen above the bandstand crashes to the floor. Blackout.*

SCENE THREE: AFTERMATH

IRENE, *a bit under the weather, her costume on the wilt, walks across the space. She carries a balloon and from her mouth dangles a blow-out snake novelty. Once or twice her foot twists in its high-heeled shoe, and she inadvertently blows the snake out.* ROBINSON *and* LES, *still in fancy dress, are making for the table carrying a chair each and cans of beer. They put down the chairs.* LES *sits as* IRENE *arrives.*

LES: Been to powder your horrible-looking face, have you?

> *She blows the snake thing in his face and stands there. Pause.*

Well, what d'you want?

IRENE: A chair would be a start, lover.

LES: Sit on your ring.

ROBINSON: Please take mine.

> *She mouths a surprised 'Oh!'*

LES: He means the chair.

> *The gallant* ROBINSON *exits for another.*

IRENE: Isn't it nice to find someone with manners?

LES: Manners, spanners.

> *She sits.*

IRENE: [*as if he had asked*] A drink? Oooh, yes please.

LES: You've got a bagful of tickets.

IRENE: You're so thoughtful.

LES: Get it yourself.

IRENE: You should get a job in the filims, Les.

LES: Yeah?

IRENE: With your charm, you could do all the David Niven parts.

LES: That pansy!

ROBINSON: [*returning with a chair*] Panzers?

LES: Ees. Pansees.

IRENE: A lady would say: Aren't they some kind of flower?

ROBINSON: Carved hunks off the rump of Belgium, the Panzers.

LES: Do you ever talk about anything but the bloody War?

IRENE: Let him talk about what he wants to talk about, Les.

ROBINSON: You have ice, don't you, Irene? I've ordered for you.

IRENE: Thank you, Mr Robinson.

ROBINSON: Herbert, please.

LES: Tah, Herb.

IRENE: I was telling Les, Herbert, that he's got more manners than David Niven. Joking, of course. [*To* LES] Look at you—slumped over your grog like some metho drinker at the Methodist Mission.

LES: God save us from wives.

IRENE: That's not very nice, Les.

> LES *looks surprised.*

God has taken Herbert's.

LES: Taken her bosom to his great bosom in the sky.

IRENE: Les!

LES: Irene!

> *They fall quiet as the* WAITER *deposits her drink.*

IRENE: I think we ought to change the subject.

ROBINSON: It's alright, really.

LES: I'm for that.

ROBINSON: Old scars heal tougher than skin itself.

LES: Let's change the subject. When we first arrived in Malaya our Medical Officer treated us to the good news that ninety-six per cent of the native sheilas had VD.

IRENE: [*pointedly ignoring this*] How far have we come, Mr Robinson, as a Navy man?

ROBINSON: At a guess—about halfway.

LES: A few days later he changed it to ninety-nine point nine per cent. Wonder who carried out the investigations?

IRENE: Do you miss her, Herbert?

ROBINSON: Miss Muriel?

LES: Boiling hot and he tells us to roll down our sleeves.

ROBINSON: Will you think it amiss of me if I say no?

IRENE: Of course not.

LES: *And* button down our shirts *and* tuck our strides in our socks.

ROBINSON: You see, I was away a good bit of the time.

LES: That way the malarial mosquito will find no flesh exposed.

ROBINSON: It got so we hardly knew each other.

LES: Signed an agreement with 'em, have you?

IRENE: Sounds a bit like Les and me.

LES: Promised not to have a go at our hands and faces, have they?

IRENE: He hardly knows me anymore. Does not have a clue.

ROBINSON: You grow apart.

LES: Take that man's name, Sergeant!

IRENE: Twenty-three years married.

ROBINSON: It's a long time.

LES: The soil of Malaya is infested with hookworm. The pest is ubiquitous. Meaning what? shouts someone.

IRENE: Perhaps too long.

> *Into a green spotlight steps an Australian Army officer, played by the* COMIC.

COMIC: Take that man's name.

IRENE: I met Les at the Trocadero in 1949.

ROBINSON: I met Muriel when she was with the WAAF.

COMIC: It enters one's body through the soles of one's feet.

IRENE: They've pulled it down now. Put up an art gallery.

COMIC: Works its way round one's bloodstream.

IRENE: They pull down all the good places.

COMIC: Into one's bowels.

LES: Arseholes.

COMIC: Take that man's name.

IRENE: Sometimes I go into the city, I don't know where I am—it's like another planet.

COMIC: Causing a slow, lingering death.

ROBINSON: When I first knew Muriel she was a blonde.

COMIC: Prevention is the only cure.

ROBINSON: God knows how she managed it—with rationing and whatnot. But she did.

COMIC: All men therefore will be issued with a pair of wooden clogs.

ROBINSON: She dyed it.

COMIC: These to be worn to the showers and back.

ROBINSON: I found out quite by accident, of course.

LES: Why don't we wear our boots or our sandshoes?

ROBINSON: She took great pains, did Muriel.

COMIC: Take that man's name!

ROBINSON: With her appearance.

LES: Take a piss, Sergeant, fall over and drown in it.

IRENE: She was pretty, then?

COMIC: Because, you clod, men wearing boots or sandshoes all the time will contract tinea, and tinea spreads.

IRENE: I mean, she must have been.

ROBINSON: Oh, you know.

> *The* COMIC *exits.* LES *starts to mime walking in clogs.* IRENE *may have removed her shoes and he could be using one or both of them. The others chat on regardless.*

IRENE: She was a WAC?

ROBINSON: WAAF—Air Force.

IRENE: And you were in the Navy?

ROBINSON: Gave us something to talk about—the differences.

IRENE: When I met Les the War was over.

ROBINSON: Nineteen fifty, didn't you say?

IRENE: Forty-nine.

ROBINSON: By then it was all over bar a good bit of the shouting between Muriel and me—except there were the children to think of.

IRENE: Many?

ROBINSON: Four.

IRENE: You didn't muck round, did you, Herbert?

> LES *reaches the green pin spotlight. The other lights fade.*

LES: So every mug hobbled round on these bloody clogs for a month or so. Never learnt how to use 'em. Fell off the bastards regularly a hundred times. Came into contact with acres of contaminated Malayan soil. And refused to die. Every one of 'em. Refused to die a slow, lingering death or a fast, unlingering one, either from hook-bloody-worm or the Venus Demilo disease known to lavatory walls the world over as VD.

IRENE: [*in the darkness*] And what do you think you're doing, Les Harding?

LES: Eh? A dance, just doing a—

> *The green light fades out. The lights come up.* LES *walks back.*

Didn't that stripper have shithouse legs?

IRENE: I thought she'd come into the conversation somewhere.

LES: If she'd been a painting, though, you'd have to say she had a pretty classy frame, eh, Robbo, eh?

> ROBINSON *smiles unenthusiastically.*

Now if you was her I'd get you a drink, no worries.

IRENE: That just about sums up our relationship in a nutshell, Herbert.

LES: And chairs, any amount of 'em—though three'd probably do the trick.

IRENE: If I wasn't me, he'd approve.

LES: Three chairs. I'd lay you across—by you, I mean her—I'd lay you across 'em, rip off the last veil and give you one, eh Robbo, bit of alright, eh, she'd be, that stripper?

IRENE: Big talk for someone who lost the lead out of their pencil years ago.

LES: What'd he say her name was?

ROBINSON: Randy Stone.

LES: Randy Stone! Well, there's a name to fit the deed.

IRENE: If you want to know, I found the whole thing a bit distasteful.

LES: Did you now? And how about you, Captain?

ROBINSON: Well, a man does get past it, you know.

LES: Not me, boy. I'm like a good suit. I last forever.

IRENE: I've noticed.

LES: What d'you mean, you've—

He stands as the WAITER *crosses with a tray of drinks.*

There's that Jap waiter.

IRENE: He's not Japanese.

LES: Up ya slant eyes, you foreign devil.

The WAITER *exits without responding.*

IRENE: Sit down, Les!

He sits.

If you want to know, he's Malay.

LES: And I'm Gough Whitlam.

IRENE: His name's Puteh.

LES: That what it is, is it? What sort of a name's that? Puteh.

IRENE: [*with foreboding*] Please, Les—don't.

LES: Robinson is a man of culture, aren't you, Robbo? Always ready for a bit of a poem.

He stands.

> The waiter's name was Puteh,
> It's said he had a beauteh,
> I ran into him one night,

Holding it tight,
And saying, How about have a root, eh?

IRENE *glares at him.* ROBINSON *coughs.*

Not to your taste, Robbo? [*Seeing* IRENE*'s look*] Who are you staring daggers at?

IRENE: Les is a bit of a poet, Herbert, and wants us all to know it.

ROBINSON: Yes. We were playing billiards the other day when he held forth for my benefit.

IRENE: He's in great demand. Especially at the end of year works party. Recites 'Eskimo Nell'.

LES: I can do the straight stuff, don't worry.
There was movement at the station
For the word had got around
That the colt from Old Regret—

IRENE: Can it, Les.

LES: That's how I won her, you know.

IRENE: You're a worse bore than a white ant.

LES: You are dainty as a flower,
And with each passing hour—

ROBINSON: Can I get you another drink, Irene?

LES: Her name's Irene, by God she is a peach.

IRENE: Will you shut up?

ROBINSON: Can I get you both a drink?

IRENE: Yes, please, Herbert. [*Fossicking in her bag*] Oh, here, let me.

ROBINSON: No no—couldn't possibly.

She holds out some tickets. He refuses them and exits.

LES: I'll take those for after.

He tries to snatch them.

IRENE: You do that!

She hurls them at him.

LES: Here, what's eating you?

She says nothing.

Well, come on—out with it.

IRENE: What do you reckon?

A brief pause.

LES: How about tonight we—?

IRENE: No.

> *He shrugs and sets about picking up the tickets.*

LES: Bloke in my cabin says he and his missus get into one of the life-boats. Says it's alright up there. [*Pause.*] Be like that time we did it in the shelter shed at the North School. Ha! Got chased along the Ballarat Road by the caretaker. [*Pause.*] We'd been dancing, remember? At St Sebastian's. The silly old cow hurled a broom at me, remember? [*Pause.*] Alright—clam up.

> ROBINSON *returns with the drinks.*

Irene and I are just remembering a few shags we had in the old days, Robbo.

ROBINSON: [*embarrassed*] Oh, yes. Ha!

IRENE: [*thumping the table*] You're nothing but a—but a—

LES: An animal. You're nothing but an animal, Les Harding.

IRENE: You are.

ROBINSON: If you think I should go…?

IRENE: No, please.

LES: I'm not good enough for her these days, Robbo. Can't crack the jackpot.

IRENE: He's not always like this.

LES: What I need's a couple of plums in my gob like you, then I might stand a chance. The truth is I haven't been good enough for her for years.

IRENE: Jesus!

> *Long pause.*

ROBINSON: Enough ice, Irene?

IRENE: Yes.

ROBINSON: Good.

> *Long pause.*

LES: Particularly nasty weather.

ROBINSON: Pardon?

LES: Are you sure you want me to repeat it?

IRENE: Don't bother.

LES: *Tickle your arse with a feather.*

ROBINSON: Oh no, we've been lucky, considering—though it could get a bit blowy later.

LES: He says—

IRENE: I heard him.

LES: He says it could get a bit blowy later. I wouldn't mind a good blow.
Later.

IRENE: And I wish I could give it to you.

LES: Yeah?

IRENE: Yeah. To the head with a hammer.

LES: Now, now.

Pause.

ROBINSON: Getting back to Muriel—

LES: Muriel! I thought her name was Randy.

IRENE: We're talking about the late Mrs Robinson deceased, Les—that's
if you're capable of holding a civilised conversation.

LES: RIP. Rest In P—

ROBINSON: In all fairness to her, she did do a marvellous job with the
children.

IRENE: They can be a bit of a handful.

LES: Can't we all, haw haw!

IRENE: Especially four of them.

LES: Four cods?

IRENE: Kids!

ROBINSON: With me gone a lot of the time it can't have been easy for her.

LES: You're the one talking about handfuls.

ROBINSON: One's a doctor.

LES: He'll be raking it in.

IRENE: No thought of becoming a ship's doctor?

ROBINSON: Heavens, no.

IRENE: The doctor on board's a Paki, Les says.

ROBINSON: But he'd be British trained.

> *The green light slowly comes up on the* WAITER *as he starts piling
> chairs on a table top. He is dressed as a Japanese soldier.*

IRENE: That firm Marge worked in the office for, Les—that was British,
wasn't it?

LES: [*quietly*] There's that Jap again.

ROBINSON: Then there's Sarah. She's in the Bodleian at Oxford.

IRENE: That'd be nice.

ROBINSON: Roger, Sarah, Mark and Chocko.

IRENE: Chocko?

LES *rises stealthily and stalks towards the* WAITER.

ROBINSON: That's our family name for Elizabeth. From 'chocolate'. Used to gorge herself on them. No stopping her. Mark went off the rails for a time. Drove Muriel to distraction. Fortunately he straightened out. I say, Les old son—

He rises and starts after LES. *A crossfade leaves us with only the green light.*

LES: You yellow-bellied dwarf!

IRENE: Les!

LES *charges the* WAITER *and butts him with his head, which sends the* WAITER *flying. Melee and confusion, with lighting effects to match.*

LES: Ya dirty mongrel dingo bastard!

ROBINSON *grabs* LES.

WAITER: This man has been attacking me the whole voyage.

ROBINSON: I'm terribly sorry, old man, seems to think you're a Jap.

He leads LES *back to the table.* LES *is calm but bug-eyed, quiet but quietly mad.*

IRENE: I'm sorry, Puteh.

WAITER: Any breakages will be taken from my wages.

IRENE: Here. [*She dredges some money from her bag.*] I'm afraid Les is a little drunk.

WAITER: You should be telling him, madam—that jealousy is a curse.

He exits stiffly, disdainfully.

ROBINSON: He could do with a brandy, I think.

IRENE: What's got into you, Les?

LES: [*still in a daze*] You know who taught me every dirty poem I know?

IRENE: I think he should be in bed.

LES: Sharkie Raymond. You know what happened to him? He died. You know how he died? A Jap hit him in the side of the head with a sixteen-pound sledgehammer.

ROBINSON: I'll give you a hand with him.

LES: Do you know where he lies?

ROBINSON: Come on, old son.

They attempt to walk him out. He shrugs them aside.

LES: Konyu. And do you know how deep? A bloody foot. One lousy foot was as deep as they'd let us dig. And when it pissed down rain the soil washed away and you'd see arms and legs sticking up stiff as the day we—stiff as the day we—

He can't finish. They lead him off. Blackout.

SCENE FOUR: A LITTLE BIT OF THE SPECIMEN'S BRAIN

McLEOD *and the* WAITER *share the dippy bird speech as* LES *paces the cabin.*

WAITER: Tarawa, where four thousand five hundred Japanese resisted the Americans.

McLEOD: Burma, where three hundred and four POWs died for every mile of track laid.

LES: Sssh! Mustn't wake the others, McLeod, but can you keep this under your hat?

He looks about him.

WAITER: Tarawa, where only nineteen prisoners were taken. They were those too wounded to resist or those buried under the dead.

LES: I did damage tonight, son, real damage.

McLEOD: Three hundred and four corpses for every mile.

LES: The brave Japanese! Joke, McLeod, joke. All I did was breathe on the cunt and he went to water.

McLEOD *and the* WAITER *shift into less public, less statistical utterance.*

McLEOD: Duckworth set himself up as an expert. Knew all about it. After malaria you get cerebral malaria.

WAITER: Today the enemy planes flew overhead from early morning.

McLEOD: Duckworth got cerebral malaria.

LES: Not that I killed him.

McLEOD: Didn't know where he was.

WAITER: They hope to annihilate us by Christmas.

McLEOD: Thought it was a hot day at Bondi.

LES: I didn't kill him. Not yet.

McLEOD: Ran into the jungle and died at the bottom of a ravine.

LES: Just showed him what was what, that's all.

WAITER: The food for today: one sardine between five men, one handful of dried vegetables, two *go* of large beans, five *shaku* of rice.

McLEOD: Ten seconds to the bottom of the ravine—three days to climb out. We let the maggots have him.

> LES *stops pacing.*

LES: Stroke of luck, getting this, eh? A uniform, McLeod. Nearly complete. The boys'd like that.

WAITER: There has been much shelling and no place of safety.

McLEOD: You won't only get malaria, he said. You'll get ulcers, scabies, beri-beri, gingivitis, dysentery, vitaminosis.

LES: You'll tell 'em, won't you, McLeod?

WAITER: All the grass and roots have been eaten already.

McLEOD: You'll get conjunctivitis, dermatitis, colic debility.

LES: Les Harding doesn't scab on his mates, right!

WAITER: They plan to annihilate us by Christmas.

LES: Les Harding doesn't scab!

> *Blackout.*

SCENE FIVE: BREAKFAST, LATITUDE 30° LONGITUDE 143°

Breakfast chimes sound over the loudspeaker. Lights up on LES *and* IRENE *at the breakfast table. A teapot, two cups.*

IRENE: It's pulverised. The tea. Green tea pulverised into a powder. Then they whisk it with whisks and serve it—with, I might add having a look at your posture, sitting there like a poached egg on the wilt—with elaborate formality, in a small room. [*She drinks some tea and refers to a brochure.*] Thick, they serve it. So thick you can stand your whisk in it I suppose, ha ha, to make a little joke, Les, to make a little—'Course, you probably won't notice, but in Japan cooking's an art form. They don't just dump food on your plate higgledy-piggledy.

LES: No, they hang it on the wall like a picture.

IRENE: They do it like a flower arrangement. A bit of this and that.

LES: And never enough of either.

IRENE: Tastefully, that's how it's done, with an eye to the colour combinations, tastefully arranged in all sorts of bowls and cooked right there in front of you.

LES: I can hardly wait.

IRENE: Which worries me a bit, I mean, if it's cooked right there on the spot it'll all take time, won't it? We might want to be out drinking in the cherry blossom and Shinto shrines and the Yamaha piano factory far and away the largest in the world, not to mention the statue of the Great Buddha at wherever it is in gold leaf and green jade. [*She drinks.*] We've got a tight itinerary, after all.

LES: Tight—half your luck.

LOUDSPEAKER: Would anyone with fancy dress costumes still outstanding please return them to Mrs Hicks on C Deck.

IRENE: Catching those bullet trains might present a few problems with the language difficulties and whatnot.

LOUDSPEAKER: I repeat, there are still some fancy dress costumes outstanding. These should be returned to Mrs Hicks on C Deck between eleven and twelve this morning. Thank you.

IRENE: You took yours back, I suppose.

LES: I suppose I did.

IRENE: Either you did or you—

LES: I did.

IRENE: One hundred and twenty-five miles an hour they travel at, those trains, and you get pushed on by the bottom if you're not careful.

LES: An Australian, name of Les Harding
        Was packed on a train like a sarding…

IRENE: The children in the streets look like tiny porcelain dolls.

LES: His doctor, a Paki,
        Said not too much *sake*…

IRENE: Well, so the brochures say.

LES: But he drank all he could and died farding.

IRENE: Must get a slide of the Imperial Palace for Marge and Stan and a duty-free tape recorder. Sanyo's fairly reliable, isn't it, a fairly reliable brand? Or a National.

LES: What's wrong with an AWA, for Chrissakes!

IRENE: We didn't come all this way to buy what we could buy in our own backyard now, did we? Anyway, it's cheaper.

    He grunts moodily.

More tea? [*She pours him another cup.*] And please try and stay off it today. You're looking seedier and seedier.

Pause. He stands, picking up a knife.

LES: It was during this conversation that I secreted a knife on my person.

He goes. She stands.

IRENE: A short time after, I noticed that the nailfile was missing from my handbag.

She gathers up her bag and goes. Blackout.

LOUDSPEAKER: Last Night Out festivities at eight. A plea from the Entertainment Officer: Everyone up for our last night together. That's tonight at eight. Last Night Out festivities.

SCENE SIX: LISTEN TO THE BAND

Reveille is heard. Lights come up on the COMIC *playing a trumpet.* HARRY *is at the drums.*

COMIC: Recognise it? Reveille. What's a mug like me doing playing reveille to mugs like you? To get you up, right, to get you up—get the message, get the message. *On your bloody twinkle toes, the lot of you,* for an evening three-step, last night out—take it away, Harry.

They perform, for example, 'Slow Boat to China', the COMIC *singing,* HARRY *playing to a tape. Fairy lights perhaps.* IRENE *and* ROBINSON *dance. The song ends, they clap and head for the table.* LES *arrives with drinks.*

There'll be a short break now, ladies and gents, while Harry and I exit for a drop of amber Enos.

They go.

LES: Well! No flies on you two—no sooner do I shoot off for the fizzies than you're up and into it.

IRENE: Don't tell me Les Harding's jealous?

LES: Jealous? If I thought he'd take you off my hands I'd toss in a year's wages as dowry.

IRENE: I'm sure that'd hardly be enough to keep me and Herbert in the style to which he is accustomed.

LES: It's done us alright, hasn't it?

IRENE: Now if you two gentlemen'll excuse me—

LES: I'll go paint my horrible head. Why bother? [*As* IRENE *exits*] Ask 'em for a paper bag and I'll punch eyes in it for you.

ROBINSON: [*sitting*] One of these mine?

LES: Yeah, the one with arsenic.

ROBINSON: Cheers.

They drink.

She's quite a dancer.

LES: Mmm.

ROBINSON: You can't be too bad yourself.

LES: Yeah, I make Fred Astaire look like he's got corns.

ROBINSON: There's something about the old-time dancing.

LES: What do you reckon?

ROBINSON: I don't know—just something.

LES: Not the lovey-dovey, cheek-to-cheek stuff, I hope.

ROBINSON: At my age?

LES: With my wife! Poetry in motion—that'd be your line, eh, Robbo?

ROBINSON: I dare say you might be right.

LES: I dare say. You're a queer sort of a bloke, aren't you?

ROBINSON: Oh?

LES: And you wanta know something?

ROBINSON: What's that, old man?

LES: I don't trust you.

ROBINSON: Look. If it's about dancing with Irene—

LES: You've been sent, haven't you?

ROBINSON: I've been what?

LES: I should have got onto it sooner. A high-ranking officer teaming up with a nobody like me. That's no everyday occurrence, you know.

ROBINSON: I don't get you.

LES: You're keeping an eye on me, aren't you? Beer. When you're a Scotch and soda man from way back. No. Don't give me the runaround. I've seen you. That's what you drink when you're not keeping tabs on me.

ROBINSON: Which proves precisely what?

LES: You're still in the Service. Not retired at all. That's all front, the retired bit. You've been sent.

ROBINSON: Don't be bloody pathetic.

LES: That first night out when I was spewing me heart on the waters— who'd come up and make friends with a bloke who was vomit from toecaps to tossle?

ROBINSON: I thought I'd offer a bit of advice.

LES: The RSL keeping an eye on its members, is it? Because they happen to be going to Japan?

ROBINSON: Either you're drunk—

LES: Cool, calm and collected, mate.

ROBINSON: —or off your head.

LES: As the light of day.

ROBINSON: That or the malaria coming back.

LES: I can see through you like a ghost, don't worry.

ROBINSON: And I'm Chief of Naval Intelligence, am I? It's 1944 and you're a coast watcher gone over to the other side.

LES: I dunno what you are, mate, I dunno what you are—but you're wasting your time 'cause Les Harding doesn't scab on his mates. You can tell 'em that—*Les Harding doesn't scab.*

ROBINSON: I think I better go. Say goodnight to Irene for me.

LES: Yeah, go on, go. Make your report, you Pommy officer bastard.

ROBINSON leaves. The COMIC returns with trumpet to do a Satchmo.

Off to the radio room.

COMIC: Dig, man. Here comes 'Mack the Knife'.

LES: Semaphore—flashing bloody mirrors.

The COMIC sings the first verse of 'Mack the Knife'. He rubs fingers over lips and does a mock Satchmo scat. He stops to mop his brow and drain spit from the trumpet into a handy glass.

LOUDSPEAKER: Passengers are reminded that they must have filled in their disembarkation cards and handed these, together with their passports, to the purser by ten tomorrow morning.

The COMIC continues his song.

LES: [*standing*] It wasn't my idea!

IRENE: [*returning*] What wasn't?

LES: This trip!

IRENE: This trip? We're having a lovely time. Where's Herbert?

LOUDSPEAKER: [*over the trumpet*] On berthing in Yokohama, passengers' luggage will be found on D Deck near the snack bar.

A foghorn sounds, along with the trumpet and singing.

LES: It wasn't my idea!

Blackout.

SCENE SEVEN: ALONE AM I

We hear a nailfile grating on a knife. The green spotlight comes up on McLEOD. *In the spill we see* LES *on his bunk, dressed in singlet and trousers, sharpening the knife.*

LES: The first one I see, McLeod. The first one. [*Pause.*] They didn't discriminate, did they—so why should I? [*Pause.*] I tell you, McLeod, I'll be down that gangway and right into it. They won't know [*testing the blade*] what hit 'em. [*He puts the knife down, stands and goes to the handbasin. He picks up a toothbrush.*] Smiling I'll be, a white, cheesy grin. [*Cleaning his teeth*] Remember how we used to clean our fangs, McLeod? Finger. With some crushed charcoal. [*Holding up the toothbrush*] This—nobody thinks twice about having one. Takes it for granted. And razor blades. Rare as hens with dentures. Now. Fair dinkum, McLeod... [*gargling*] it's like there'd never been a war on. [*He gets the uniform jacket from under his mattress.*] Two hours, son. Yokohama. When I come down the steps it'll be like this... [*He slips it on and buttons it up.*] That'll put the wind up 'em. Shirt. Forgot the shirt and tie. [*He finds them.*] Kim Foley, Ernie King, Ted Gamble. In captivity, McLeod, dead in bloody captivity. Beaten shitless, starved, diseased—bloody skeletons—so bloody light you could toss 'em round like feathers— five and six stone. There's a bit of equalising called for, I tell you, and I'm it—I'll let the bastards know a thing or two, see if I don't. [*Pause as he finishes dressing.*] Sat on it, McLeod—I've sat on it thirty years. Burns a man up inside. There's a lot of forget in me but not much forgive. The first one, I tell you. He's gone. And as many as I can get after him and that's a bloody promise. Sharkie. Hit on the head for a bit of sport, for a bit of bloody—and you, McLeod.

McLEOD: Dead.

LES: Gavin McLeod. Dead.

McLEOD: D.E.

LES: A.D.

      LES *comes to attention, then stabs forward with the knife, bayonet-fashion. Blackout.*

SCENE EIGHT: YOKOHAMA BLUES

A foghorn blares shorts and longs. Confusion. The SHIP'S OFFICER *is heard screeching.*

OFFICER: Don't *panic*. Please, there's no need to—No, madam, nothing's happened. Just hurry along, that's the spirit. Will you all stop *panicking*. No, no. Hurry along, please, just organise your luggage and—don't *panic*. No, sir, no, a man has not tried to kill anyone, so just hurry along and don't—

> *A light comes up on* IRENE. *She sits on a suitcase. Around her is a scatter of cabin trunks and cases.* ROBINSON *approaches.*

ROBINSON: I've ordered some tea.

IRENE: What are they doing to him?

ROBINSON: I can't say. He's… below.

IRENE: Why? He never so much as mentioned it—never.

ROBINSON: Sometimes that's the way it happens.

IRENE: But why? Why didn't I know?

ROBINSON: You can't blame yourself.

IRENE: I didn't think. I mean Stan and Marge just gave us the tickets. An anniversary present. The tickets and the suitcases. He could have said something then, but he didn't.

ROBINSON: I wouldn't worry. He'll pull through alright.

IRENE: He wanted us to take the old ones. He thought the new ones might get knocked off.

ROBINSON: The suitcases?

IRENE: I've never seen him like that before.

ROBINSON: Fortunate he didn't do himself an injury.

IRENE: The knife. He could have stabbed someone. God knows where that came from.

ROBINSON: It was touch and go there for a moment.

IRENE: If only I'd have known.

ROBINSON: You couldn't have known—no-one could have.

IRENE: I should have remembered.

ROBINSON: I don't think even he had any inkling.

IRENE: I should have said, No, we won't go, we'll go to Suva instead, or Bali. [*Pause.*] We'll fly home, won't we—they'll let me take him home?

ROBINSON: Sure to. Probably exchange the tickets.

IRENE: What did they think he was, a tourist attraction? I don't know how they can. Did you see them?

ROBINSON: I'll see if the tea's coming, shall I?

IRENE: No, please—

ROBINSON: Of course.

He sits again.

IRENE: Taking photos. What did they think he was—?

ROBINSON: Ar—

He gets up as the WAITER *approaches with tea.*

IRENE: He never let me know.

Blackout.

SCENE NINE: DRUM POEM TWO

Green light comes up on LES *in a strait jacket, locked in his cabin.* HARRY—*and maybe others—thread percussive effects through* LES's *gigantic word stream.*

LES: Went like a dream, McLeod. Seven yellow fuckers in one blow. Blood all over the joint. Yabber yabber. The babble of foreign tongues. Scared shitless they were. Knees like Aeroplane Jelly. Les Harding drives a hard bargain, McLeod. Through the gut. Drives it. Through the foreign gut like carving Sunday dinner, Sunday at home. (When'll we ever get back, and how many of us?) Twenty to hold me down and add another ten to that to cart me off. I can't tell you how good it felt. And singing the 'Maori's Farewell'—which old Shark taught me, like much else—something we Anzacs sing by tradition on leaving the country and I never had a son to teach it to (only managed a daughter and that a fluke after what…) to teach it to like it was taught to me by word of mouth—that's something he opened my eyes to. Les, he says:

A comely young widow named Ransom
Was ravished three times in a hansom;
When she cried out for more
A voice from the floor
Said, Lady, I'm Simpson not Samson.

Two hundred years, he says, if it's a day, word of mouth, one hundred years old if it's a day, fair dinkum word of honour, do you see what I'm driving at, I can't tell you how good it felt.

He suddenly changes position and has faint glimmers of his situation.

What's all this for, McLeod? Eh? What?

He discovers the limiting effects of the strait jacket and goes into a rage. He ends up kneeling.

Water! [*Shouting*] Iwantsomewater, Iwantsomewater, Iwantsome...

It becomes a chant, then falls away. He slumps against the bunk. Silence.

Craigee? You awake, Craigee? What d'you reckon—we'll ever get out of this one, eh? What d'you—? [*Pause.*] Hey, Sharkie, Shark—

It was on the good ship Venus,
By God you should have seen us,
The figurehead was a nude in bed
Sucking a red-hot—

Pause.

Penis.

He launches himself into a mad twirl, clutching his stomach.

Acute appendicitis. I was lucky. They still had some anaesthetic. I came to in the hospital compound. They were all dying there. You could tell that. None of 'em would eat. An English boy was taking weeks to die. Maybe that was Jimmy. He had eyes you couldn't look into. Trembled whenever he heard a Jap voice. I was the only one recovering. Eighteen and he'd seen the lot. I watched a blowfly crawl out of his arse. Slowly. All the time in the world. And he lay there in a coma with his mouth open and another one crawled out his mouth. Along his tongue. Feeding on him. I told 'em all to eat. Eat like the Jesus. Just rice. They couldn't hold anything down. Bring it near them, they'd chuck. Chuck nothing. Pus and bad air. The sweet stench of—I made myself eat. No matter what. And the bloke next to me gurgled a bit, twitched a bit, wheezed—I kept eating. I took a look and kept eating. He'd died. I turned over and ate. And later I took his boots. I had none. I took his...

He speaks more slowly, more consciously.

Boots, McLeod, boots were a racket—and you reckon we were better than they were. Fifteen hours a day on hot rock as sharp as shit, barefoot, and the bloody criminal element sitting on two and three pairs—the criminal element and officers—and you reckon we were better than they were. We were disgusting. Kaley—cunts come in all colours—at Changi, Kaley'd buy your stools from you if you had dysentery. Buy 'em. Whinge his way into hospital. Say they were his. Anything for the sweet cop. That officer—a bag of peas and two bags of sugar that didn't get to us. They had batmen! Jokers being turned out of their beds—down with dysentery, beri-beri, couldn't beat a lame goose in the egg and spoon, skinny as all shit, would not cast a shadow at sunset—turned out for work parties for a clean shirt and someone to put sugar in their tea. Fifteen hours a day in heat like hell. That's right—they had it—sugar. And three eggs to our one! And fish. And more meat in a sitting than you or I saw in a month! What do I know? I know there's more than one way to make a cunt of yourself, that's what I know—eyes you couldn't look into.

Another change of pace and tone.

And he told us about it once, one
hundred and thirty-four of the wounded they couldn't
carry when the retreat started from Parit Sulong,
so they waited for the Japs
and the Japs just tied 'em up,
knelt 'em in the middle of the road and machine-gunned the lot,
and Jimmy just got it through the chest,
lived,
and his mate lived too,
and Jimmy was lying on top of him and telling him to keep
still but he wouldn't, the pain was too much,
and the Japs saw him moving and threw Jimmy off him into the
    stormwater ditch
and shot shit out of his mate,
and he lay there watching the Japs bayonet anything that moved
but even then a couple lived,
and then they got out the petrol and doused the corpses and you could
    hear the wounded

doggo experts
pleading to be shot or slit, anything but that,
and they lit the whole heap
and when the flames died down they drove over the
remains in trucks, backwards and forwards, making sure,
and he lay there in the ditch under some weeds
and got his eyes you couldn't look into,
and when they stamped out singing their songs he lay there,
couldn't move,
shocked out of his tiny,
and the moon rose,
moonlight on the road with nothing moving, nothing
moving
just the smell of burnt flesh
and then out of the jungle
later
there's this stream of wild pigs
and dogs
at one with each other, allies,
and they started eating, started…
eighteen,
eighteen, just a boy…
at eighteen the worst thing I could have remembered
happening was not eating two days in a row,
trow that always had holes in
and being sent out every morning before it got light
down to Dynon with my handcart
ten years old
to get what I could get 'cause there was no work,
and once we got evicted so we went down four doors and
broke into this place where a bloke had gone west with
his wife and kids,
and lived there,
and everyone gave us a hand,
and after it was round to Tiger Sutton's,
the old man was always round to Tiger Sutton's
washhouse,
always a brew in the bathtub,

and everyone got pissed,
and no landlord would have got out alive,
and that was alright except the old man got snaky
and hit the old lady one across the mouth the...

He returns to his first manner.

Mouth. The lower half of his face was shot away. They'd stitched his tongue to his shirt. Stop him from swallowing it. Needle and thread. Stitched with—And another had a point five anti-tank bullet in his gob. Between teeth and jaw. The blood and pus. These were blokes you talked to. Lied to. How do I look—no mirrors at Pudu—How do I look, I just got engaged, see. As beautiful as ever. That's good. You see, I just got engaged. You see, I'm going with this girl.

There was a young girl from Cape Cod, said Sharkie,
Who thought babies were fashioned by God, said Sharkie,
It was not the Almighty, said Sharkie,
Who hiked up her nightie, said Sharkie,
'Twas Roger the lodger, the dog, said Sharkie.

The Dutch East Indies, says Duckworth. Chief source of the world's quinine. The Dutch East Indies, he says, chief source of the world's quinine, have been overrun by the Japs. The Japs, says Duckworth, have enough quinine for nine hundred and ninety years. *Ashita*, say the Japs, tomorrow—*ashita*. Except *ashita* never came. After malaria you get cerebral malaria. Duckworth got cerebral malaria. Didn't know where he was. Ran into the jungle. Thought it was a hot day at Bondi. Ran into the jungle and died at the bottom of a ravine. We let the maggots have him. Ten seconds to get to the bottom, three days to climb out. Ravines steeper than the prices at Maxim's. *Mother Becton*. McIntosh had a copy. The most thumbed book in camp. Recipes like poems. Melt one tablespoon of olive oil. Peel and quarter the tomatoes. Mix with the chopped onion, carrot, celery, liver, ham and tongue. Beat the slices of veal until they are very thin. Add the marsala. Pound the anchovies. Trim the fat and gristle. Halve the peaches. Score the chestnuts. Roll and tie and put and pour and melt, arrange and serve—

A shift of manner.

Years of it. That's what you can look forward to, says Duckworth—what was he? St John's or something, Medical Corps. Vitamin B tablets. Easiest thing in the world to manufacture. The Japs have got billions. I never asked, easiest thing in the world to manufacture. Since they won't give us any, says Duckworth. Starts with a faint discomfort. Since we live on a rice diet, he says. Leads to chafing, the skin round the scrotum splits, peels, chafes. Since they won't even give us the rice polishings they throw away, says Duckworth, a spoonful per day, even that would be a valuable source, he says, of vitamin B. Spreads to the inner thighs. Rice balls, says Duckworth, that's its name. And you can look forward to years of it.

He moves about restlessly.

Thirty seconds and I'd be thirty yards behind the others. Beri-beri. Slows you down. Swells you up. My toes stuck out like purple teats on a goat's udder. Slosh slosh. When they saw me coming, the Nip guards'd draw a cross on the ground. You'll be dead tomorrow. *Ashita mati mati.* Up your arses, you lumps of lard. The beri-beri fluids sloshing round my chest cavity. Legs like purple balloons. Chest like a milk can rattling on the back of a truck. They'd mime a man drowning. Up your arses, you lumps of lard. Up you… [*Pause.*] You always checked your shit. Read it for signs. [*Pause.*] It was during this conversation that I secreted a knife on my person.

He sits on the edge of the bunk. The WAITER *(as Captain of the Dippy Birds) sets up the fourth and last dippy bird, threading his spiel through some of the following. He also places the four dippy birds in position—one in each corner of* LES's *cabin. They nod away in perpetual insanity. Still seated,* LES *composes.*

> There was a young fool from Dimboola
> Who spent a long month in the cooler,
> Under cover of dark
> In Victoria Park
> He'd been measuring his tool with a ruler.

Pause. He recites with great serenity.

> Bob Menzies stood up for Australia,
> He'd painted his arse like a dahlia,
> The colour was fine,
> Likewise the design,
> The aroma—ah, that was a failure.

Pause.

The sweet stench of gangrene.

Pause.

Orderly, the boat—too late, mate, bring the shovel. If two hundred men, McLeod, evacuate forty times a day and there are only two orderlies with half a dozen bamboo bedpans to cope with the day's eight thousand calls, what are you up to your ankles in by five o'clock?

Pause. He stands and steps forward.

This urinal was built by Bob Fox, and we call it Bob Fox's piccolo. A pleasure to piss into. A twenty-four-foot length of bamboo, the bulkheads cut away, holes between the divisions, two forked sticks to support it, one higher, one lower, the slight angle being for drainage purposes. Bob Fox's piccolo, and fifteen men can play it at once. A pleasure to...

And the onlookers tell how Eskimo Nell
Lay smiling and aloof,
With the strength of ten in her abdomen
And a vault that was bulletproof.

She could take a jet (and not get wet)
Like the flush of a water closet,
And she gripped his cock like the forged-steel lock
On the National Safe Deposit.

Now Red-Eye Dick could not come quick,
He planned to reserve his powers.
He had it in mind to grind and grind
For at least a couple of hours.

But she lay for a while with that subtle smile,
Then her vice-like grip grew keener,
With a gentle sigh she just sucked him dry
With the ease of a vacuum cleaner.
With a gentle sigh—with the ease of a vacuum cleaner.

He suddenly changes tone.

Jesus Christ, McLeod, *what are they fucking doing to me?!*

He seems screwed up with pain. He speaks in a rush.

One bloke—photos were rare—had a dirty scrap of paper and he comes up and shows me. Little Jan, it's got written on it. And below that, Little Billy. Nice kids, eh, he says. Hey, mate. Nice kids! Jesus! This is the middle of the night. Give us a hand. You look up. Somebody's hung themselves from a crossbeam. Better off out of it. Better off out of it. Otto was off his brain. Maybe he wasn't. It's just a scrap of dirty paper. What's the use, he yells. He's in hospital by this. And he rips the drip out. Tears it out. But they calm him down and reckon he's mad and rig the drip up again, saving his life. I won't go crook no more, he says. Started out a thirteen-stone brute. He's seen the light, they reckon. Then in the night he quietly pulls it out again. A rugby player. Wasn't twenty— wasn't twenty years old—when they shovelled dirt on a five-stone skeleton. Jesus, McLeod, what are they fucking doing to me?! What are they fucking...? Three hundred and four corpses for every mile of track.

He calms down, changing to considered, factual delivery.

Eighteen different diseases at once. Ulcers was one, scabies: two, beri-beri: three, malaria—what are they doing to me, McLeod?—four, dysentery: five, gingivitis—McLeod, McLeod—six, vitaminosis: seven, conjunctivitis: eight—I'm on holiday, McLeod, just on— colic: nine, debility: ten, dermatitis: eleven, something: twelve, something: thirteen, something: fourteen, something: fifteen—I had eighteen, McLeod, at once—eighteen something, eighteen something, seventeen something, sixteen something, fifteen—How many started with D? Dermatitis, debility, dysentery, D, D, D... What are they up to, I'm on holiday, I'm on—It was during this conversation that I secreted a knife on my person.

Pause.

Konyu, Chungkai, Tampie, Tarsau, Hintok, Hin—
    A prisoner of war from Hintok
    Was famed for the length of his cock,
    The granite was hard,
    And one day the guard
    Made him drill himself into a rock.
—into a—Tamarkan, Kanburi, Kinsayok, Tamuan. Six stone seven. I felt like a new man. What you up to, Parky? Sssh. Come on, come

on, what are you up to? Sssh. The prick's made a rag doll—ssh—looks like Battlegong. He's off his head. Sssh. Eh, Parky—he's sticking slivers of bamboo into it. In the really bad time, jokers would collapse on the latrine and fall in—at least one of 'em drowned—too weak to scream. You missed half of it, McLeod.

From the bandstand, HARRY *begins to counterpoint* LES's *monologue.*

HARRY: Les Harding is still in Larundel.

LES: The best half—the last half.

HARRY: Couldn't handle it.

LES: When it was all over the Japs painted a sign on the roof: 'PW Camp 21—608 Men'. You know what that's for, said Bubbles, so they'll know how many blondes to drop.

HARRY: It's not that human beings cannot bear too much reality. It's that reality is too much to bear.

LES: The Americans flew over. It started raining fruit salad and vitamins. Crates of chocolate, tinned meat…

HARRY: It's one thing to say human beings are not fit for this world—and another to say this world is not fit for human beings.

LES: November the second. Melbourne Cup Day. We ran the Siam Sweepstakes. Official placings: Starvation first, Bludger second, *Benjo* third.

HARRY: The point is not to suffer the world but to change it.

LES *is trapped among the dippy birds, thinking, perhaps, that* McLEOD *is one of them;* HARRY *and the others speak from the bandstand, maybe sharing the lines. Percussion, flutes under.*

LES: He made me stand there holding up his rain-sheet to dry. They'd just marched in from down the line and were going further. Two-star Corporal Yomito. I stood there swaying.

HARRY: When an airliner crashes there is wreckage strewn on either side for a mile. We are all human wreckage and there is not one place on this earth we have not walked.

LES: It caught fire. I was out of my mind from the beri-beri. Slowed right down. He saw it before I did and kicked me into the flames, snatching the sheet from me. I lay there, hardly moving. His boot had left a hole in my swollen leg. I didn't feel the fire burning into the flesh. Just heard distant sizzling as the fluids escaped.

HARRY: Les Harding couldn't handle it. It all comes back.

LES: They scraped me out—potatoes out of the embers. I stood there swaying as he rained blows on me. I didn't feel a thing. In the corner a bottle of vitamin B tablets poked from the top of his pack—danced like palm trees in a mirage—flowers on a cloud—

HARRY: They gather samples, investigate the parts, scrape metals, discover where the fault lies: crashes have causes. All crashes have causes.

LES: I walked in a dream—the ghost of a shoplifter in Myers haunting the scene of the crime—time had stopped for everyone but me. When they left that night two-star Corporal Yomito lacked his vitamin B supply. I lived in a floating world.

HARRY: We are wreckage strewn across a planet—evidence of some monstrous crime against ourselves.

LES: I sat up all night eating them.

HARRY: The century of disasters.

LES: The gait and limbs of an elephant.

HARRY: Les Harding took the 1974 *Women's Weekly* Cherry Blossom Cruise.

LES: Then it happened.

HARRY: He couldn't handle it.

LES: I dragged myself to the latrine and pissed solid for ten minutes.

HARRY: The 1974 *Women's Weekly* Cherry Blossom Cruise.

LES: I stayed there. I played Bob Fox's piccolo for two and a half days.

HARRY: The 1974 *Women's Weekly* Cherry Blossom Cruise.

LES: I started to empty out—first the chest, then the thighs—I had thighs like a human being again.

HARRY: The 1974 *Women's Weekly* Cherry Blossom Cruise.

He continues the chant under LES*'s voice.*

LES: Knees the size of footballs to knees the size of knees. A new man. I was well again. A skeleton. Six stone seven. I can't tell you how good it felt. I was well again! A new man! I was well again.

We leave LES *to his institutionalised future.*

THE END

NOTES AND GLOSSARY

The author made use of a number of written sources in researching material for *The Floating World*, noteworthy among them being Ray Parkin's *The Sword and the Blossom* (London, The Hogarth Press: 1968) and Russell Braddon's *The Naked Island* (London, Laurie: 1966). *A Treasury of Anzac Humour*, ed. Roger Fair (Brisbane, Jacaranda Press: 1965) also proved useful.

Aeroplane Jelly, a brand of jelly crystals whose advertising jingle has achieved the status of a family favourite with many Australians.

AIF, the Australian Imperial Force. The First AIF was a special volunteer force formed for overseas service in World War I. It was re-formed as the Second AIF for service in World War II.

Amberley, Royal Australian Air Force base, Queensland; the home base of the F-111 aircraft.

Ascot Vale, a Melbourne racecourse.

benjo benjo (Japanese), to excrete.

biyoke (Japanese), ill.

Changi Gaol, the major Singapore gaol, on the north-east tip of the island, used by the Japanese for prisoners of war after the fall of Singapore in 1942.

Chungkai, a construction camp in the southern section of the Burma-Thailand railway.

Collins Street, Melbourne's most fashionable central city street.

dags, sheep droppings that cling to the fleece.

Digger, a form of address derived from the camaraderie of servicemen returning from the trench warfare of World War I. In World War II it came to mean an Australian soldier.

Dromana, a holiday resort on the eastern side of Port Phillip Bay.

Dynon, a railway freight yard, Melbourne.

Gallipoli, Australia's first major military encounter: the battle at Anzac Cove in the Dardanelles in 1915 between the Australian and New Zealand Army Corps and the Turkish forces.

Gemas, a Malay town on the main road running south-east to Johore, where General Gordon Bennett, commanding the Australian Division, established a defence position in 1942. In a two-day battle in January 1942 following close on the defeat at Slim River (q.v.) the Australian 2/30th Battalion repulsed the Japanese forces thrusting south to the headquarters of the Australian Division in Johore, defending Singapore. It did much to revive morale at a difficult time and raise hopes that the Japanese advance had been halted.

gibber, a type of stone found in the desert.

Herbert Adams, a brand of meat pie sold in Victoria.

Hintok, a primitive river camp halfway along the Burma-Thailand railway, the site of the Pack-of-Cards Bridge constructed by prisoners from green timber and bamboo: so named because it collapsed three times under construction in 1943. Two thousand prisoners and coolies built it in 17 days; 31 men were killed in falls from the bridge and 29 were beaten to death there. The survivors suffered a severe cholera outbreak at the Hintok camp.

Kanburi, the southern end of the Burma-Thailand railway.

Kinsayok, a camp on high ground north of Hintok on the Burma-Thailand railway.

Kokoda Trail, a 240-kilometre mountain track crossing the Owen Stanley Range in Papua and reaching a height of over 1,800 metres. In August 1942 Japanese forces began an attack on Port Moresby from the landward across the Trail but were held by Australian forces who in November 1942 began the offensive by pushing the enemy back over this high, wet, forested terrain.

Kota Baru, a town on the Kelantan River in north-eastern Malaya near the Thai border, possessing an airfield; the site of the Japanese landing in December 1941.

Konyu, a river camp south of Hintok on the Burma-Thailand railway which suffered a high mortality from malaria, dysentery and cholera.

Larundel, Larundel Mental Hospital, Melbourne.

MacArthur, General, Commander of the US Forces in the Far East during World War II; he was created Supreme Commander for the Allied Powers in order that he might undertake the signature of the Japanese surrender in Tokyo Bay, 2nd September 1945.

Mascot, Sydney's Kingsford Smith Airport.

Mersing, a town on the east coast of Malaya where General Bennett set up defences in 1941 for the trunk road and railway between the north-east and Australian Division headquarters in Johore.

Mo, **Roy Rene**, known on stage as Mo McCacky; Australia's most famous vaudevillian between the 1920s and the 1940s.

Moonee Ponds, a lower middle-class suburb of Melbourne, made famous by the comedian Barry Humphries as the home of Edna Everage.

Myers, Melbourne's largest department store.

Queenscliff, a holiday resort on the western side of Port Phillip Bay.

ready-mix truck, a truck carrying cement ready to pour.

ridge, **ridgy-didge**, true, right (possibly from a facetious pronunciation of 'right' as 'ridge-it').

Slim River, a river on the west coast of Malaya which forms the border between Perak and Selangor. In January 1942 the Japanese invasion from the north culminated in the Battle of Slim River, in which its bridge was defended by the Combined Surreys and Leicesters, the Argylls, the Ghurkha Rifles and the Australians. Their failure to stop the advance was a bitter blow, alleviated a few days later by the repulse at Gemas (q.v.).

smash and grab, rhyming slang for scab, one who betrays his fellows.

Sorrento, a holiday resort on the eastern side of Port Phillip Bay.

Straits of Johore, the narrow sea passage between Singapore and Johore Bahru, the adjacent tip of Malaya; here the thin defence line in 1942 between Singapore and the invading Japanese forces.

sweet cop, a sinecure.

TAB, Totalisator Agency Board, a chain of State-established off-course betting shops.

Tamarkan, a construction camp on the Burma-Thailand border, on the Burma-Thailand railway.

Tampie, a camp established in 1943 south of Konyu on the Burma-Thailand railway.

Tamuan, a prison camp and hospital in Thailand just south of Kanburi on the Burma-Thailand railway.

Tarsau, a construction camp on the Burma-Thailand railway where a hospital was established.

Trocadero, a popular Melbourne dance hall.

Velvet, an old-established brand of household soap.

Women's Weekly, Australia's most popular illustrated women's magazine. One of its features is a cut-price world cruise offered annually to its readers, the *Women's Weekly* World Discovery Tour.

Jonah

BASED ON THE NOVEL BY LOUIS STONE

MUSIC BY ALAN JOHN

BOOK AND LYRICS BY JOHN ROMERIL

Diane Smith as Pinky Partridge, Peter Carroll as Mr Packard, Michele
Fawdon as Clara Grimes, Alan David Lee as Arthur 'Chook' Fowles,
Valerie Bader as Miss Giltinan, Simon Burke as Jonah Jones,
Geraldine Turner as Mrs Yabsley, Wayne Scott Kermond as 'Waxy'
Collins and Lynne Emanuel as Ada Yabsley in the 1985 Sydney
Theatre Company production of *Jonah Jones*. (Photo: Brett Hilder)

Jonah was commissioned and first produced under the title *Jonah Jones* by the Sydney Theatre Company at the Wharf Theatre, Sydney, on 26 October 1985, with the following cast:

JONAH JONES	Simon Burke
MRS YABSLEY	Geraldine Turner
ADA YABSLEY	Lynne Emanuel
PINKY PARTRIDGE	Diane Smith
ARTHUR 'CHOOK' FOWLES	Alan David Lee
'WAXY' COLLINS	Wayne Scott Kermond
CLARA GRIMES	Michele Fawdon
HANS PASCH	Tony Taylor
MR PACKARD	Peter Carroll
MISS GILTINAN	Valerie Bader
FROGGY / PARSONS / MODEL / ARNOLD / MR HUTCHIN	Tony Taylor
CONSTABLE CASSIDY / MR PARTRIDGE	Peter Carroll
MRS BOLAN / MRS WATKINS	Valerie Bader

Director, Richard Wherrett
Assistant Director, Wayne Harrison
Musical Director, Michael Tyack
Musical Staging, Ross Coleman
Designer, Roger Kirk
Lighting Designer, Nigel Levings
Sound Designer, Colin Ford

A second production by the State Theatre Company of South Australia was directed by Neil Armfield. In 1991, the ABC recorded live (and put to air) Neil Armfield's STCSA production as an audio cassette featuring all of the numbers and some linking dialogue. Both productions employed great Australian actors. Louis Stone's novel *Jonah* was first published in 1911. It is set in the inner suburbs of pre-World War One Sydney. This musical version ends with that war being declared.

JR

CHARACTERS

JONAH, the benighted hunchback hero of the piece

ADA, the girl he gets pregnant, and whom he marries

YABSLEY, her mother, the matriarch of Cardigan Street

PASCH, an immigrant bootmaker who employs Jonah but lives to rue the day

CHOOK, a mate of Jonah's who falls in love with

PINKEY, a friend of Ada's (new to the area when the story starts, she and Chook will get by in the fruit and vegetable trade)

WAXY, a member of Jonah's push who later does jail

Other notable characters:

PACKER, a Boot King who refuses to employ Jonah but is finally bought out by him when Jonah adds production to retailing activity

MRS BOLAN, who runs a ladies only bar, frequented by Ada

CLARA, who teaches piano, plays organ at the dual wedding of Jonah to Ada, Pinkey to Chook, and who Jonah does a line for

GILTINAN, works at The Silver Shoe and ends up partnering Jonah

Minor characters:

Pinkey's father MR PARTRIDGE, CANON VAUGHAN who weds the couples (Jo and Ada, Pinkey and Chook), CASSIDY, a policeman who arrests Waxy, the wife of Bob Watkins. It's assumed these roles are doubled by the actors; or drawn from amongst the musicians. Ray, child of the Ada-Jonah liaison, is an unseen but not insignificant influence.

If the presence and choric oomph of a much larger cast is feasible, ample pretexts for employing them are implicit in the script.

SETTING

Multi-locational. There are street scenes; shop scenes; scenes set at Circular Quay; a factory scene; a Paddy's Market scene; a recruiting rally. Jonah's Silver Shoe Emporium is a major location. Cremorne Point likewise.

PART ONE

SCENE ONE

A tableau of Sydney street life in 1905.

MRS YABSLEY *enters, pushing a pram, and slowly the figures in the tableau become animate.*

YABSLEY: Here's a riddle for you:
　　I'm a daughter with a mother, and a mother,
　　And I'm the mother of a mother all in one…
CHORUS: How come?
YABSLEY: I'm a daughter to my mother,
　　But a mother to a mother,
　　'Cause my daughter's recently become
　　The mother of a son!

> JONAH *enters, carrying a wine bottle and wearing a cobbler's apron. He is on an errand. He is caught staring at the pram.*

Like it? One of me well-to-do customers give me the pram after hearing of my daughter's predicament. S'pose you're all wondering—has the kid got a hunch like his father?

> *She pulls back the hood of the pram.*

JONAH: Shirts and sheets? A cauliflower?
YABSLEY: I'm doing me deliveries. And the shopping, the kid's elsewhere.

> *The* CHORUS *enjoys the humour of this. His malevolence evident, bottle in hand,* JONAH *silences them in song.*

JONAH: [*sung*] Kid's a bastard, I'm a bastard
　　　　Nothing like the bastard from the bush
　　　　A city bastard, the Bastard King
　　　　Of the Botany Road Push!
YABSLEY: If you think Jonah's out of the Bible think again
JONAH:　I'm not!
YABSLEY: If you think Jonah's out of the Bible
　　　　You're liable to be in for a shock
CHORUS: (You're liable to be in for a shock)

JONAH: Noah wouldn't park
          Me in his ark
YABSLEY: He's a nightmare by day
JONAH: I'm a devil after dark!
YABSLEY: One of those faces
CHORUS: (If you think Jonah's outta the Bible)
YABSLEY: A mixture of races
CHORUS: (If you think Jonah's outta the Bible)
YABSLEY: Is that a trace of the Yid?
CHORUS: (You're liable to be in for a shock)
JONAH: A street Arab, as a kid!
YABSLEY: Or is there a touch of the tar?
JONAH: Tah for what? Night I was born it was into a shoebox and dumped
    at Redfern railway station.
          [*Sung*] Kid's a bastard, I'm a bastard
          Nothing like the bastard from the bush
          A city bastard, the Bastard King
          Of the Botany Road Push!
    She's planning to take me to court! I got you pegged.
YABSLEY: Pegged wrong! Take you to court? Why bother? You don't
    earn enough mending shoes part-time for Pasch to keep yourself in
    beer and cigarettes, let alone a wife and kid. 'Course if smoking,
    drinking, spitting and swearing was hard work, he'd die a rich man!
JONAH: Who fathered me's what I want to know!
YABSLEY: You were born out of Wedlock and Misery Guts—two nags
    that never yet won a race!

        YABSLEY *exits with her pram.*

        JONAH *back-pedals through the* CHORUS *to the rear.*

CHORUS: [*sung*] Jonah didn't live in no whale
          Jonah didn't live in no whale
JONAH: No fear
CHORUS: Jonah lived in Sydney
          Didn't he?
JONAH: Too right
CHORUS: And it's a Sydney Sat'day
          Sydney Sat'day
          Sydney Sat'day night!

The street scene becomes a gloomy interior.

PASCH *is in his shop with* CLARA, *a customer.*

PASCH: A singer. I always wanted to be a singer.
> '*In einem bachlein helle, da schoss in froher eil*
> *Die lanische...*'

CLARA: Schubert.

PASCH: Yes.

CLARA: '*Die Fourelle*'.

PASCH: 'The Trout'. As a boy I ran away from home and joined a travelling opera company. Here I am, boots and shoes, trapped in the trade my father whipped into me.

CLARA: [*aside*] You complain of having a trade?

PASCH: A trade I hate.

CLARA: [*aside*] Try being prevented from ever having a trade, forced instead to earn a pittance here, a pittance there, the way a lady must. Embroidery. Giving piano lessons.

JONAH: Here's ya plonk and ya change, Dutchy. Don't drink it all at once.

On entering, JONAH *hands* PASCH *his wine.*

You'd be the Kling and Wessels?

CLARA: Kling and Wessels, I'm comfortable in nothing else.

PASCH: My assistant.

JONAH: Can't he find 'em for you? Hopeless. We don't often get shoes of Kling and Wessels quality round here.

CLARA: How much?

JONAH *hunts up a package.*

JONAH: I just do the work. He handles the money matters.

CLARA: [*aside*] Money matters a great deal.

PASCH: Ladies soled and heeled—two and six.

CLARA: Isn't two shillings your standard rate?

JONAH: He thinks anyone who can afford Kling and Wessels must be rolling in it.

CLARA: Sadly, not so.

JONAH: Two bob, Dutchy. And if you're worried about the sixpence I'll work it off some other way, that's how much of a pleasure mending your Kling and Wessels was.

PASCH: Bohemia. I came from there. To the Cooktown goldrush. Here I stand, my homeland a fading dream.

CLARA: [*aside*] An exile?

PASCH: Gold!? Bah! I found nothing!

JONAH: Often has trouble finding me wages, but I'll say this for him, at least he'll employ someone with a hunch.

CLARA: [*aside*] Amongst the poor of Sydney I too lived like an exile.

A factory hooter sounds. CLARA *goes.*

JONAH *hat-racks the apron and takes down his vest.*

PASCH: You finishing work?

JONAH: Packer's siren, Dutchy. Saturday night, ain't it?

VOICES: [*sung*] A flurry of colour
        A hurry of sound and sight
        A worry of people
        Caught in the glare of the light
        It's a Sydney Sat'day
        Sydney Sat'day
        Sydney Sat'day night
        City of a million stories
        City of a million stories
        Only one happening tonight.

CHORUS *has returned to mask the shop.*

CLARA *is seen amongst the crowd. Looking back, she spots* JONAH, *and he her. A brief moment soon lost.*

SCENE TWO

Street lights light Botany Road, Waterloo, 1905.

High up is a sign over factory doors, 'Packer Boot and Shoe Pty. Ltd. Est. 1867'.

ADA *and* PINKEY *enter below, through the doors.*

ADA & PINKEY: [*sung*] Fresh from work wearing
        Our gladrags
        Bit of money staring
        Up from our handbags
        Rouged cheeks, something with the hair
        Watch out for us we're on the tear
        Two of Packer's girls (on Botany Road)

Two factory girls (on Botany Road)
Two factory girls
Prettier than diamonds
Brighter than a string of pearls.

Music plays under.

CHOOK *and* WAXY *(members of the Push) have spotted the girls.*

WAXY: Hey, Ada. What name's the new donah go by?
ADA: What's it to ya?
WAXY: Nothing—but she's got Chook in a flap.

CHOOK *has locked eyes with* PINKEY.

PINKEY: Are you walking in your sleep?
CHOOK: I am. And don't wake me.
PINKEY: Get a move on or you'll miss your bus.
ADA: Waxy and Chook, Pinkey. Two of the local ne'er-do-wells.
CHOOK: Pinkey, eh?
PINKEY: Chook, eh?
CHOOK: Headed where?
ADA: Nowhere you're going.
CHOOK: I'll come with you, you look lonely.
PINKEY: Not with that face!
CHOOK: What's her story?
ADA: New to the area, just started at Packer's, I'm showing her the sights.
    You two aren't one of 'em.

The girls begin their promenade past the shops.

ADA & PINKEY: [*sung*] There's a freedom working in the factory
            There's a freedom
            To do with earning your own
            We been slaving—seven to six
            In a factory
            At least we're not dawn to midnight
            Slaving in the home
            Packer's girls
            Two factory girls
            Two factory girls
            Prettier than diamonds
            Brighter than a string of pearls.

CHOOK *has filched the comb from* PINKEY's *hair.*

WAXY: Hey, lady! Your head's on fire!

CHOOK: Her ginger hair escapes from the comb and flows like a red river down the back of her neck.

PINKEY: Give us me comb.

CHOOK: Me pulse quickens. I'm seized by an insane desire to kiss the white flesh, pale as ivory.

ADA: You ever seen a mouth open that wide?

PINKEY: Did once—a circus elephant yawning!

ADA: Blow your trumpet, Chook.

PINKEY: Sound your horn.

CHOOK *leads a lament.*

CHOOK: [*sung*] God, I'm crook
　　　　Off me tucker
　　　　Through the fence
　　　　Down the chute
　　　　Up the creek

PINKEY: Got it here

ADA & WAXY: He's in love

CHOOK: Got it here

ADA & WAXY: It must be love

CHOOK: Fading fast
　　　　Like I won't last the week
　　　　God, I'm crook (must be love)

PINKEY: God, it's shocking (must be love)

CHOOK & PINKEY: Must be love!

WAXY *and* ADA *are sceptics concerning 'love'.*

ADA: He's a fighter.

PINKEY: That all he does?

CHOOK: Not me only talent.

ADA: He also filches chooks outta people's backyards.

WAXY: Last week it was Eileen McGurty.

ADA: Before that Nell Corcoran.

CHOOK: This is the full catastrophe!

ADA: Keep talking, Chook, and your jaw'll fall off.

PINKEY: That's if I don't smack it off for him first.

CHOOK: Love's flames lick me innards!

WAXY: Can't she give it lip.

CHOOK: The lips! Thought of 'em sends a shudder through me aching limbs. And I'm...

Instrumental builds as the lyric continues:

PINKEY: [*sung*] Fading fast?

CHOOK: Like I won't last the week

ADA & WAXY: Must be love

CHOOK: God, I'm crook

PINKEY: God, it's shocking (must be love)

ADA & WAXY: They call it the Doctor

CHOOK: (They call it the Doctor)

PINKEY: It's more like a Curse

ADA & WAXY: (The man's getting round)

CHOOK: I'm getting round
         Like I'm liable to burst

PINKEY: Like you're parched of hunger?

CHOOK: Like I'm starving of thirst!

ADA & WAXY: Tip is, it gets better

CHOOK: I'm getting worse
         God, I'm crook (must be love)

PINKEY: God, it's shocking (must be love).

CHOOK: Me nostrils have caught the smell of her flesh and the perfume's mounting to me brain like wine. [*To* PINKEY] Your comb, Your Majesty.

PINKEY: Thanks for nothing.

CHOOK: This isn't nothing. It's...

JONAH *has entered.*

JONAH: [*sung*] A Sydney Sat'day

CHORUS: (A flurry of colour
        A hurry of sound and sight)

JONAH: Sydney Sat'day

CHORUS: (A worry of people
        Caught in the glare of the light)

JONAH: A Sydney Sat'day night!

WAXY: City of a million stories

CHORUS: City of a million stories
        (City of a million stories)

JONAH: This one's happening tonight!

ADA: Well, if it isn't the man of my dreams.

PINKEY: You mean nightmares, don't ya?

JONAH: Learn the art of speaking when spoken to.

CHOOK: Gidday, Jo.

JONAH: Chook.

WAXY: Gidday, Jo.

JONAH: Waxy.

ADA: Whatcha want?

JONAH: Who looks after the kid when you don't?

ADA: Me mum—

JONAH: Like hell. I seen her doing deliveries outta some pram!

ADA: It's the kid's pram!

JONAH: Kid weren't in it!

ADA: Hasn't been near me for months, suddenly comes over all concerned about the kid. What happened? You grow a heart in your hunch?

JONAH: The old dame's at me to marry you.

ADA: Who says I'd have you?

JONAH: Tell her to keep off me back

> PINKEY *laughs.* JONAH *glares at her.*

ADA: Meet the kid's father—

JONAH: Your kid could be anyone's. Ain't I right?

CHOOK: Yeah, Jo.

WAXY: Yeah, Jo.

CHOOK: Ada's slept with Waxy.

WAXY: And with Chook.

JONAH: And no end of others.

PINKEY: They're thick as thieves.

ADA: They are thieves. This way, Pinkey, there's more to Botany Road than the hoi polloi.

CHOOK: 'I did but see her passing by, but I will love her till I die.'

> CHOOK *watches* PINKEY *disappear out of sight.*

JONAH: Snap out of it, Dreamboat—we got sport. Parsons' nose is asking to be broken.

> *The scene darkens.*

> *The* PUSH *sing and stage 'A Push Routine'. As they 'travel', other male* CHORUS *members join them.*

PUSH: [*sung*] A fight a night, we kick, cut, bite
We dunno right from wrong
But we know left from right
Give you a hard time
Just for fun
And out of spite
The Push
Watch out for your windows
The Push
Watch out for your windows
The Push
Watch out for your windows
Watch out for your life!
Watch out
The Push is out to-night!

The PUSH *promenades,* JONAH *taking the lead.*

JONAH: I'm Jonah the Boot the Boot the Boot
(The boot to smear your smile)
Jonah the Boot the Boot the Boot the Boot
If I walk on your ribs (he walks a mile)
Jonah the Boot the Boot the Boot's (hard as nails)
Cracking ribs (is like snapping twigs)
Like crushing snails!

Well, well—look who it isn't. I heard right—he's been drinking. Five months hard labour's what Shorty got 'cause this animal spilled his guts to the law.

WAXY: Parsons alright.

CHOOK: Daring to show his face.

JONAH: The rat's finally appeared out of the drainpipe he's been hiding in. Hey, Parsons! You ever hear tell of a copper boiler?

PARSONS: What copper boiler?

PARSONS, in drunken circles, has entered. JONAH *and the* PUSH *fan out.*

CHOOK: He don't mean something you use to boil up a copper.

WAXY: This ain't a prayer meeting! Biff him on the boko! Finish him in one act!

CHOOK: He means a copper boiler—

WAXY: Outta the washhouse—
CHOOK: Of the house—
WAXY: Next to your house!
JONAH: Ever meet a lag as put the jacks on a pal and got him five months
hard in the pool for lifting a copper boiler?
PARSONS: I never put no-one away to the traps!
JONAH: Then the fairies must have done. Sorry to have bothered you.

> JONAH *makes to leave but it's a feint. He swivels like a dancer*
> *punching* PARSONS *to the ground, then delivers a massive kick as*
> *the others close in.*

JONAH: [*sung*] Sticks and stones'll
          Break your bones but
          Jonah Jones'll—
          They call me
          The Boot
PUSH: Jonah's the Boot the Boot the Boot
JONAH: The boot to smear your smile
PUSH: Jonah's the Boot the Boot the Boot the Boot
JONAH: If I walk on your ribs I walk a mile
PUSH: Jonah the Boot's a hard man
JONAH: I am—hard as—nails
          Cracking ribs
          Is like snapping twigs
          Or crushing snails.

> PARSONS *is out to it on the ground.*

And don't try lagging us for this. Do so—you won't be talking after.
CHOOK: He ain't talking now.
WAXY: You don't think we've stoned him, do you?
JONAH: You're not dead, are you, Parsons? See. But you will be if you
keep singing songs to the traps.

> *A police whistle. They look around.*

Nit, you larks! Time we was running the lanes.
CHOOK: Scatter!

> *They exit, running.*
> *Crossfade.*

SCENE THREE

Sarah Bolan's Bar.

CLARA *is playing piano.* ADA *and* PINKEY *are being served.*

CLARA: [*sung*] Sarah Bolan's women-only Bar
        Where women are
        Served strong drink disguised
        As light refreshment…

ADA: More our style, eh Pinkey, Sarah Bolan's Bar, better known as the Ladies' Sanctuary.

PINKEY: Why so?

BOLAN: No men allowed. The new piano player is showing us what she can do…

      PINKEY *and* ADA *take the drinks* BOLAN *is offering.*

PINKEY: Me father'd kill me.

BOLAN: Your father wouldn't get his head in the door, I'd see to that.

ADA: There's been blokes come in here trying to hunt up their wives or girlfriends and guess what?

PINKEY: What?

BOLAN: They've woken up six weeks later still in hospital.

ADA: Cripes. The pram! Me mum must be here.

YABSLEY: Ada Yabsley!

      MRS YABSLEY *enters.* ADA *hides her drink behind her back.*
      PINKEY *follows suit.* YABSLEY *does likewise.*

What brings you to this den of ill repute?

ADA: What about you?

YABSLEY: Sarah's been looking after the kid while I do me deliveries.

BOLAN: She's resting up for the journey home.

YABSLEY: That's my story, what's yours?

ADA: We ducked in here to, um—

PINKEY: Get away from a bloke making a nuisance of himself.

ADA: You know what Chook's like. Anything in skirts.

YABSLEY: Chook!

ADA: Pinkey. Me mum.

YABSLEY: Mrs Bolan. Ada's cobber Inky—

PINKEY: Pinkey.

BOLAN: Howdy-do.

YABSLEY: Well, I hope you're not leading me daughter towards the demon drink, Inky.

ADA: Pinkey! Are you deaf as a post?

YABSLEY: 'Cause when a woman, Inky, takes to the drink, she's taking a short cut to hell. [*Showing her drink*] I'm just having one because I'm here.

> *The girls produce their drinks.*

ADA: Us too!

CLARA: [*aside*] This was how low I'd sunk. Playing piano in a wretched ladies-only tavern.

> *A song and dance routine ensues.*

ALL: [*sung*] In praise of drinking
>>> In praise of drinking
>>> In praise of drowning your sorrers
>>> Keeping the horrors
>>> Of all your tomorrows at bay
>>> In praise of drinking
>>> In praise of drinking
>>> In praise of whisky, brandy, beer and gin
>>> Champagne, schnapps and tokay!

CLARA: In Sarah Bolan's Bar for Women
>>> Someone was always singing

ADA & CLARA: In praise of getting stinking
>>> Meanwhile thinking
>>> All sorts of nice thoughts
>>> Just why nots and I oughts
>>> In praise of drowning your sorrers

ALL: Keeping the horrors
>>> Of all your tomorrows at bay
>>> In praise of drinking
>>> In praise of drinking
>>> In praise of whisky brandy beer and gin
>>> Champagne schnapps and tokay!

> CLARA *stops playing.*

YABSLEY: Joining us in a cordial, are you, dear?

CLARA: [*standing*] I'm sorry, Mrs Bolan, I don't think—

BOLAN: Is it the money?

CLARA: No.

YABSLEY: Is it us?

CLARA: I fear I'm not cut out for this line of work. [*Aside*] But what sort of work was I cut out for?

> *Blackout.*

> *Musical bridge to:*

SCENE FOUR

A street.

ADA, PINKEY *and* MRS YABSLEY *are at the pram, heading home.*

YABSLEY: Will you look at that moon.

ADA: It's hanging over Redfern.

YABSLEY: Nah. Waterloo.

ADA: Nah. Zetland.

YABSLEY: Whatever your point of view, up the hill we go. Cardigan Street, Pinkey. Here's where your sons, if you have sons, Ada did, end up dodging policemen before they're in long trousers.

> [*Sung*] They're dirty, they're dark, they're dingy
> That's the houses
> The men look mean, the women sad
> The brats: the brats are whingey
> Oh, it's hard making ends meet

TRIO: On Cardigan Street
  On Cardigan Street
  Making ends meet.

YABSLEY: As for your daughters, before their bones are set your daughters are mothers.

ADA: You keep harping about it.

YABSLEY: I'm not harping.

ADA: You'd think I was the only woman ever had a kid without being married.

YABSLEY: All I'm saying is that's how it is round here.

> *A police whistle offstage.*

See what I mean, that'll be the Push up to no good, half the street's drunk, the other half wishes it was, people look hungry...

> [*Sung*] Too many of 'em, even halved

ADA: That's the dogs
YABSLEY: The cats die young, they're skin and bone
              The rats: even the rats look starved
              It's hard making ends meet
TRIO: On Cardigan Street
              On Cardigan Street
              Making ends meet.
YABSLEY: Though from what I hear the rich don't have it so easy either.
       Misery ain't choosy who it visits—or how long it stays.
ADA: The rich don't have it half as hard as we do, do they, Pink?
PINKEY: Wouldn't say so.
YABSLEY: More clothes poles than a hat-rack's got hooks.
PINKEY: What?
YABSLEY: Me backyard. Look at it, and look at me, gone ten on a Sat'day
       night and I'm still on me pins.
ADA: She should try seven to six at Packers, eh?

       They sing as YABSLEY *parks the pram.*

       [*Sung*] It's dirty it's damp an' dingy
YABSLEY: Packer's Factory?
ADA & PINKEY: [*sung*] Yeah—the hour's are long the money's bad
              The boss, the boss is stingy
              Oh, it's hard winning the toss
              When you got a boss—
YABSLEY: But I ain't got your talents for factory work so it's the wash-
       board, the clothesline and mangle for me.

       Lines of washing drop into view.

       [*Sung*] Consider the widder
              Always lifting the lid'a
              The boiling copper
              Or rub a dub dub
              With washboard at tub
              Scrubbing shirts
              Or making the mangle run proper
              All me days are Mondays
              Sat'days Sundays
              All of 'em Mondays
Since I started taking in washing, which widows do to get by…

YABSLEY & ADA: [*sung*] Flatirons lined up
        Like soldiers
        On me stove
        Me arms up to the shoulders
ADA: Maroon from the heat
YABSLEY: I'd call 'em mauve
        All my days are Mondays
PINKEY: Sat'days Sundays?
        All of 'em Mondays?
YABSLEY: This much is true
        Hands Reckitts Blue!
        Hello, someone's in a hurry.

High up, CHOOK *and* WAXY *are running.* JONAH *stops them.*

JONAH: Where's the fire?
WAXY: I'm running 'cause Chook's running.
JONAH: And why's he running?
CHOOK: Why do you bloody think!

The sound of police whistles again heard. All three throw their hats over the fence. They leap it, slither down the long drop, ending up in the Yabsley backyard.

YABSLEY: Trouble, your middle name is Jonah.

The PUSH *look forward. It's* MRS YABSLEY. *They look back and up; the police on their trail. They're trapped.*

We thought we heard something un-towards coming towards us.

The three intruders cower against the back fence.

A voice from above:

CASSIDY: You there, Mrs Yabsley?
YABSLEY: Yes, constable.
CASSIDY: All's well?
YABSLEY: Right as rain, what's the ruckus?
CASSIDY: The Push have hospitalised that bricklayer Parsons. Worse than animals they are.
YABSLEY: Couldn't agree more.
CASSIDY: Goodnight then.
YABSLEY: Goodnight.

Pause as, high up, CASSIDY *moves away.*

ADA. Go see to the child—and fetch that jug of beer from inside. The rest of you can start looking like you been here all night, which is what I'll tell Cassidy if he comes back.

WAXY: Thanks, missus, you're a sport.

YABSLEY: Little Waxy Collins, who six months ago went to Sunday school so often they thought he'd end up a parson.

WAXY: I dunno nothing about no Parsons, do I, Chook?

YABSLEY: Chook, who used to come to my house regular to borrow a spoonful of dripping for his mother and butter wouldn't melt in his mouth. Pinkey Partridge, meet Arthur Fowles. And, what do you know, the Devil himself.

JONAH: Whose idea was this?

CHOOK: Dunno. But lucky we had it.

PINKEY: You again.

CHOOK: Would you care to dance?

PINKEY: There ain't no music.

CHOOK: Looking at you's music enough for me.

YABSLEY: And me seeing a marriage in me teacup this morning.

JONAH: Here we go.

YABSLEY: Here we go what?

JONAH: Marriage. You're at me to marry Ada, aren't you?

YABSLEY: I'm not talking about you and Ada, I'm talking about them. [*She indicates* CHOOK *and* PINKEY.] Stuck on each other or I'm Ned Kelly.

PINKEY: I'll help Ada fetch the beer.

CHOOK: I'll join you.

WAXY: Did somebody mention a beer?!

WAXY, CHOOK *and* PINKEY *exit to the Yabsley house.*

YABSLEY: When'd that happen?

JONAH: Just now, for all I know.

YABSLEY: Which is how it happens: the feelings—creeping up on us, out of the blue. Can't be bought. Can't be seen. Half the time we ain't even got a name for 'em. But there's nothing finer when you have them than the feelings. 'Course you wouldn't know—you got none.

JONAH: I got feelings!

YABSLEY: You? Ha hardee ha!

JONAH: Even a dog's got feelings.

YABSLEY: For fighting, you bet. Dumped at birth with a hunch on your back and now King of the Push. That you got a feeling for, for knocking round the streets with a bunch of mudlarks as can't look a policeman in the eye. But for Ada? Want you to marry her? I want you not to! Some catch you'd be. Why add a bad marriage to the sum of human misery, I say.

JONAH: You say it.

YABSLEY: But you don't believe a word? You listen up, young man, 'cause—

Music under.

—I'm telling you straight, in my philosophy a man and a woman don't get married 'cause they have to; they want to, and they want to 'cause they've suddenly dreamed a whole lotta things they never thought possible before! He can't be with her, and she can't be with him, without the ground opening up. The only time to even think about marrying's when you feel there's something wrong.

JONAH: Is that right?

YABSLEY: Inside ya!

[*Sung*] If all you are is warm on the idea
And the question's popped, say no fear
You'll wait until you're feeling ill
Till you're…

She dances.

Light as a feather
Weak as a tear
Mad as a hatter
Silly as a goose that's drunk on beer
Never get married till it gets you!
Never get married till it gets you!
Never get married till it gets you here
'Cause here, is where, it gets you.

And out here sooner or later, in Ada's case sooner, but I won't hear a word against my daughter, and never from the likes of you.

The others have returned and harmonise.

[*Sung*] Many's the contract (signed in the dark)
That can't stand the light of day
Many's the bargain (bought at the sale)

Never gets worn, gets given away
Many a candle (casts a poor light)
Some apples (are rotten although they look ripe)
Some ships (are best left to pass in the night)
Never get married till it gets you!
Never get married till it gets you!
Never get married till it gets you here!
'Cause here, is where, it gets you.
This I know: if the feeling ain't there the game ain't worth the candle.

The cry of a baby is heard.

ADA: Nothing wrong with the kid's lungs, eh Joe?

JONAH: But what else is wrong with him? Scatter!

JONAH *tries to exit. Music and voices pin him there.*

CHORUS: [*sung*] You hear that cry
Something moves, something stirs
Something moves inside you, you dunno why
What is it, what is it?
What is it about that cry?
The thought occurs
It's not just hers
The kid's also yours!
Rock is rock and mud is mud
Rock is rock and mud is mud

YABSLEY: (He's calling to you, Joe)

ADA *has fetched the swaddled child.*

JONAH: [*sung*] It's like an axe between the eyes
A bolt out of the blue
Like lightning outta the empty skies

CHORUS: What'll you do?
What'll you do?
Rock is rock and mud is mud
Rock is rock and mud is mud

JONAH: But this is my own flesh my own blood

CHORUS: Your own flesh and blood
And it's...

JONAH: His back's straight as a die!

ADA: What'd you expect: a monkey on a stick?

JONAH *holds the child up.*

JONAH: Little bugger's giving me a grin.

ADA: [*to* JONAH] You may not be a picture. Don't mean the kid has to be the same.

CHORUS: [*sung*] It's a Sydney Sat'day…

JONAH: When a man meets the first thing that's ever looked at him without seeing his hunch, missus, what's that feeling called?

YABSLEY: You having it, Jo?

CHORUS: [*sung*] It's a Sydney Sat'day
Night
It's a city of a million stories
City of a million stories
This one's happening tonight!

Tableau: CHOOK *and* PINKEY *together;* ADA, JONAH *and* YABSLEY *with the child;* WAXY *drinking beer from the jug.*

Crossfade.

SCENE FIVE

A church.

CLARA GRIMES *is at the organ as* CANON VAUGHAN *enters.*

CLARA: Canon Vaughan, whilst working in the slums of London, had acquired progressive ideas. Canon Vaughan, on arriving in the colony, had proceeded to annoy his new congregation by treating the poor of his flock with the same kindness and consideration as the rich. The first Saturday of every month, Canon Vaughan married unmarried working-class couples at Trinity Church, on the cheap, no questions asked.

CANON: You may enter.

CHOOK *and* JONAH *enter.*

CLARA: Because the usual church organist felt herself above such things, the job of playing organ at these dubious unions fell to me.

CHOOK: What price that for a mouth organ?

JONAH: You'd need a throat big as a bellows to play it.

CLARA: The coarse talk of these once-a-month wedding parties was a trial but what sustained me was the thought of the fee I'd receive. Set aside, by year's end it would be enough for a new bag and gloves, or a new pair of shoes.

JONAH: [*to* CLARA] How are the Kling and Wessels?

CLARA: [*aside*] The hunchback—where had she seen him before?

JONAH: Your shoes.

CLARA: [*aside*] That lane, off Botany Road, where the shops were as poor as their owners were mean.

JONAH: I'm the bloke who mended them.

> YABSLEY *enters with pram and* WAXY.

YABSLEY: Sssh, Jo, you're on hollow ground.

CANON: Are the young ladies…?

YABSLEY: Yes, Your Honour.

WAXY: They're bringing up the rear.

JONAH: Let's get it over with… eh, Chook?

> ADA *and* PINKEY *enter.*

CLARA: [*aside*] All afternoon there'd be a dreary procession of couples. All afternoon my mind would crowd with thoughts of how things had been, and how they were now…

> CHOOK *and* PINKEY *are exchanging vows.*

[*Aside*] Once I'd been rich. And attended parties, soirées, balls. Once I'd been engaged to be married. But now the only world I knew was ever-present poverty, pressing in on me…

> *Before the* CANON, ADA *and* JONAH *replace* CHOOK *and* PINKEY *as the couple taking their vows.*

[*Aside*] To be poor, like these folk, was a burden, but to have been rich once, then overnight made poor, that was truly a cross to bear…

> JONAH *and* ADA *have completed their vows.*

> *A musical round-off from* CLARA.

> *The wedding party exits.*

> CLARA *stands. The* CANON *pays her a fee.*

SCENE SIX

Exterior.

PASCH *sings above the Yabsley backyard:*

PASCH: [*sung*] She told me her age was five and twenty
        Cash in the bank, oh yes she'd plenty

I like a lamb believed it all
I was an em-u-gee…
In Trinity Church I met my doom
Now we live in a top back room
Up to my ears in debt for rent-ee
I was an em-u-gee…

Below, the newlyweds arrive from church.

Jonah. You didn't invite me to your wedding. I know why. I'm Bohemian. People think I'm German. To some not even Schleswig-Holstein is a country. But I came, anyway! And I sang. For you.

PASCH *has climbed down.*

JONAH: What's that you're carrying?

PASCH: Sausage. A wedding party without food?

BOLAN: And what's a wedding party without drink?

WAXY: Look what fell off the back of a brewery dray!

WAXY *and other* WELLWISHERS *roll on a keg.*

YABSLEY: What's this string of boots doing in me backyard?

WAXY: Ain't it a custom—throwing old boots at the newlyweds?

ADA: So much for getting married on the sly, half the street must be here.

BOLAN: And the other half's on its way.

PINKEY: You was, none of you, supposed to know we four were getting hitched!

The dunny door opens. MR PARTRIDGE *(Pinkey's dad) comes out.*

Cripes!

CHOOK: What?

PARTRIDGE: [*to* PINKEY] Why, Liz? Why?

PINKEY: It's me, Dad.

PARTRIDGE: Why'd you get married in secret?

PINKEY: And have you kill us?

PARTRIDGE: You coulda told me.

CHOOK: I think I can explain, Mr Partridge—

PARTRIDGE: This him, is it?

CHOOK: Have a beer, Mr Partridge. Chook's the name.

CHOOK *offers* PARTRIDGE *a beer. He realises it's an empty glass.*

I'll just fill this up for you.

PARTRIDGE: Here.

PINKEY: Blow me down with a feather! Have a look, Chook. Me mum's long gone—but me dad's come good with…?

PARTRIDGE: Twenty quid!

PINKEY *hands the notes to* CHOOK.

WAXY: Whatcha gonna do, Chook?

CHOOK: Take it to Paddy Flynn's two-up school. Double or nothing!

PINKEY: Like hell.

PARTRIDGE: Me daughter'll have a say in how it's spent or she's no Partridge.

PINKEY: Five quid's key money and rent in advance on that empty shop I was showing you.

CHOOK: That's five.

PINKEY: Six is going for some furniture, crockery and bedding, so's we can live behind the shop.

CHOOK: Leaves nine.

PINKEY: Eight on fruit and veg to stock the shop: I'll sell from there and you can hawk the streets as usual.

ADA: You got it all worked out, Pink.

CHOOK: No she hasn't, there's a quid left over.

PINKEY: With that I'll buy a new hat!

WAXY: Liking married life, Chook?

CHOOK: Wouldn't swap it for quids!

PASCH: He was an em-u-gee…

YABSLEY *takes focus.*

YABSLEY: I used to hope when Ada got married there'd be a party in this backyard Cardigan Street wouldn't forget in a hurry. Looks like me wish has come true. [*A toast*] To marriage!

ALL: To marriage!

YABSLEY: To husbands, Mrs Bolan?

YABSLEY *and* BOLAN *do a patter song and dance.*

YABSLEY: Husbands husbands

BOLAN: Husbands husbands
        There's all sorts, there's even
        Some that's willing to keep yer

YABSLEY: There's them that smashes the furniture
        And them that smashes you

YABSLEY & BOLAN: Why? Only 'cause you're cheaper…

BOLAN: (Your husband, how is he?

YABSLEY: Hasn't done a tap for twelve years.

BOLAN: No?

YABSLEY: That's how long he's been dead.

BOLAN: And it's been your luck not to marry again?

YABSLEY: That's the luck I've had…)

YABSLEY & BOLAN: Husbands husbands
　　　　　　　Husbands husbands

BOLAN:　They're like a wart (a what?) a wart
　　　　　Upon your nose

YABSLEY: You're stuck with it!

BOLAN:　Scratch it (squeeze it)
　　　　　Try to please it (what's the point?)
　　　　　When you got one of those (warts?)

YABSLEY & BOLAN: *Husbands!*

YABSLEY: All husbands are beasts, Mrs Bolan.

BOLAN: Must be why so many of 'em get round with horns on.

　　They involve others in a dance.

YABSLEY & BOLAN: Husbands husbands
　　　　　　　Husbands husbands

YABSLEY: They're like the wind (the what?) the wind
　　　　　When it blows it blows—like the weather
　　　　　(You have to wear it)
　　　　　And whenever (you think) you just can't bear it
　　　　　Remember this

YABSLEY & BOLAN: It's one of Mother Nature's iron laws
　　　　　　　Everybody's husband, everybody's husband
　　　　　　　Everyone's husband's every bit as bad
　　　　　　　As yours!

　　The music ends.

　　JONAH *awkwardly takes focus:*

JONAH: I'll give youse a song, if you're game.

　　He hands sheet music to YABSLEY.

YABSLEY: I can't read writing, let alone dots on a page, what's it say, Ada?

ADA: Ada.

YABSLEY: Eh?

ADA: 'Ada'. That's the title.

JONAH: It's the latest novelty tune.

YABSLEY: Well, what do you know—?

ADA: Did you learn this for me, Jo?

JONAH: Mighta done.

>   ADA *sings,* JONAH *plays mouth organ.*
>
>   CHOOK *and* PINKEY *dance a sort of bridal waltz.*

ADA: [*sung*] Yes I've strayed-a with a maid, it's true
>   Been waylaid-a in a glade-a or two
>   Played-a lover's game but haven't paid-a sou
>   Wouldn't trade-a minute now I've made-a blue
>   Oh, Ada Ada Ada, I'm afraid-a loving you

JONAH: (You give me goose bumps)

ADA: Ada, I'm afraid-a loving you

JONAH: (You turn me head round)

ADA: Ada, I'm afraid-a loving you.

YABSLEY: Make it a barn dance, Jo, progressive.

>   *All dance,* JONAH *plays,* PASCH *leads the song.*

PASCH: [*sung*] Oh, Ada Ada Ada, I'm afraid-a loving you
>   (You give me goosebumps)
>   Ada, I'm afraid-a loving you
>   (You turn me head round)
>   Ada, I'm afraid-a loving you…

True. I'm not your father. All I did was take you in, age of seven, and teach you a trade, but why make a speech when a song will do?

>   *The 'Ada' chorus continues, with* JONAH *on mouth organ.*

ADA: Looks like you got a party Cardigan Street won't forget in a hurry.

BOLAN: All's well…

YABSLEY: That ends well.

>   *A backyard tableau.*
>
>   *At a window, high up,* CLARA *sings:*

CLARA: [*sung*] All's well that ends well—makes it a play
>   But when no happy ending hoves in view for you
>   What's there to say…?

>   *The lights darken. A thunder clap.*

YABSLEY: God save us, rain! And me thinking I could hang out sheets after you dragged your carcasses home!

WAXY: Get the keg outta the weather!

CLARA: [*sung*] But what ends—one week ends
   Monday morning—another one starts

  CHORUS *forms as the scene changes.*

  What ends?

CHORUS: Nothing ends
   One week ends
   Monday morning
   Another one starts.

SCENE SEVEN

Pasch's shop.

PASCH *is buffing a large custom-built orthopaedic boot.*

PASCH: It's not Friday or is it?

JONAH: Try Monday.

PASCH: What you doing here?

JONAH: Work.

PASCH: Monday's quiet.

JONAH: What you telling me? How about Tuesday?

PASCH: Some work may come in then. Some on Wednesday. Thursday I may have enough for you to do—half a day.

JONAH: Half a day! Whatcha thinking, I got half a kid to feed?!

PASCH: It'd be different if people wore their shoes out more quicker. But look how much time they spend sitting down. It's to save shoe leather. Round here there isn't the trade. People are poor.

JONAH: So why aren't we doing outdoor finishing for Packer way Bob Watkins does?

PASCH: Piecework!

JONAH: You could get it in. We'd do it. I'd do it!

PASCH: I'm a tradesman! I want nothing to do with factory production. Custom-built and repairs.

JONAH: Custom-built!?

PASCH: Don't remind me.

JONAH: You're holding the last custom-built job you did. Four bloody year ago, a special bloody shoe for a bloody cripple back from the Boer bloody War with one bloody leg shorter than the other.

PASCH: And he wouldn't bloody pay!

JONAH: Do you bloody blame him?! You made it so bloody heavy he couldn't bloody walk. Some tradesman, you!

> JONAH *has grabbed the boot and looks ready to clout* PASCH. *He lets it drop.*
>
> *Music is building.*

PASCH: Does this mean you won't be in on Friday?

JONAH: That's the long and the short of it!

PASCH: There isn't the work!

JONAH: No. And what there is, I been doing! I'd turn up Fridays and Sat'days and go like stink on a mound of repairs thinking that's how hard you were at it the rest of the week. Not so. I sweat, you sit on your ring, who gets the money?!

PASCH: I pay the going rate.

JONAH: I know what I get. And the rest? What's not glug glug glug going down your Bohemian throat is into your pocket, right!

CHORUS: [*sung*] When you're down you're down you're down
But are you out?
Does a drowning man, down on his uppers
Drown without a shout?

JONAH: So that's the lie of the land and
What I didn't understand was
I've been the reason you've survived
The sweat of my brow's what's kept you alive
I come to you now 'cause suddenly I've
Got a kid to feed!
And it's like I never done you a turn
Well, could be it's you I don't need!

[*Aside*] Next time I'm in here, Dutchy, I'll be dancing on your grave!

SCENE EIGHT

Cut to the interior of the 'Packer Boot and Shoe Pty. Ltd. Est. 1867'.

ADA *and* PINKEY *sing as* PACKER *watches them and others arriving at work.*

ADA & PINKEY: [*sung*] Clattering, clakking
    Chattering, yakking
    Down a dreary, weary, bleary street before first light
    Crammed, jammed
    Grabbed, jabbed
    In a crowded tram, not home till night
    Seven to six, working for a living
    Lace it, wrap it
    Seven to six, working for a living
    Paper it, pack it
    Seven to six, living in a working world…

As the factory whistle sounds, work starts.

    Stamp it, stack it
    Lace it, wrap it, paper it, pack it
    Working for a living
PACKER: A hundred pair an hour
    Give me more but never give me
    Less than that
ADA: Tired, like you think you'll drop
    What you're facing's the sack if you stop
PINKEY: You lift your head, try to snatch a word above the din
    If the foreman catches you…
VOICE: [*offstage*] Hey!
CHORUS: You know he'll dob you in
    Seven to six, seven to six
    Working for a living
    Seven to six, seven to six
    Working for a living
    Seven to six
    Working for a living (lace it, wrap it)
    Seven to six
    Working for a living (paper it, pack it)
    Seven to six
    Living in a working world!

A rest whistle sounds. The workers relax.

ADA & PINKEY: Elbows aching, swollen wrists
    Stiffened fingers that won't make fists

ALL: You lift your head, you try to snatch a word above the din…

    JONAH *has entered. The back-to-work whistle sounds.*

    It's like God's backed you for a place
    And somebody else for the win
    Seven to six, working for a living
    Seven to six, working for a living
    Seven to six
    Living in a working world
    Living in a working world
    Seven to six, working for a living (lace it, wrap it)
    Seven to six, working for a living (paper it, pack it)
    Seven to six
    Living in a working world
    Living in a working world

PACKER: A hundred pair an hour, give me more
    But never give me less than that
    A hundred pair an hour, give me more
    But never give me less than
    A hundred pair an hour, give me more
    But never less than that
    You're living in a working world!

    JONAH *is with* ADA *asking for* PACKER. ADA *indicates where* PACKER *stands, dealing with* MRS WATKINS.

PINKEY: What's Jo doing here?

ADA: Trying for a job.

PINKEY: Jo? Here?

ADA: Something about outdoor finishing.

JONAH: I'm looking for work, Mr Packer—

PACKER: I'm busy, son.

JONAH: I said I'm looking for… Sorry.

    PACKER *gives him a hard look and turns back to* WATKINS.

PACKER: Eight shillings.

WATKINS: Eight? Bob told me ten a batch. These uppers are the last lot
    of piecework you'll be getting from him, Mr Packer. The TB. The
    quacks have sent him to the mountains. I reckon next time I see him
    he'll be wearing a coffin.

PACKER: Eight shillings, take it or leave it.

JONAH: Hang on, word is your going rate's ten.

PACKER: The man's been sick. His workmanship's gone downhill.

JONAH: I'd say that work's as good as you'll get.

WATKINS: Really, Jo, I'm only too glad of the eight shillings, heaven knows I need it.

JONAH: And you pocket the other two bob, ya swine.

PACKER: What did you call me?

JONAH: Hands off or have 'em ripped off.

PACKER: You got thirty seconds to be out the door.

JONAH: Wanta try putting me out?

> JONAH *has picked up a hammer from a bench.*

PACKER: Put that tool down or I won't just have you put out the door I'll have you put through the courts.

JONAH: The man who makes a margin sweating working men and women—he'll have me for theft! [*He throws the hammer down.*] I came here looking for work.

PACKER: I wouldn't bother.

JONAH: I won't. A hunchbacked bastard, slotted in a shoebox and dumped at birth. But what's that make you, Packer?

ADA: Knew something like this would happen.

JONAH: The richest man in all of Waterloo and Zetland, but you'd thieve the pennies off a dead man's eyes.

PACKER: Out! [*To the workers*] And what are you lot staring at?!

> JONAH *starts to exit.*

WATKINS: That's telling him, Jo.

JONAH: Yeah. And it got you your two bob, did it?

> ADA *and the other workers resume work.*

CHORUS: [*sung*] When you're down you're down you're down
>> But are you out?
>> Does a drowning man drown
>> Without so much as a shout…?

> *Crossfade.*

SCENE NINE

A street.

JONAH *is pushing the pram. He encounters* CHOOK *working a fruit and veg barrow (and certain prospective employers, voiced by the* CHORUS*).*

JONAH: [*sung*] Game's rigged!

CHOOK: Play it crooked—cop the yard with Shorty

JONAH: Try to play it straight

CHOOK: And you can't get a look-in

JONAH: How's a man get his start?
           How's a man get his break?
           They know how to break your heart
           Every step you take…

VOICE 1: (Not on your life, Jones)

JONAH: And it's not whether you're willing to work
           Or not…

VOICE 2: (On your way)

JONAH: And it's got
           Nothing to do with the skills you got
           You'd bust your guts
           But no, you're just
           One more pair of hands
           That nobody wants to know
           And so

CHOOK: Sorry, but the answer's

CHORUS: (Sorry, but the answer's—)

JONAH: Sorry, but the answer's: No!

I been the length of Botany Road. Not a scrap of work to be had. Sank as low as carting the kid with me thinking some mug might take pity on me.

CHOOK: Kid looks fine.

JONAH: Yeah, but his dad's nosing the bottom of the barrel.

CHOOK: Cabbages! Apples!

JONAH: I seen Chinamen in jobs.

CHOOK: Watch what you say about the celestials, Li Shou Cheng's a mate. Rhubarb and Curly Kale!

JONAH: One place I front, they're filing out on strike. Me? I can't land a job, let alone take a walk! Death's breathing down me back left side. Starvation's coming in on the right.

CHOOK: Can't see nothing, Jo.

JONAH: Ha ha. Caught Packer frauding Bob Watkins' wife. He's got TB.

CHOOK: Packer?

JONAH: Bob! She thinks she's seen the last of him.

CHOOK: At least you got your health.

JONAH: Has his tools up for sale.

CHOOK: You thinking of—?

JONAH: Buying them? If only. Yeah, and starting up on my own, only I got an angel's hope in Hell of shelling out seven quid. Pigs can fly and there's a revolving door I can go through and come out minus me hump!

CHOOK: A question of luck, mate.

JONAH: Mine's out, if it was ever in!

CHOOK: [*sung*] There's the horse that wins the race
    There's the horses that lose the race
    There's the difference
    What's the difference?

JONAH: You're saying the difference is luck?

    CHOOK *demonstrates with the pram.*

CHOOK: There's the kid, there's the cliff
    The but and the if
    There's being there at the right time
    (If only you were)
    There's being there in the right place
    (But you weren't)
    There's the difference

JONAH: A helluva difference

CHOOK: The difference is luck…
    There's having a silver spoon in your gob
    At birth

JONAH: There's getting a mouthful of mother's mitt
    With your mother's milk
    'Cause that's all you're worth!

CHOOK: There's the bloke who makes the boot

JONAH: There's the bloke who puts it in

CHOOK: There's the difference
    How come there's a difference?
    I tell you the difference is luck.

Next Monday Pinkey and me set up shop, she'll sell from there, I'll keep hawking the streets. Sitting pretty, how come?

JONAH: [*sung*] Her old man's twenty quid

CHOOK: I had the unadulterated good fortune to marry someone whose old boy had more than one and a kick in his kick.

JONAH: So, failing a stroke of luck, what's the answer, rob a bank?

CHOOK: Precisely my point:

> [*Sung*] Some bloke, he robs the bank
> Some bloke, he owns the bank
> That's the difference
> How come there's a difference?
> I tell you the difference
> The difference is purely a difference of *luck*!

And the great thing about luck is…?

JONAH: Dunno, but you're gonna tell me.

CHOOK: It changes.

JONAH: Thanks for that.

> WAXY *enters in a new hat.*

CHOOK: Cabbages! Apples! Waxy? You have a win on the nags? Cop it, Jo. Our boy's got a new lid.

WAXY: Thought I'd smarten up me rig-out. You two getting married's made me Leader of the Push.

> CASSIDY *the cop has entered.*

Didn't seek the office, but the rest of the blokes, you know, thought I was the next in line. Some seek greatness…

CASSIDY: Others have it thrust upon them. Leader of the Push? You? A fortnight back a fella called Parsons was bashed near here, says the Leader of the Push did the kicking, grievous bodily harm—

WAXY: It weren't me… it was…

> JONAH *and* CHOOK *eye him warily.*

Fair cop, Cassidy, give us the bracelets. You got your man.

> WAXY*'s hat falls off as* CASSIDY *handcuffs him and leads him away.*

JONAH: Hey! His hat!

CASSIDY: Where he's going he'll be inside most of the day.

> JONAH *picks up the hat.*

JONAH: That coulda been me.

CHOOK: Or me. Fact it wasn't has to mean—

JONAH: What?

CHOOK: Our luck ain't all bad.

JONAH: Says you. Where Waxy's headed at least he'll be fed.
CHOOK: Cabbages! Apples! Tamats! You're in need of a quid.
JONAH: Seven of 'em, to be precise.
CHOOK: Pawn the hat.

>   *Music in as* CHOOK *and* JONAH *go their separate ways.*

>   *Crossfade to:*

SCENE TEN

A lamplit kitchen in the Cardigan Street house.

YABSLEY *with a pinchbar.*

YABSLEY: [*sung*] Those who by omens and stars
>   Are struck
>   Will tell you it's Fortune
>   Will tell you it's Luck
>   Have you noticed too
>   The solemn nods
>   When someone declares
>   It's all
>   Rise or fall
>   In the lap of the gods?
>   Yes, life's a gamble
>   A punt, a risk
>   But the smart have an art—
JONAH: What art's this?
YABSLEY: They even up the odds!

>   JONAH *and* ADA *have entered to see* YABSLEY *levering up a floorboard.*

They always have something up their sleeve, and it ain't a rabbit like a conjurer bloke I seen once.
JONAH: We ain't so down on it you have to rip the floorboards up for stove wood.
YABSLEY: You tried to get put on at Packer's?
JONAH: Yeah.
YABSLEY: You wouldn't last a week in a place like that.
ADA: He didn't last a minute.
JONAH: Packer's an animal.

ADA: And you're not?

JONAH: Grrr.

ADA: Saying our prayers now, are we?

> YABSLEY *is kneeling, one arm down the hole.*

YABSLEY: A bloke like Jo needs to be his own boss. Seeing as he's got his heart set on earning a living—seeing what he needs is the wherewithal—

ADA: An old widow...

YABSLEY: That's me.

ADA: ... has saved up her threepences and sixpences, turns 'em into gold coins, wrapped 'em in newspaper and dropped 'em through a crack in the floor for safe-keeping, just like that play you and I saw.

YABSLEY: Exactly like that play you and I saw. It's what give me the idea.

JONAH: Of what?

YABSLEY: Of dropping my gold coins through a gap in the floorboards for safekeeping. Only...

> YABSLEY *is alarmed. There's nothing there.*

JONAH: What?

YABSLEY: They're missing.

ADA: You really have some gold coins?

JONAH: You coulda put 'em in a bank, you goose!

YABSLEY: Goose yourself. You put it in and you put it in, and when they got enough they close the doors, and Smartypants in the waistcoat with the sterling silver winkers is next heard of in Argentina living happily ever after.

ADA: She don't like banks.

JONAH: Better her way right?

ADA: And have some rat thief filch her savings.

YABSLEY: The rats! They've boned the paper for their nests. Dragged the coins away with 'em. Here's one.

JONAH: Give us a go.

YABSLEY: Here's another. I'll fetch that hook thing I use on the cobwebs. If twenty quid can set Chook and Pinkey up in a shop, what I got oughta see you right...

> YABSLEY *exits.*

> JONAH *continues the hunt. Focus on* ADA.

ADA: [*sung*] Being rich'll be a wonder
    We'll have a castle
    Horses
    Servants serving
    Big meals
    I'll go to racecourses
    Drink wine
    Eat eels
    Boat on a lake
    Read romances
    Dance
    All night
    Through the castle
    With a loved one
    Candles, fires
    Floor like a draught board
    Being rich'll be a wonder
    Being rich'll be a wonder…

JONAH: Twenty-nine quid!

ADA: You can't buy a castle with twenty-nine quid!

YABSLEY: Not gonna.

JONAH: It's a fortune.

YABSLEY: No. It's half a quid for every year I've drawn breath, but I'm calling it your start.

The lights fade as music continues under.

SCENE ELEVEN

Early morning. Pasch's workshop.

PASCH *enters below. He stares as though at the shop opposite.*

PASCH: All night percussion. Then I wake up and realise it is hammering. I look out: banners going up—

Banners drop into place.

I mean down. Repairs. Repairs to what? 'While U Wait'. While U wait? Must be a foreigner. There's no Y and no O in the U. I wonder what country? 'Soled and Heeled'! 'Boots and Shoes'!

He exits for a closer look.

High up, PINKEY *enters with handbills.* PACKER *enters opposite.*

PINKEY: Here y'are! Here y'are! Read all about it, Mr Packer!

PACKER *takes a handbill.* PASCH *enters.*

PASCH: Handbills? What is this waste of money?

PINKEY: [*going*] Not a waste—a saving.

PINKEY *exits.*

PASCH: Such prices.

PACKER: Gent's boots: soled and heeled, two and eleven. Women's shoes: soled and heeled, one and eleven. Competitive pricing. Child's: eleven pence.

PASCH: Gent's is always three and six. Women's, two and six. Child's, one and six. Like on my sign. A band? Why?

PACKER: It's no ordinary shop. A funeral, do you think?

PASCH: Whose?

PACKER: Whose indeed?

Below, the workshop.

YABSLEY, CHOOK *and* PINKEY *are transforming it.*

YABSLEY: Across the ceiling, twisted into rope, coloured tissue paper. Brightens the place up.

PINKEY: Down one side, a row of chairs.

CHOOK: In front of the chairs, a strip of carpet.

YABSLEY: Ada's idea.

CHOOK: Pinkey chose the colour.

YABSLEY: Red.

PINKEY: Homey.

PACKER: A crowd is looking in through the window.

PASCH: I can't look.

PACKER: A woman's entering.

It's ADA. *Soon* JONAH *will appear.*

She's taking off her shoes. She's putting them on the bench and sitting down with some other people who have their shoes in hand. A man's entering. He's taking up her shoes. He's starting work on them then and there.

PASCH: That must be—

PACKER: It is. It's—

PASCH: Service 'While U Wait' and—

OTHERS: We're 'While You're Waiting'!

PASCH: Who is the man who's come to snatch the bread from my mouth?!

JONAH: Only trying to put a bit in my own, Dutchy!

ADA, YABSLEY, PINKEY *and* CHOOK, *all shoeless, are reading magazines.*

PASCH *climbs down to the shop below.*

Above, PACKER *leads the* CHORUS *in a song.*

One by one, YABSLEY, CHOOK, ADA *and* PINKEY *receive mended shoes.*

CHORUS: [*sung*] Big and small
We're all
Treading water
Fighting for air
Life's not luck, life's fighting to not go under
Fighting to get your share!
It's a dog-eat-dog
Bite-or-get-bitten kind of world
You step on or get stepped on

JONAH: For some it's a stairway to paradise

PACKER: Others don't find that stairway
No way—do they
They
Just don't get on!

CHORUS: 'Cause it's a dog-eat-dog
Bite-or-get-bitten kind of world
You step on
Or get stepped on…

JONAH: Like me set-up, Dutchy?

PASCH: [*sung*] Money you may one day have
In plenty
But never your heart's content!
For like a dog
You did bite
The hand that fed you!

JONAH: So far a chapter, but I'm in it!

PASCH *departs. Night is falling.* PACKER *remains high up.*

PACKER: The boot trade is a strange beast, Mr Jones, with a great beauty at its heart. Think about it: people don't just wear boots and shoes, they wear them out. Every step someone takes is taking them one step closer to buying their next pair of boots or shoes.

JONAH: Or to having the old pair repaired.

PACKER: Good for you, you mend shoes. Good for me, I make shoes. That's the great beauty of the boot trade.

> PACKER *(a string of boots and shoes around his neck) slides down a pole to join* JONAH.

JONAH: You don't remember me, do you, Packer?

PACKER: Should I?

JONAH: Maybe better you don't.

PACKER: Closed down the opposition, I see.

JONAH: Pasch? A blue mouldy. Couldn't race a snail up a wall.

PACKER: And it's a fair go on Botany Road.

JONAH: Betcha!

PACKER: Every man for himself.

JONAH: Pasch wouldn't put in the hours or move with the times. Is that my fault?

PACKER: Jonah the Boot.

JONAH: That's me moniker.

PACKER: First in the suburbs to use a city gimmick: 'Repairs While U Wait'.

JONAH: Someone had to—I got there first.

PACKER: First on the road with the new advertising.

JONAH: It gets 'em in.

PACKER: And the new prices.

JONAH: Gets 'em in even better.

PACKER: All repairs, something and eleven.

JONAH: People get a penny back they think—

PACKER: They're getting a bargain.

JONAH: You don't think much of me cut-price tactics?

PACKER: Just the opposite. You're the talk of the trade. A man making good, in a hurry. I take my hat off to you, but have a question. What if staying big meant having to get bigger?

> PACKER *casts the string of boots and shoes upon the bench.* JONAH *keeps working.*
>
> *Music under.*

JONAH: They don't look like they need mending.

PACKER: Samples.

JONAH: You're wasting your breath.

PACKER: But you have thought of stocking your shop?

JONAH: And will—soon as I've saved enough tin.

PACKER: Ar, money! You mend shoes, Mr Jones. But you only make money when someone brings you their shoes to mend. I, sir, make shoes, but only make money when those shoes end up on people's feet. Those who help bring about that result can themselves make money while I'm making money. A hundred pounds worth of boots and shoes, this quality, yours. Are you the man I been hearing about or not?

YABSLEY *enters with the pram.*

JONAH: Paying how?

PACKER: Not how. Paying when. Not at seven days, not at thirty days. At ninety days.

JONAH: You'll stake me a century's worth of boots and shoes, three months to pay?

PACKER: Hmm.

JONAH: I can charge what price I like?

PACKER: All I want is my hundred pound ninety days hence.

JONAH: Stock of my choosing?

PACKER: From this range.

JONAH: What's to stop me walking off with your stuff?

PACKER: Turn your back on a going concern? I don't see that's a risk. It's more me investing in your future. Credit, Mr Jones. I give it where and when I think it's due.

Music under.

PACKER *climbs back to the upper level.*

YABSLEY: Jonah spent a pound on brass rods and glass stands and cleared the first batch inside a month at one and six per pair profit. His next order was for two hundred pounds worth of stock.

PACKER: In no time he was operating a flourishing retail trade.

JONAH: So that's how you do it!

PACKER: Credit. It's a lever.

YABSLEY: He was like a rock, prised from the ground and set rolling.

PACKER: [*sung*] Men make money!
     They make money!
     By making money: a weapon!

JONAH: Pasch's old shop! When I get too crowded in here, missus, I'll put a girl on. Do me repairs from here and me retail opposite. Two-Shop Jonah they'll call me.

YABSLEY: And in time they did.

JONAH: [*sung*] So far a chapter, but I'm in it
And really the sky
Forget the sky
Not even the sky's the limit…

A musical shift.

YABSLEY *passes the child from the pram to* JONAH.

YABSLEY: Jonah's dream…

JONAH: Seven years, Ray, and I'll have clawed me way along Botany Road. Nine: I'll have reached the end of the suburbs and be casting an eagle eye on the city itself. And will I give those bigwig downtown traders a run for their money! A shop big as four or five shops put together, the whole shebang, floor to ceiling, boots and shoes. Boots and shoes clinging to brass rods like swarms of bees—boots and shoes hanging from the rafters like bunches of grapes. Fittings'll glisten with varnish. Everything'll be new, and kept new, or else. The smell of leather'll clog the air. Signs. I'll give 'em signs that'll have people's heads turning in the trams and trains to see what he's dreamed up next. On the roof, Ray, there'll be another sign: a giant glittering silver shoe! Jonah The Boot's 'Silver Shoe Emporium'.

The pram has risen, strings of boots and shoes cascading from it to form a silver rainbow on high.

Above the pram, a large silver shoe crowns this glittering leather trade nativity scene.

And at night, Ray, me sign'll be lit up with a row of electric bulbs. You'll see it for miles.

ADA *enters and will take the child.*

ADA: [*sung*] And what do I do
While this dream's being brought about?
I fit where in your scheme of things?
Do I get a say over what the next day brings?

JONAH: You can stop working, dear heart.

ADA: It won't be to sweat in some shoe shop, that's flat!

JONAH: We're surviving—you can stay home! Look after Ray.

ADA: Give him the attention you never had?

JONAH: Yeah.

YABSLEY: You sure you know what you're doing, Jo?

JONAH: I'll be a legend and me store'll be a retail landmark.

> JONAH *sounds a long note on his mouth organ for Ray.*

> CLARA *appears at her window.* PACKER *too will be seen up high.*

CLARA: [*sung*] Music (ar, music)

CHORUS: Music (ar, music)

CLARA: Music soothes the savage beast
It's brandy to the damned the way
Religion's whisky to the priest
At least
That's what they say
But is it the music that makes the piper want to play?

PACKER: Money (ar, money)
Money (ar, money)
Moolah makes the world go round
You who pay the piper
You really make the sound...
The world works, and only works, that way!

CHORUS: But is it money or music?
Music or money?
That makes the piper want to play?
What gets us on our feet
To face each coming day...

> PASCH *enters below.*

PASCH: You have snatched the bread from my mouth!

JONAH: How? By trying to put a bit in me own! By wanting for my kid a childhood I never had?
[*Sung*] So far a chapter, but I'm in it!

YABSLEY: Sydney
Nineteen hundred and five

CHORUS: City of a million stories
City of a million stories
Only one happening tonight!

END OF PART ONE

PART TWO

SCENE ONE

Afternoon. The Silver Shoe Emporium, 1914.

A group of employees sing a jingle. They surround a 3D likeness of Jonah (a cast member or model). This 'toy' (a puppet cobbler) will come to life.

CHORUS: [*sung*] Jonah's the Boot the Boot the Boot
        The boot the boot or shoe
        When only the best will stand the test
        Or get you through
        Jonah the Boot the Boot the Boot the Boot'll
        Fit your feet
        Guarantee it—Regent Street
        Sign of The Silver Shoe

JONAH PUPPET: Where the little man tap tap tap
        Tap taps
        At a shoe last.

JONAH: The verdict?

GILTINAN: It's a good likeness, except…

JONAH: Except?

GILTINAN: It's missing one thing…

JONAH: And what's that, Miss Giltinan?

GILTINAN: Your hunch.

JONAH: My sentiments exactly. Me trademark hunch is a key part of the legend. The latest with the newest. That's The Silver Shoe!

JONAH PUPPET: [*sung*] Where the little man tap tap tap
        Tap taps
        At a shoe last.

JONAH: Give it a hunch and I'll install it in the front window.

    CHORUS *exits with the* JONAH PUPPET *revealing* PACKER, *a rolled-up contract in his hand.*

PACKER: Jonah Jones in miniature.

JONAH: Miniature that gizmo is, small I ain't.

PACKER: No. The downtown traders are predicting you'll be in George
    Street by Christmas. You're a phenomenon.

JONAH: I'll be telling the world me next move when I want the world to
    hear it. You've read the paperwork? I'll be buying big lots and big
    lots means big money.

PACKER: I have to be interested.

JONAH: 'Course you do, 'cause...

> [*Sung*] It's a dog-eat-dog
> Bite-or-get-bitten kind of world
> You either step on
> Or get stepped on!

PACKER: It's the name
> Just what are you at?

JONAH: What's my game
> Are you asking me that?
> What it's always been, Packer—survival
> Sink or swim and I'm for swimming!

PACKER: But the name!

JONAH: What's in a name?

PACKER: That's what I'm saying
> What's the game—
> You're playing?

JONAH: You're in a hole—we both know it
> The Yankees can land an article in Australia as good as yours
> Ten per cent cheaper than you can make it
> That's from New York
> Not San Francisco!

PACKER: It's a trade war
> They're selling cheap to send outfits like mine to the wall
> With the Australian manufacturer out of the picture
> They'll charge retailers like yourself the earth.

JONAH: So you do appreciate how I might benefit from keeping you
    alive? Me idea's simple...

> [*Sung*] Thirty lines made to my designs and specifications
> Available to the public nowhere but The Silver Shoe
> House lines, I'm calling 'em...

PACKER: It's an unusual request

JONAH: I'm an unusual man
           My reckoning is that contract'll make me your biggest customer
           And worthy of special consideration
           You've read the paperwork
           You don't want to fall in with me plans, others will…

PACKER: 'Cause as we know…
           It's a dog-eat-dog
           Bite-or-get-bitten world!

JONAH: You got it in one

PACKER: The Americans have the advantage of a bigger home market

JONAH: If it's so big, why ain't we exporting to it?
           It ain't as if Australians don't grow shoe leather
           It ain't as if Australians dunno how to make shoes
           It ain't as if ships don't sail the Pacific
           God save me
           You ain't put a new machine in your place for twenty years!

PACKER: But the name!

JONAH: Your name ain't material to me
           What happens to my name is!
           I want
           Stamped on every sole
           Jonah Jones
           And the sign of The Silver Shoe

CHORUS: Stamped on every sole
           Jonah Jones
           And the sign of The Silver Shoe!

PACKER: But they'll be Packer shoes! My shoes!

JONAH: Yeah, but with my name on them!

PACKER: Why?

JONAH: So putting 'em on and taking 'em off, people'll remember you
    don't get shod shoddy at The Silver Shoe.
           [*Sung*] So next time they want their footwear needs taken care
           of they'll come here

PACKER: Where the little man tap tap tap
           Tap taps
           At a shoe last?

JONAH: Think what you will about me tactics
           I measure 'em by whether they work or not

Heard of the boomerang?
I want customers returning time after time…

PACKER: You want the name Packer to disappear

JONAH: You're doing that anyway without my help
I'm offering you a way to save the family firm…

PACKER: You're assuming I have no choice

JONAH: A blind man on a galloping horse could see that you can't?

PACKER: And if I don't need your money?

JONAH: Do fish need water? Do horses need hay?

PACKER: You're a hard man

JONAH: Or is life a hard game to play?
Have you signed?

PACKER: What do you think?

JONAH: Good, 'cause this is eating into my day…

CHORUS: Money—ar, money
You can wield a fist full of fives
Better than the handle of a pick
A knife, a broken bottle
The paling off a fence
They pale before the damage done
By pounds, shillings and pence!

JONAH: That's what I think, Packer
And that's something you taught me nine year ago!

Blackout.

SCENE TWO

Thunder and rain. Early morning light.

CHOOK *and* PINKEY *enter high up, shielding their heads with sacks.*

CHOOK: Weather you wouldn't send an umbrella into.

PINKEY: Lucky we don't have one, eh?

Below, the CHORUS *is gathering as buyers and sellers at Paddy's Market.*

CHOOK *and* PINKEY *shake rain off their sacks and will join the crowd below.*

CHOOK: [*sung*] It fair gives a man the hump

> I'm choking on swallowed pride
> It fair gives a man the hump

PINKEY: (What's eating you?)

CHOOK: It eats a man up inside
        How'd I have the hide to have the hide
        To do it to you?

PINKEY: (Do what?)

CHOOK: (Force you to marry me.)

PINKEY: (Forced to the altar? I broke a heel rushing there.)

> CHORUS *figures start loading* CHOOK *and* PINKEY*'s sacks with fruit and vegetables.*

CHORUS: Parsnips, carrots, spuds, fresh beet
        Parsnips, carrots, spuds, fresh beet

CHOOK: You're skinny as a stake
        I'm driving you into the ground
        It's me job to make you happy
        I've done what?

PINKEY: (What have you done?)

CHOOK: I've done you down
        (I've seen string beans carrying more condition than you got.)

VOICE 1: (Beautiful beans!)

CHOOK: It's 'cause I bean stringing you
        Along with the idea
        That one day soon we'll be in the clear
        Plain sailing from here
        But it's just an idea
        And ideas are cheap…

PINKEY: (So are radishes.)

CHOOK: But the real thing's
        Real dear…

PINKEY: (I got two only complaints. First, you talk too much.)

CHOOK: (Second?)

PINKEY: (You're standing on me foot.)

CHOOK: It fair gives a man the hump
        I'm choking on swallowed pride

PINKEY: (I've remembered a third! You keep singing the same God-awful tune!)

When I scan the rows for what's tiptop
My eyes get to you
That's when they stop

VOICE: (Ripe tamats!)

PINKEY: Way I see it:
You're the best in the market

VOICE 2: (Delicious apples!)

PINKEY: You're the pick of the crop

VOICE 3: (Iceberg! Cos!)

PINKEY: Lettuce be clear, my dear
I go choko

CHOOK: (Choko?)

PINKEY: Get biffed on the boko
Being here with you, old bean

VOICE 4: (Scarlet runner!)

PINKEY: I go bananas

VOICE 5: (Bananas?)

PINKEY: Like heroines in dramas
You're the King of Fruit and Veg
And I'm the Parsley Queen
So mind your peas and cues

CHOOK: (They're squashes.)

PINKEY: We're our own bosses
Watch where you're putting your pawpaws
I forget, I'm sold

CHORUS: You may squeeze her, she's yours!

PINKEY: Love's its own celery
And I'll beetroot to you, will—

CHOOK: I'll beetroot to you, will—

PINKEY: I'll be true to you, will
You be true to me?

VOICE 1: (Rockmelons!)

VOICE 2: (Best in the market!)

PINKEY: Everything's—

VOICE 1: (Apples!)

CHOOK: (Apples? It's raining cats and dogs—)

PINKEY: You're a—

VOICE 3: (Peach!)

PINKEY: We make a nice—
VOICE 4: (Pear!)
PINKEY: We got each other
So a word in your—
VOICE 1: (Cauliflower!)
PINKEY: Ear, my dear:

Their sacks are full. They dance with them.

Love's its own celery
And I'll beetroot to you, will
CHOOK: I'll beetroot to you, will
PINKEY: I'll be true to you, will
You be true to me?

*A thunderclap. They look upwards, then sit on the sacks for a bit,
hoping the weather might improve.*

CHOOK: You deserve better.
PINKEY: Me sitting on a cushion and every half an hour a cocky on a
spring comes outta the wall and plonks a Mintie in me mouth? It ain't
gonna happen!
CHOOK: No, and it gives me the hump.
PINKEY: We got food on our table, a roof over our heads, and each other.
It's more than most!
CHOOK: But far less than some.
PINKEY: Here we go: 'Jo's the posh end of Regent Street and where
are we?'
CHOOK: Where we started nine year ago, doing what? Working ourselves
to the bone. Why? So's we can get up tomorrow and do it all again.
Lugging sacks in the cold morning air's killing you.
PINKEY: I consider myself in the pink! Whingeing won't get this lot to
the shop—walking will!

They shoulder the sacks.

CHOOK: I'm getting us a horse and cart.
PINKEY: If wishes were horses…
CHOOK: Beggars would ride, I know, well as sure as I stand here—
PINKEY: Keep walking.
CHOOK: Your days as a beast of burden are numbered. Three miscarriages,
beloved, is something I have trouble living with!

PINKEY: Some women are built that way. Like it or lump it!

> CHOOK *and* PINKEY *exit humping their sacks.*

SCENE THREE

The Silver Shoe. Day.

ADA *comes down the stairs.*

ADA: [*sung*] I thought being rich'd be a wonder
>> I'd have a castle, horses
>> Servants serving big meals…

JONAH: What you look like is a servant dressed up. Going where?

ADA: Out.

JONAH: You ain't even washed your grimy neck.

ADA: How someone with your back can talk about the necks of others
I do not know.
>> [*Sung*] I thought being rich'd be a wonder
>> I'd read romances
>> Dance all night
>> Through the castle!

JONAH: That's right, start a scene in front of me staff and customers.

ADA: Can you spare one and six?

JONAH: Any other woman'd take an interest in a man's business.

ADA: Name one besides me who'd be fool enough to marry you?

JONAH: I s'pose making a silk purse outta a sow's ear can't be done.

ADA: No more than you can make a man out of a monkey on a stick.

> JONAH *doles her out some money.*

Ooo, look. The Boot King keeping his wife on a shoestring. One and
six. All me own. Ar, Miss Giltinan. He tells me you're a hard worker.
I don't have to work. I married money.
>> [*Sung*] I thought being rich'd be a wonder!
>> Well, it ain't! Castle I got's The Silver Shoe!

> ADA *exits, watched by* JONAH *and* GILTINAN.

JONAH: Uncanny. I saw those galoshes were beginning to sweat. Time
to mark 'em down, I thought.

GILTINAN: If you look at the price tag—

JONAH: I did, and saw you already had, that's the uncanny thing. How
in step with my thinking you are.

GILTINAN: On that topic, I got sacked at me last job for speaking me mind. I trust you're not gonna repeat the act.

JONAH: It's because you speak your mind I hired you. And I'd be a fool not to listen to me Head of Ladies Sales, so fire away.

GILTINAN: This plan you got of shifting The Silver Shoe to the city.

JONAH: That's my plan, is it?

GILTINAN: The deal you're striking with Packer suggests as much.

JONAH: You're not just a pretty face.

GILTINAN: I'm not a pretty face so don't go smarmy on me. Where others wouldn't have, you give me a go, so gratis I'll give you a piece advice. Easy to sympathise with wanting to move downtown.

JONAH: And teach those stuck-up bigwig city retailers the meaning of real competition.

GILTINAN: But I've worked half me days in the city, Mr Jones, and it ain't what it was. Where's the people these days? Moving to the new housing, getting to work in the new trains, going where the new factories are. It's like you say…

[*Sung*] Where there's people there's feet

JONAH: Where there's feet there's shoes

GILTINAN: We oughta be there!

JONAH: That's where the trade is!

GILTINAN: (People are leaving the city for the suburbs, and where are they gonna shop?)

JONAH: [*sung*] Where they've always shopped
            Where it's cheapest…

GILTINAN: (But also where it's handy.)
            Sydney ain't just urban, it's sub-urban out there
            It's expanding, a spread, a sprawl
            And the best way of taking
            Your share of the bacon
            Is to some way service it all!
        (What I'd do…)

JONAH: (If you were me…)

GILTINAN: (Is realise shelling out getting an emporium one up from this ticking over in the city could get four or five Silver Shoes up and running in key go-ahead suburbs.)

JONAH: (A ring of Silver Shoe stores?)

GILTINAN: (Here'd be Headquarters.)

      [*Sung*] Where there's people there's feet

JONAH: Where there's feet there's shoes

GILTINAN: We oughta be there!

JONAH: That's where the trade is!

GILTINAN: The people are the clue, Mr Jones

      Stick with the people, Mr Jones

      And neither you nor The Silver Shoe

      Can put a foot wrong…

(That's what I'd sing if I was musical.)

JONAH: (And were to put it in a song?)

GILTINAN: Although a mere minion, Mr Jones

      In my opinion, Mr Jones

      To ensure taking

      The Silver Shoe's share

JONAH: Of the boot trade bacon

GILTINAN: It'd pay

      To keep in step with the trends of the day…

    Music continues.

My hunch is Bondi Junction'd be the spot for a store. Leichhardt, Glebe, Balmain…

JONAH: Double Bay?

GILTINAN: It may seem sleepy but its time'll come.

JONAH: Don't move into the city, surround it?

GILTINAN: Let the know-nothings tear each other to ribbons trying to be Boot King of the City, you make yourself Boot King of the Suburbs and we'll see who's bigger.

JONAH: One to put in the brain box, Miss Giltinan.

GILTINAN: Starve the lizards!

JONAH: What have they done to you?

GILTINAN: Customer we got's giving us more trouble than a cat's got fleas.

JONAH: Reluctant to see someone leave The Silver Shoe without leaving us their money.

GILTINAN: Yes. We'll just try another hundred pair or so.

    A musical sting.

    JONAH *sees* CLARA *coming forward.*

JONAH: I know her. Kling and Wessels.

CLARA: Kling and Wessels…

JONAH: Told you.

GILTINAN: She's comfortable in nothing else.

CLARA: I'm com-for-table in nothing else!

An ASSISTANT *is following, arms laden with boxes.*

JONAH: Alas, Miss Grimes—

CLARA: You know my name?

JONAH: Once mended your shoes for you. Kling and Wessels they were then too. And you played organ at my wedding.

CLARA: Did I?

JONAH: Though whether I should thank you for that I dunno.

CLARA: Your assistant here's been telling me—

JONAH: And it is the case.

CLARA: I've worn my last pair of Kling and Wessels.

GILTINAN: Done for.

JONAH: Bought out by the Americans who promptly closed 'em down.

CLARA: How's that possible?

JONAH: It's the way of the world. The boot trade's a cut-throat game. You can put those back on the shelves. I'm Mr Jones.

The ASSISTANT *exits.*

GILTINAN: Mr Jones owns The Silver Shoe.

JONAH: It owns me, more like.

CLARA: From King of the Push to Boot King. Mother and I have followed your career in the newspapers. A 'from rags to riches story'.

JONAH: I wouldn't believe all you read in the papers, it ain't done with mirrors. Hard work's how it happened.

The CHORUS *wheels the* JONAH PUPPET *forward.*

CHORUS: [*sung*] Jonah's the Boot the Boot the Boot
   The boot the boot or shoe
   When only the best—the best—will stand the test
   Will stand the test—or get you through
   Jonah the Boot the Boot the Boot the Boot'll
   Fit your feet
   Guaranteed—Regent Street
   Sign of The Silver Shoe…

JONAH: Sure to get the kiddies in, eh Miss Grimes? And today's squaw-kers, as we say in the trade…

GILTINAN: Are tomorrow's walkers.

JONAH PUPPET: Where the little man tap tap tap
        Tap taps
        At a shoe last...

JONAH: That's more the ticket. First time they forgot the most interesting thing about me—me hunch.
        [*Sung*] It ain't a pretty thought I know
        But the oddities of nature
        Seem to fascinate most of the people
        Most of the time.
I once dreamed all this, Miss Grimes, a shop big as four or five shops put together, floor to ceiling boots and shoes, now I've got it. Two whole suburbs I've clawed me way through. Here I am, the posh end of Regent Street.

CLARA: And now?

JONAH: Time for a new dream perhaps. My card.

He hands her his business card.

GILTINAN: God gave humanity feet—

JONAH: But Jonah Jones will put those feet in shoes!

CLARA: Your motto?

JONAH: And I'd hate for you to think me less than a man of my word. Tell you what, Miss Grimes, I'll do you a pair of shoes, handcrafted, same price as a pair of Kling and Wessels—

GILTINAN: You can't—

JONAH: I can't and still make me margin's what Miss Giltinan means. What she doesn't know—get a seat for Miss Grimes—is that I have a favour to ask of you.

    GILTINAN *does his bidding.*

You are still teaching kiddies piano in that house of your mother's below Cardigan Street?

CLARA: Yes.

JONAH: It's my son. Ray. Once my only sunshine. He's becoming a real street Arab.

CLARA: Like you once were.

    JONAH *whistles—someone brings a measuring slide.*

JONAH: Worse than I ever was. Seeing you, it struck me: music might be the making of him.

CLARA: They do say it soothes the savage beast.

JONAH: Who better than you to teach him?

CLARA: My instep's the problem.

JONAH: So I see. A high instep. A sign of great beauty.

> GILTINAN *arrives with a stool.* CLARA *sits.* JONAH *kneels to measure her feet.*

CLARA: Perhaps. All I know is it makes buying shoes a nightmare.

JONAH: I don't normally make to order, low margins high turnover's the name of my game, but a foot like yours deserves a special last shaped to suit.

CLARA: Custom-built? Beyond my budget, alas.

JONAH: You must watch your pennies.

CLARA: In the hope that somehow the pounds will mount up—I'm afraid they never seem to.

JONAH: I'll do a deal with you, Miss Grimes. A pair of shoes as good as, and the same price as, a pair of Kling and Wessels, if you'll take Ray in hand as a pupil. What do you say?

GILTINAN: You're getting a bargain there.

CLARA: You mean, no fee?

JONAH: The fee per lesson would be on top of that.

CLARA: Oh, yes, well…

> JONAH *stands and assists* CLARA *to her feet.*

JONAH: What say we discuss the boy's musical future when you come for your shoes, let's say a week from today.

CLARA: A week from today. In black.

JONAH: It's the most serviceable shade.

> CLARA *bows to exit,* JONAH *watching her go.*

GILTINAN: Thank God. For a minute there I thought you'd kissed your business nous goodbye and were stuck on that stuck-up piece.

JONAH: A little mutuality, Miss Giltinan, that's all.

> *Music under.*

[*Aside*] Christ, it was like the beginning of an illness on the verge of become a raging disease.

CLARA: [*aside*] I stared ceilingward. Brass canisters hurried along wires their cargo of notes and coins destined to end up with the man I'd just spoken to.

JONAH: [*aside*] A picture of the old woman flashed through me head telling me years ago…

    A flashback: YABSLEY, PINKEY *and* CHOOK *appear.*

YABSLEY: The feelings, Jo. Can't be bought. Can't be sold. You can't even see 'em, but there's nothing finer than the feelings when you have 'em.

JONAH: [*sung*] It's like an axe between the eyes

YABSLEY: A bolt out of the blue

JONAH: Like lightning outta the empty skies

YABSLEY: What'll you do?

CHORUS: What'll you do?

CHOOK: God, you're crook

            God, it's shocking

            Must be—

JONAH: Miss Grimes!

    YABSLEY, PINKEY *and* CHOOK *vanish as* CLARA *turns back.*

I dunno what I was thinking. Here I am asking you to teach me boy piano. I don't have one. A good shoe I can tell by the smell of the leather, but pianos? Can I enlist your advice, without it I'm a blind man buying a painting.

CLARA: A request easily accommodated.

    A musical bridge jump-cuts to:

SCENE FOUR

A piano showroom.

HUTCHIN *is squiring* CLARA *and* JONAH.

HUTCHIN: Welcome to Kramer Kramer Kramer and Hutchin, Mr Jones. Pianos upright. Pianos squat. Pianos grand. To the left, to the right, pianos. The largest piano showroom in the Southern Hemisphere.

JONAH: So many—

HUTCHIN: I know. We've had to have the floor reinforced.

JONAH: Miss Grimes will be teaching my boy piano.

HUTCHIN: So she says, and for that you'll need an instrument.

JONAH: Correct.

HUTCHIN: Do you play yourself?

JONAH: Mouth organ. Means I know a good tune when I hear one, but a piano, there I've put myself in Miss Grimes' capable hands.

VOICE: [*offstage*] Telephone.

HUTCHIN: Excuse I.

    HUTCHIN *exits briefly.*

JONAH: Kramer Kramer Kramer and Hutchin. He's…?

CLARA: Hutchin.

JONAH: You don't think my boy's too young?

CLARA: Not if he has the gift.

JONAH: The gift?

CLARA: Of music.

JONAH: That'd be something you're born with, would it?

CLARA: Mother and I go by the width of the forehead at the temples. Phrenologists call it the bump of music. You have it yourself. At a guess I'd say you're fond of music.

JONAH: Very.

    She begins to play a piano as HUTCHIN *returns.*

    The instrument she's playing?

HUTCHIN: Is the Bechstein.

JONAH: Sssh.

HUTCHIN: Pardon?

JONAH: Lower it to a roar. [*He listens for a bit.*] I ain't heard the like in me natural. The Bechstein, eh? That's its name, what's its price?

HUTCHIN: A hundred.

JONAH: You're not talking shillings—a hundred pounds?

HUTCHIN: Guineas.

JONAH: Makes a piano an expensive piece of firewood.

HUTCHIN: If money's an object—

JONAH: If it was fresh air we'd all be millionaires.

HUTCHIN: Speciality of the house: KKK and H do do a cheap line.

JONAH: Cheap's how cheap?

HUTCHIN: Fifty.

JONAH: Guineas?

HUTCHIN: Pounds. The tone's inferior compared to the Bechstein.

JONAH: Inferior? [*Aside*] She'll think I ain't good for the hundred. [*To* HUTCHIN] The Bechstein it'll be.

HUTCHIN: In instances like this Miss Grimes usually recommends the Ropp.

JONAH: The Ropp?

HUTCHIN: The celebrated Ropp. Middle of the range. In her opinion the Bechstein's wasted on beginners.

JONAH: Ray is that.

HUTCHIN: It's an instrument for artistes.

JONAH: Like her.

HUTCHIN: Like her. Eighty.

JONAH: Pounds still? Or are we back to—?

HUTCHIN: Guineas, although for special cash customers…

JONAH: You make it pounds? How's seventy-five of them sound?

HUTCHIN: Done. I'll fetch the sales slip docket book and warranty.

JONAH: Wait up. We must build a commission in for Miss Grimes. What would you think adequate?

HUTCHIN: That's taken care of.

JONAH: It is?

HUTCHIN: She's already due a commission.

JONAH: Of course. Business is business, be it pianos be it—

HUTCHIN: Shoes?

HUTCHIN *exits.* JONAH *moves towards* CLARA *who has been playing throughout.*

JONAH: That must be hard.

CLARA: It does take it out of one.

JONAH: They'll wrap it up, or whatever they do, and deliver? There'll be some stairs.

CLARA: Kramer Kramer Kramer and Hutchin know all about stairs.

JONAH: They ain't alone there. I've attracted a few in me time. And I don't suppose you're a stranger to a stare or two either, eh?

HUTCHIN *returns.*

HUTCHIN: The Ropp, Miss Grimes. We've saved Mr Jones some money.

JONAH: But your commission will still be substantial.

CLARA: You know about my commission?

JONAH: I wanted to make sure you got one.

CLARA: [*aside*] God, how sordid life can be.

JONAH: I'll call a cab and see you home.

CLARA: If it's all the same to you, Mr Jones, I'll walk from here, there's some shopping I need to see to.

JONAH: Till Thursday next, then?

CLARA: Thursday next.

JONAH: Lesson Number One. Strange, you and me, after all this time, the way people's paths cross?

On the street, CLARA *exits.*

WAXY *steps forward.*

WAXY: Passing strange, I'd say.

JONAH: What you after?

WAXY: After doing nine years for a certain party, three of them hard, a hello would do for starters.

JONAH: Consider it said.

WAXY: Who is she?

JONAH: She'll be teaching me kid piano.

WAXY: Your kid learning piano, Jonah Jones has kicked on.

JONAH: And you're down on your uppers?

WAXY: Away nine years, what a changed world it is.

JONAH: A feed—if you're hungry. A job—supposing you want one.

WAXY: A beer—for old times' sake?

JONAH: Sworn off it.

WAXY: Taken the pledge?

JONAH: Nobody finds answers to their problems at the bottom of a beer glass.

WAXY: But it's good fun looking for 'em there, eh.

JONAH: These days I don't touch a drop. And I don't give people money for drink.

WAXY: Pretty pious coming from someone whose wife's getting full as a boot at Sarah Bolan's Bar. Probably there right now singing 'I'm Just a Bird in a Gilded Cage'. Know how she feels, the cage bit anyway.

Crossfade.

SCENE FIVE

Evening.

JONAH *is travelling towards the Yabsley interior.*

JONAH: [*sung*] They're dirty, they're dark, they're dingy
        That's the houses
        The men look mean, the women sad
        The brats, the brats are whingey

YABSLEY *enters with tea for* JONAH.

YABSLEY: Oh, it's hard making ends meet
    On Cardigan Street
    On Cardigan Street.

JONAH: I ain't asking you to do it just 'cause Ada's on the drink. There's Ray, you're his favourite grandmother.

YABSLEY: Not hard. I'm his only one.

JONAH: It's also me. Wanting you out of here. It's a street of thieves.

    PINKEY *enters.*

PINKEY: For the fowls from the Fowleses. Brought you some scraps, Mrs Yabs. Gidday, Jo.

YABSLEY: Pinkey keeps me chooks in the pink.

PINKEY: Don't see much of you in these parts.

YABSLEY: 'Course not. It's a street of thieves. Pinkey's a thief, is she? Chook's a thief?

JONAH: I get news. The money you gave Floss Fairfrait for Little Johnny's medicine went on a hat—

YABSLEY: 'Cause Darkie had got out of jail.

JONAH: A hat. And a day at the races.

YABSLEY: If a woman can't have a bash when her man gets out of prison, when can she?

PINKEY: Mrs Yabs knew what the money'd go on. Willing to steal, cheat and lie is proud enough not to beg, and I know which I'd rather.

JONAH: People keep robbing her blind!

YABSLEY: Can't rob me of what I don't have! As for what I do have I don't mind sharing it.

JONAH: There's a system. Reprobates taking it in turns to prey on you.

PINKEY: You're telling her nothing!

YABSLEY: If I've got a shilling and some poor beggar's got nothing I see it as I owe him sixpence.

JONAH: You'd give the Devil himself a handout.

PINKEY: Some say she did, giving you your start.

JONAH: Some are so used to lying they couldn't stand straight if God turned 'em into picket fences!

YABSLEY: You've pulled yourself up by your bootstraps, Jo, but nobody's perfect, not even you.

JONAH: So I'm wasting me breath?

YABSLEY: He's heard how often Ada frequents Sarah Bolan's. Wants me to go live at The Silver Shoe. That backyard plum tree's me, Jo. You'd have to cut me off at the roots.

PINKEY: And if I can be permitted my sixpence worth, that's a bit Ada's story.

JONAH: Then I'll be going.

CHOOK *enters with flowers for* YABSLEY.

CHOOK: Gidday, Jo. How's—?

JONAH: Ada? Don't ask. The Silver Shoe? A success, thanks for asking.

JONAH *exits.*

YABSLEY: He's found out Ada's taken to the drink. But as I'm fond of saying, if a woman does that she not only takes a short cut to Hell but chances are some man's driving her there. Told those two way back: the feeling's gotta be right between a man and a woman or the game ain't worth the candle.

> [*Sung*] Many a candle casts a poor light
> Some apples are rotten although they look ripe
> Some ships are best left to pass in the night
> Never get married till it gets you
> Never get married till it gets you
> Never get married till it gets you here—
> Or trouble's sure to find you.

Cuppa tea, Chook?

CHOOK: Please. We got news.

YABSLEY: Pregnant?

PINKEY *nods.*

Here's hoping, my girl.

YABSLEY *hugs* PINKEY.

Crossfade.

SCENE SIX

The Silver Shoe in a darkened state.

JONAH *is perched on top of the stairs.* ADA *(drunk) is arriving home.*

ADA: [*sung*] Ada Ada
     Ada, I'm afraid-a loving you

You give me goosebumps
Ada Ada
Ada, I'm afraid-a loving you
You turn my head round…

A light snaps on upstairs.

JONAH: Has a man got a right to know where you been all day? Not that you need tell me. Bolan's, right?

ADA: [*sung*] In praise of drinking
In praise of drinking
In praise of getting stinking

CHORUS: Meanwhile thinking

ADA: All sorts of nice thoughts
Just why nots and I oughts
Keeping the horrors of all my tomorrows at bay…

JONAH: And you been going there behind me back for months.

ADA: Try years.

He descends the stairs.

JONAH: I thought I had done with the no-good loafers I used to know, but in marrying you I married me past.

ADA: [*sung*] The past that we dwell on so fondly
Was it really that wonderful?
I wish you were me past!
But me past, you ain't.

JONAH: I'm your husband.

ADA: [*sung*] Husbands husbands
Husbands husbands…
You're me past, me present and me future and I'm a bird in a gilded cage.

JONAH: You're a millstone round me neck!

He drags her upstairs.

CHORUS: [*sung*] Sticks n stones'll
Break your bones
But Jonah Jones'll…

JONAH: You ain't going out making my name mud! I got a reputation to uphold! And you got a son in there waiting to be fed.

ADA: Ar yes, our Little Ray of sunshine! Will there be light at the end of this tunnel?

SCENE SEVEN

Chook and Pinkey's shop, some days later.

PINKEY *is singing.*

PINKEY: [*sung*] God, I'm crook
Off me tucker
Through the fence
Down the chute
Up the creek
Got it here, got it there.

    She sneezes as CHOOK *enters.*

CHOOK: Caught ya.
PINKEY: Singing?
CHOOK: Sneezing.
PINKEY: Ain't you gonna 'God bless' me?
CHOOK: God don't bless the likes of us, if he did I'd have twenty quid
    and we'd be laughing.
PINKEY: Twenty quid?
CHOOK: Jack Ryan's horse and cart's for sale.
PINKEY: We ain't got twenty quid.
VOICE: [*offstage*] Shop!
PINKEY: Li Shou Cheng for the crates.
CHOOK: I'll do it.
PINKEY: Like hell you will. I run the shop, you hawk the streets.
CHOOK: It's Thursday.
PINKEY: Your afternoon off. And you're the last thing I want underfoot,
    so spend threepence and get thee to the picture show. Coming…

    PINKEY *exits.*

CHOOK: I took the hint, but never did go to the picture show… it was
    more like getting trapped inside one!

    CHOOK *exits. Music under.*

SCENE EIGHT

The flat above The Silver Shoe. The day of the first piano lesson.

ADA *is in a nightdress.* JONAH *is holding a brown paper-wrapped bottle.
Somewhere offstage Ray thumps piano keys.*

JONAH: Hidden, in the bloody piano! For Godsake, woman! I can't turn me back? Who give you the money, I'll wring their neck.

ADA: I give me the money.

JONAH: You've pawned something? Your clothes!

He's checked her wardrobe.

ADA: Buy the kid a piano but you'd begrudge me the air I breathe.

JONAH: No spending money till you stop spending money on drink.

ADA: It's me medicine.

JONAH: Your medicine's doing without. You heard the doctor!

ADA: A meaner man than you never trod the earth!

They become aware that CLARA *is witnessing this.*

JONAH: I had hoped to spare you the sight.

ADA: I won't introduce myself, Miss Grimes. He says I ain't good enough to meet the likes of you.

ADA *exits.*

CLARA: She seems…

JONAH: A wreck? You ain't wrong. Cheap brandy, Miss Grimes. I just now discovered she's pawned her clothes to buy drink. Without me knowing it, it's been going on for years.

CLARA: The nearest and dearest are often the last to know.

JONAH: Nearest and dearest? Ada and me? I'm at my wits' end and feel if I don't talk to somebody, get it off my chest, I'll burst. Could we meet? At the Quay, say? After the boy's lesson?

CLARA: If you think I can—

JONAH: Help? You can. Ray's in there waiting for you, Miss Grimes.

CLARA: So I hear.

JONAH: Quiet, boy! Well…

CLARA: Lesson Number One.

Music as they exit separately.

SCENE NINE

A street. Day.

CHOOK *is describing his afternoon off.*

CHOOK: I would have gone to the Thursday matinee except walking to the tram a black cat crosses me path.

A musical sting.

Not that I take much notice. Too immersed in me worries.

> [*Sung*] How's a man get his start
> How's a man get his break
> When they know how to break your heart
> Every step you take.

At which point a second black cat hoves into view.

The musical sting repeats.

But still I think nothing of it. Me mind's on the twenty quid I don't have…

> [*Sung*] And it's not whether you're willing to work or not
> You'd bust your guts
> But no, you're just
> Another pair of hands
> That nobody wants to know!

But when seconds later a third black cat happens onto the scene…

A third sting.

… a kind of religious sensation spreads through me whole constitution. Maybe Lady Luck's telling me something.

> [*Sung*] When you're down you're down you're down
> But are you out?
> Does a drowning man drown without so much as a shout?

He counts his money.

For me bank that's what would have been tram fares, that's what would have been me ticket to the picture show, and that's what I'm gonna buy stock with at tomorrow's market. Give fortune no excuse for neglecting you is my motto, and…

He tosses a coin.

Heads it was!

> [*Sung*] Casting caution to the winds
> I make straight for Paddy Flynn's
> Two-Up Emporium!

Crossfade.

SCENE TEN

The flat above The Silver Shoe.

CLARA *is teaching Ray. Piano discords under.* ADA *enters singing.*

ADA: [*sung*] Square peg, round hole
       Right actor, wrong role
       Like a cart driving the horse
       The sweet's arriving before the main course
       Like an ape wearing trousers
       Like a two-headed face
       In a word, I'm a word
       Outta place.

CLARA: C D C—C D C.

ADA: A D A, Miss Grimes, Ada. I feel awful dressed this way, but I can't dress for company. He's taken all me clothes to stop me going out.

CLARA: He told me you pawned them to get money for drink.

ADA: Heard that, did you? What else have you heard, 'cause there's two sides to every story. Two sides. What a lovely purse—

CLARA: Isn't it? And it's lasted me a good long while. Quality tells.

    ADA *picks up* CLARA*'s purse.*

ADA: You keep playing, Ray, your father's paying for this.

CLARA: C B C—C B C.

ADA: Have you also heard I'm kept under lock and key? And how by starving his wife he squeezes a few more shillings into his bank account.

CLARA: [*aside*] She's going to steal money from my purse.

ADA: Once King of the Push now a Boot King, but nothing's changed, same brute he always was.

CLARA: How much money did you take?

ADA: What money, Miss Grimes?

CLARA: What's that in your hand?

ADA: For me medicine.

CLARA: For your drink you mean.

ADA: For some of us the drink is medicine. It's the only happiness I know. One and six, Miss Grimes, we could call it a loan.

CLARA: And if Mr Jones finds out?

ADA: He won't, unless you tell him.

CLARA: [*aside*] Why not let her have the one and six? Poor devil. If she
wants to die of the drink who am I to stand in her way?

ADA: Run your mother a message, Ray, there's a good boy.

> CLARA *laughs.*

Whatcha laughing at?

CLARA: You. Me. I find us amusing. You've gone to the demon drink.

ADA: It's the only thing that keeps me going.

CLARA: In my way I'm just as lost.

ADA: Perhaps you should play something, Miss Grimes, in case Jonah's
downstairs and notices Ray's stopped his lesson.

> CLARA *plays.*

The Silver Shoe. I don't belong here, do I?

CLARA: [*aside*] And me? Do I belong where I've ended up?

ADA & CLARA: [*sung*] Square peg, round hole
>> Right right actor
>> Wrong wrong role
>> Like fish out of water
>> Wild birds trapped in a cage
>> Kept under wraps in the wings
>> Never on stage
>> Always the bridesmaid
>> Never the bride
>> Pretty as a picture to look at
>> Turned to stone inside
>> Square peg, round hole
>> Right right actor, wrong wrong role
>> When clocks are going backwards
>> When water's flowing uphill
>> We'll come into our own then it's like knowing
>> We never will!
>> Was there for us
>> Ever a time, ever a tide?
>> Pretty as a picture to look at
>> Turned to stone inside.

> *Blackout.*

SCENE ELEVEN

The sounds of Circular Quay.

WAXY, *on high, swigs from a bottle.*

WAXY: I spotted 'em at the Quay, him and the piano teacher. Not much going on by way of entertainment, I thought I'd take a closer look.

Down below, CLARA *and* JONAH *feed gulls.*

JONAH: My money's done Ada no good.

CHORUS: Money—ar, money.

JONAH: I shoulda done us both a favour and left her in Cardigan Street. Human happiness, Miss Grimes, it's an elusive thing.

CLARA: Mine, oddly, is a similar story. Human happiness again proving an elusive thing.

JONAH: Do we look for it in the wrong places?

CLARA: My father drank to excess, speculated unwisely, and suicided. From a once distinguished once landed family, Mother and I found ourselves overnight forced to join the poor of this great city. Genteel poverty, Mr Jones, consists of pretending not to notice how poor you are. Mother's rather better at pretending than I am.

CHORUS: Money—ar, money.

JONAH: If it helped I could offer you a cashier's job at The Silver Shoe. A take-home pay of two pound ten.

CLARA: More per week than I earn in a fortnight, yet I dare not accept. I've been raised a lady and a lady must earn a living, when earn a living a lady must, in a ladylike fashion. I give lessons. Piano and embroidery.

JONAH: Offer's open.

CLARA: Mother would die before seeing me in a shop. Trade is not ladylike.

JONAH: A ferry ride, Miss Grimes, at least let me shout you that.

CLARA: Why not? I so rarely glimpse the Harbour.

WAXY: They caught the Cremorne Point ferry. And so did I.

CHORUS: Is it money or music, music or money.
　　　　That makes the piper wanta play?

They exit. PASCH *enters below, a blind beggar.*

PASCH: [*sung*] There's having a silver spoon in your gob

At birth
There's getting a mouthful of mother's mitt
Mit your mother's milk
'Cause that's all you're worth
There's he who makes the boot
There's he who puts it in
There's the difference
How come there's a difference?
I tell you the difference
Is all just a matter of luck.

At the ferry rail above, JONAH *and* CLARA *see* PASCH.

JONAH: The man they say I ruined. If I beat him it was because I was the better man at the game.

CLARA: You don't feel sorry for his plight?

JONAH: He took me in, taught me a trade, but you wouldn't have such a sentimental way of looking at it if you were dumped at birth and grew up with no-one caring whether you lived or died. He got his money's worth outta me, with interest. [*To* PASCHA] Singing tunes for ferry passengers, eh Pasch?

PASCH: Is that you?

JONAH: Eyes not what they were? Pity. Here, for the tune you give us.

JONAH *tosses some money below. Someone gathers it for* PASCH.

PASCH: Give me back the shop you stole from me!

JONAH: Stole ain't the word and you know it.

PASCH: Give me back my business!

JONAH: Keep a civil tongue in your head.

PASCH: Keep your cursed money!

JONAH: You're frightening the lady.

PASCH *sings a curse as he flings the coins.*

PASCH: [*sung*] You are a rich man
            But not for the opium in China would I be in your shoes
            Money you may have in plenty
            But never your heart's content
            The great gods shall mock you for like a dog you did bite
            The hand that fed you!

JONAH: He makes out I'm a cruel man. It's the game that's cruel.

JONAH *and* CLARA *move away.* PASCH *cavorts.*

PASCH: [*sung*] Fate, luck or fortune
        Spin of the wheel
        Fall of the numbers
        Luck of the deal
        Fate, luck or fortune
        Destiny's gate
        Hinges on chance, but
        Slams shut on the late
        Nations rise against the odds
        Sparrows fall
        We're all in the lap of the gods
        The playthings
        Of fate!

The gate to the ferry has shut.

SCENE TWELVE

The space functions as The Silver Shoe (where ADA *will appear), a two-up school (which* CHOOK *enters) and Cremorne Point (where* CLARA *and* JONAH *take the view).*

CHORUS: [*sung*] A dollar heads, a dollar heads
        Half a dollar heads
        Get set, get set, what do you set?
  Fair go!

      CHOOK *surveys the knot of gamblers looking up to follow the rise and fall of the coins.*

CHOOK: All me life I've been haunted by the idea of sudden riches falling outta the sky and into me lap. Still I hesitated. Pink had made me swear off the two-up. But something drew me on and I joined the magic circle adding my voice to the others.

CHORUS: [*sung*] A dollar heads, a dollar heads
        Half a dollar heads
        Get set, get set, what do you set?
  Fair go!

      The CHORUS *follows the second toss of the coins while* CLARA *and* JONAH *appear on high.*

JONAH: Been reading me spring mail-order catalogue, have you?

CLARA: These patent leather pumps, seven and eleven post-free, they'll sell like hot cakes.

JONAH: Me loss leader. Cost me more than I sell 'em for but it gets 'em in. Factory hands, waitresses, dressmakers, bits of girls that'll do without to doll 'emselves up. They're the sort I want.

CLARA: The sort you want?

JONAH: The sort The Silver Shoe wants. The sort I want's a different story.

Focus shifts below.

CHOOK: Three times the spinner threw heads and three times I backed him in. But success had shaken the spinner's nerve and he fumbled the kip. Change your tack, I thought. A dollar tails.

CHORUS: [*sung*] A dollar tails a dollar heads

        Half a dollar tails

        Get set, get set, what do you set?

Fair go!

They follow the toss-up.

JONAH: You're a grown woman, Miss Grimes. And I'll square with you. We both know the way of the world.

CHOOK: Tails it was. The spinner had lost the kip.

PADDY: Come in, spinner!

CHOOK: And I'm on me feet!

JONAH: At the Quay I offered you a job. Fact is, it ain't all I want to offer you.

CHOOK: As if obeying an instinct I walk to the centre of the circle, sling Paddy Flynn the five bob required, and prepare to chance me arm.

JONAH: Time was I thought I knew all there was to know about women. Then I met you.

CLARA: Please, you mustn't.

JONAH: I have to, don't you see?

CHOOK: I place the pennies on the kip.

PADDY: What do you set?

JONAH: I can't ask you to marry me because I'm married to Ada.

CHOOK: The lot. Everything.

JONAH: But I can ask you to be my mistress.

CHOOK: With the skill of an old gaffer I send the browns upward into the dome.

The PLAYERS *follow the toss up and down.*

CLARA: Your kept woman?

JONAH: I'd spare no expense. A house servant, a carriage of your own. You'd have the lot.

CLARA: Everything?

CHOOK: Seven times I throw the kip and seven times it comes down—

PADDY: Heads it is!

CLARA: I know 'marriages' of the sort you propose.

CHOOK: The pile of silver in front of me has turned itself into fifteen quid.

CLARA: I know what life in such a house would be like. I'd have everything but the thing most important would be missing: the right to walk down the street, my head held high.

CHOOK: I load the kip for toss number eight.

CLARA: Throughout my adult life all I've known is shame. Ashamed of my drunken spendthrift father. Of the poverty he left mother and I to endure.

CHOOK: Half seconds seem like minutes.

CLARA: You come into my life offering—

JONAH: To change all that!

CLARA: The poverty yes, but not the shame.

CHOOK: Jack Ryan's horse and cart's hanging on this. So is being broke. I set the coins spinning into the ether.

JONAH: That's a shame then, ain't it?

CLARA: Silly perhaps. But I'd live in dread of what the servants you appointed were saying to the neighbours behind my back.

    CHOOK *tosses the kip.*

CHOOK: It's like the world's come to a standstill. Heads and I'll be laughing.

    A third focus is revealed—The Silver Shoe.

ASSISTANT: It's the boss's wife.

GILTINAN: Clad in a petticoat, Ada's appeared at the top of the stairs.

    ADA *above,* GILTINAN *and the* ASSISTANT *below.*

ADA: What right's he got to imprison me?

GILTINAN: She's been drinking.

ADA: What you staring daggers at me for, Miss Giltinan? I'll make a spectacle of myself in The Silver Shoe if I want.

ASSISTANT: Customers have noticed.

GILTINAN: Heads are turning.

JONAH: It's 'cause of her. Ada. 'Cause I'm married and can't make an honest woman of you.

ADA: Other people live in houses, real people. Not us. We live above The Silver Shoe, though that's a lie 'cause above us there's what? The sign of The Silver Shoe!

GILTINAN: She steps off the landing, coming down misses her footing and falls headlong.

CHORUS: [*sung*] The last seconds of your life
        Are slipping by
        You're letting go
        You're going to die
        That's all you know
        Those last seconds of your life
        Those last seconds of your life
        Those last seconds of your life.

> ADA *has slow-motion fallen and landed amidst the* CHORUS. *It parts to reveal* CHOOK *scooping his winnings.*

CHOOK: I am on the longest winning streak of my gambling career. What happens?

ASSISTANT: The police!

GILTINAN: Somebody fetch a doctor!

CHOOK: The johns pick this moment to raid Paddy Flynn's!

GILTINAN: Her head's facing the wrong way round.

> ADA *stands in a spotlight and sings.*

ADA: [*sung*] Those last seconds of your life
        Those last seconds of your life
        Those last seconds of a life.

> *Cremorne Point continued:*

CLARA: Music.

JONAH: Band on a passing Manly steamer.

CLARA: Is that what it is?

JONAH: Like a spot of music would you? Hang onto your hat, Exhibition Concert Model. That day at Kramer Kramer Kramer and Hutchin I got Huchin to palm it my way.

He produces his new mouth organ and plays 'Ada'.

You know I love you, don't you?

CLARA: Yes.

JONAH continues to play.

Suddenly CLARA *turns away.*

JONAH: Racing, is that your game!

He catches up to her.

I'm not gonna touch you if that's your fear.

CLARA: No, it's just—

JONAH: I wouldn't, not without you saying so.

CLARA: It's, since childhood, crowded carriages.

JONAH: Proximity to people?

CLARA: Yes, sets me on edge.

JONAH: My hunch doesn't worry you?

CLARA: Credit me, Mr Jones, with being able to see past your shape.

JONAH: To the person I am? Not everyone can, Miss Grimes. Scenery. Never knew the point of it.

CLARA: Now you do?

JONAH: Now I know it's something for people like us to stare at and feel...

CLARA: What?

JONAH: Sad.

CLARA: Sunset. Another dying day.

As JONAH *moves closer, she sings.*

> [*Sung*] I often feel the wind, the sea, the clouds
> Are more a living thing than I am
> That they breathe and I don't
> That a life is being kept from me.

JONAH: Ever thought you might be keeping yourself from life?

WAXY appears to one side.

WAXY: Strange, eh, what people talk about when they dunno they're being watched. My thinking's: 'Hunchback Boot King Seen With Mistress'. A paper might pay a pretty penny for that.

CLARA: Dusk's approaching.

JONAH: They'll be lighting me sign soon.

CLARA: And mother—

JONAH: Will be concerned?

CLARA: It is late.

JONAH: For us both. Why not embrace the life we got left?

CLARA: Is that what you're thinking?

JONAH: Ain't it on your mind as well?

WAXY: At this point the sun's rim dipped below the horizon and Sydney—seconds earlier bathed in gold and silver—melted into a blood-red sea.

> *The lights fade on* JONAH *and* CLARA.

> *Focus shifts to* CHOOK *escaping from the two-up school.*

CHOOK: As in wartime, when a man may walk unhurt amid a shower of bullets, I beat a retreat to the top floor of Paddy Flynn's. A bunch of us fight like trapped rats round a window before dropping one by one onto the roof of the stables next door. I still had 'em—me winnings. But if I'm nabbed now I can kiss the lot goodbye. Wearing the hat I'd ended up with, two sizes too big for me skull, I walk the iron roof and duck behind the signboard expecting every minute a walloper to call me down. Night falls, I give it an hour, shimmy down the verandah post and head for home. A happy man.

> CHOOK *grins triumphantly.*

> *The lights fade to blackout.*

SCENE THIRTEEN

Night. The sounds of Circular Quay.

CLARA *and* JONAH *exit down a ferry gangway.* GINTINAN *steps forward to meet them.*

GILTINAN: You were seen catching the ferry.

JONAH: Miss Grimes and I have been discussing the boy's progress, musically.

GILTINAN: It's your wife.

JONAH: What gives now?

> GILTINAN *steers* JONAH *away.* WAXY *approaches* CLARA.

WAXY: I'm onto you two, and unless paid not to, I'm going to the papers with the whole sordid tale.

CLARA: If you're suggesting whatever's passed between Mr Jones and myself is in any way, shape or form suggestive of scandal…

WAXY: That's more or less it.

CLARA: You're wrong.

WAXY: Let's let Ada decide that, shall we?

JONAH, *with* GILTINAN, *reapproach* CLARA.

JONAH: Ada's had a fall.

CLARA: She what?

GILTINAN: She's dead.

JONAH: [*to* WAXY] What you doing here?

WAXY: It's a jetty, ain't it? I'm fishing, only the big one seems to have got away.

GILTINAN *exits, saying:*

GILTINAN: I've arranged a car. I'll see how close it can get.

JONAH: You know what this means, don't you?

CLARA: Yes.

JONAH: I can make an honest woman of you. Being with you I've felt things I never thought I could feel, dreamed dreams I never thought were in me. Perhaps this means me dreams can come true!

Above, PASCH *sings as the light slowly blacks out.*

PASCH: [*sung*] Money you will have in plenty
But never your heart's content.

JONAH: Is that so, Pasch!? Is that so!?

SCENE FOURTEEN

Chook and Pinkey's shop.

PINKEY *lights a candle.*

CHOOK: So there you have it. I'm late getting home from the picture show on account of I never even saw it. Now before you flare up like a box of matches, tell me to vacate the premises, and generally do your 'nana on the subject of me and gambling, first tell me how it feels to as good as own Jack Ryan's horse and cart because, strike me pink, pinch me, tell me I ain't dreaming, is that or is that not twenty quid?!

PINKEY: Ada's dead.

CHOOK: Makes twenty quid a bit of an anti-climax.

Music under.

SCENE FIFTEEN

The Silver Shoe at night.

A candle-lit coffin and the CHORUS. YABSLEY *is keeping vigil.* PINKEY *enters with* CHOOK.

CHORUS: [*sung*] And because our mothers lay in labour giving birth
        We draw breath
        When we cop death labour digs our trench
        Labour nails the coffin
        Labour lays us in the earth.

YABSLEY: It ain't right, Pinkey.

PINKEY: I know it ain't right.

YABSLEY: She should be burying me, not me keeping watch over her coffin.

PINKEY: [*sung*] You dunno what they're looking at
        The dead.

YABSLEY: You dunno what they're seeing.

PINKEY: Are they seeing…

YABSLEY & PINKEY: … anything at all?

      CLARA *and* JONAH *arrive.*

CHOOK: I'm sorry to hear about Ada, Jo.

JONAH: We're all sorry to hear about Ada, it's a dreadful thing.

     Coming downstairs, GILTINAN *moves towards* JONAH *holding a brown paper-wrapped bottle.*

WAXY: Good, all this—means you can step into Ada's shoes, eh?

CLARA: You again.

WAXY: Why not? I'm a friend of the family.

YABSLEY: Is that Waxy Collins?

WAXY: It is.

GILTINAN: I've questioned the staff. No-one'll admit giving Ada the money.

JONAH: Who else was up there this afternoon?

GILTINAN: Apart from you? Only Miss Grimes giving Ray his lesson.

     JONAH, *holding the bottle, turns to* CLARA.

CLARA: There were pennies on her eyelids.

YABSLEY: They're to keep her eyes from coming open.

CLARA: [*sung*] You dunno what they're looking at

    The dead

    What can they be seeing?

    Are they seeing

    Anything at all?

JONAH: Was it you?

CLARA: What?

JONAH: For Godsake, woman, say something. Say you never had a hand in Ada dying and I'll kiss the ground you walk on.

CLARA: And we'll live happily ever after?

JONAH: She somehow got hold of the money to buy this.

CLARA: Stole it.

JONAH: The bottle?

CLARA: The money. From my handbag.

JONAH: You noticed you had money missing?

CLARA: I saw her take it.

JONAH: And didn't try to stop her! Righto. I see it now.

CLARA: Do you?

JONAH: Ada not going to the grave fast enough, you thought you'd give her a shove. Me. I'd started to feel something I'd never believed in.

CLARA: Is love what you're going to say?

JONAH: Talk about snatching defeat from the jaws of victory! Well, as sure as you've helped murder me wife you've murdered the best in me.

CLARA: Doesn't seem much more to say, does there?

JONAH: No.

CLARA: I've killed her. I've killed the best in you. Why don't I just go and kill myself—it runs in my family.

JONAH: Why don't you? 'Cause I fancy you ain't got the guts.

CLARA: I envy her.

JONAH: You envied her alright.

CLARA: She isn't being strangled, suffocating a breath at a time, for her it's over.

JONAH: I thought you just might have wanted me, but no.

CLARA: Well, you might have known that!

    As CLARA *leaves,* YABSLEY *approaches* JONAH.

YABSLEY: It ain't natural, Jo.

JONAH: Natural?

YABSLEY: Mothers outliving daughters.

JONAH: Is anything, is anybody, natural?! People look at me, they think I ain't got feelings. Look at me and think I'm a machine for making money—everything he touches turns to gold. Do they think I don't stand here sometimes saying: What is this place? What am I doing? For who? For what? Who do I think I am?! Don't talk to me about natural. Ada'll have a decent burial. There'll be black drapes on all the windows. The Silver Shoe'll be shut for the rest of the week.

> [*Sung*] There was a crooked man
> He walked a crooked mile
> They slashed a crooked smile
> Across his crooked dial!

He smashes the bottle. The JONAH PUPPET *starts up.*

JONAH PUPPET: Where the little man tap tap tap
> Tap taps
> At a shoe last!

JONAH: Somebody turn that thing off!

Blackout.

The Cardigan Street theme plays.

SCENE SIXTEEN

After Ada's funeral. The Yabsley house. Evening.

YABSLEY: Weren't much of a wake, Jo.

JONAH: I drew the line at hiring mourners.

YABSLEY: Street's changed.

JONAH: Has it?

YABSLEY: Time was, a death woulda brought us all together.

JONAH: Waxy came.

YABSLEY: He wanted a drink.

JONAH: Mrs Bolan came.

YABSLEY: You paid her for the drink.

JONAH: Chook and Pinkey—soldiering on.

YABSLEY: On True Love's bones they put a bit of meat and gristle.

JONAH: And do it while in the fruit and vegetable trade—funny that.

A violin from somewhere. Music builds under:

YABSLEY: [*sung*] Time was we laughed, drank, sang, even fought
      Without malice o' forethought
      In this street

JONAH: But now?

YABSLEY: People seem meaner somehow

JONAH: The past that you dwell on so fondly
      Was not all that wonderful
      Being you being young was what was wonderful
      It gave base metal the gleam of gold

YABSLEY: Time was, I read me neighbours' faces like a clock
      They'd tell me their troubles straight
      Now they tell me all sorts of lies and inventions

JONAH: All for a few shillings

YABSLEY: I don't always see through 'em

JONAH: When's this street been anything but mean?
      You've seen it through rose-coloured glasses
      And taking 'em off

YABSLEY: Hurts?

JONAH: The past that you dwell on so fondly
      Was not that wonderful
      Being you being young that was wonderful

YABSLEY: And now I've grown old?

JONAH: But like the hump I wear, you can't shrug it off, can you?
      You're back there in the old days
      With the old people, the old ways
      Even though they're gone for good, if good
      Was what they were!
      'Cause I was there and from where I stood
      There weren't too much good
      But good or not good
      The old days
      The old people the old ways

YABSLEY: Over, finished, done?

JONAH: And there's nothing as bright as the morning light
      When you're facing the setting sun!

YABSLEY: You saying life's a fraud?

JONAH: There's a lot of it about.

YABSLEY: Young, it promises you everything, only it asks you to wait, and meanwhile hands out the rose-coloured spectacles. So you wait.

JONAH: Then find you've lost your appetite. Or your teeth. Or you've forgotten what it was you were waiting for. And all the while life's been taking you for everything you've got, a day at a time.

YABSLEY: [*sung*] Life promises warmth.

JONAH: We end up cold.

YABSLEY: Yesterday, today and tomorrow?

JONAH: Base metal pretending it's gold.

YABSLEY: The past that I dwell on so fondly
                         Wasn't that wonderful?

JONAH: But you, of course, won't be told.

YABSLEY: What I know, Jo, is Ada's dead too young to meet her maker. That mothers shouldn't outlive daughters. That I've started feeling a stranger in me own street. That the world seems cockeyed, on its ear, and so much of it's stopped making sense.

JONAH: Something—being brought up an outcast—I've always felt…

   PINKEY *and* CHOOK *have entered.*

PINKEY: Coming back here, wanting to help the old girl tidy up, we heard the news.

JONAH: What news?

PINKEY: War.

JONAH: What war?

CHOOK: There's a punch-up on, read it for yourself.

   CHOOK *hands* JONAH *the paper. He scans it.*

CHORUS: [*sung*] That's right, you heard: a war is coming
                         Feet are marching, drums are drumming
                         The grim reaper's shouting something
                         Armies march in, bomp stomp bomp stomp
                         Armies march in, bomp stomp bomp stomp
                         Armies march in, bomp stomp bomp stomp—

JONAH: *Boots!*

   WAXY *enters in uniform.*

WAXY: How do you like me outfit?

CHOOK: Waxy, you haven't?

WAXY: A shilling a day beats no pay at all.

PINKEY: You ain't going!

CHOOK: I know that.

YABSLEY: That's right, Chook. Be part of the B Brigade. Be here when they go, be here when they get back, those that do.

The CHORUS *crowds around* WAXY.

CHORUS: [*sung*] He wears blue or green, khaki or grey
        And he shoots
        At one end a hat, cap, helmet or beret
        And he salutes
        At the other end, unless he's lost his legs
        He's wearing

JONAH: *Boots!*

A recruiting rally in the Domain.

CHOOK, PINKEY *and* YABSLEY *are in the crowd.* PACKER *is making a speech.*

PACKER: [*sung*] It's only an old piece of bunting
        It's only an old, coloured rag
        But many have died in its honour
        And shed their life's blood for the flag.

PINKEY: You're a stay-at-home patriot, Packer!

CHOOK: [*sung*] Capitalists, parsons, politicians
        Landlords, newspaper editors…

PINKEY: To arms! To the trenches! Your country needs you!

CHOOK: Workers! Follow your masters! Go if they're going!

PINKEY: Are you going, Packer?

PACKER: That is unpatriotic nonsense!

PACKER *spreads his arms wide. All of a sudden* CHOOK *and* PINKEY *have white feathers in their hands.*

CHOOK: What do we do with these?

PINKEY: Sign some peace treaty when it's over?

PACKER: This is a recruiting rally not a butcher's picnic!

PINKEY: A butcher's picnic's what a recruiting rally is!

CHOOK: Is that what we want? To turn women into widows?

PINKEY: Children into orphans?

WAXY *hurls a bloodied* PASCH *towards* PACKER.

PACKER: What gives?

WAXY: He's a German, ain't he?

PASCH: Bohemia. I come from Bohemia.

> *The rally breaks into chaos. The sound of bombing.* YABSLEY *is going to* PASCH*'s aid. On high, looking down, is* JONAH.

JONAH: [*sung*] I got a hunch war is
>> In my biz
>> What'll put me through the roof.

> *Escaping to higher ground,* PACKER *reaches* JONAH.

Seventy-five thousand pound for you—lock, stock and barrel!

PACKER: That's ten per cent more than I'm worth.

JONAH: You flatter yourself. It's fifteen per cent more than you're worth. Going once, going twice—

PACKER: The war! Your thinking is the war'll drag on!

JONAH: Me offer's on the table. What do you say?

PACKER: What do you think I say?

JONAH: That a yes?

PACKER: Of course it's a yes! And here's a ha-ha to you-you. The Germans? Piss and wind—it'll be over in a month.

CHORUS: [*sung*] That's right you heard: a war is coming
>> Feet are marching, drums are drumming
>> The grim reaper is shouting something.

YABSLEY: Bugger the lot of 'em. Stay at my place, Dutchy, as long as you like.

PASCH: Thank you, thank you, thank you.

> YABSLEY *is leading* PASCH *to safety.*

CHORUS: [*sung*] Armies march in
>> Armies march in
>> Armies march in…
>> *Boots!*

Blackout.

A shed door opens and car headlights shine into the lower space.

Footsteps.

GILTINAN: Packer's warehouse?

JONAH: From now on I'm Packer. One hundred and eight thousand square feet, access to the wharves on all sides. And I ain't just bought his warehouse, I've bought Packer's plant.

GILTINAN: The war'll have that going hell for leather.

JONAH: That's the punt I'm taking.

GILTINAN: I see. Moving into production, meaning I'm yet again out of a job.

JONAH: Not quite. You picked it. People are moving to the suburbs, Miss Giltinan, and The Silver Shoe should be going where they're going. A ring of Silver Shoe stores surrounding the city was your idea and I'm calling that idea your capital. I'd like you to manage that chain of stores as me partner.

GILTINAN: You think I could?

JONAH: Wouldn't say it if I didn't. I'd concentrate on production. The retail side'd be your concern, supplied from this warehouse.

GILTINAN: I'm Queen of all I survey?

JONAH: Fact is, it ain't all I got to say. In a month or two, after a fit period of mourning for Ada, I'd like you to consider extending the partnership into areas matrimonial.

GILTINAN: Gasp, swoon.

JONAH: I'm serious. Forget me shape, I'm a man, despite it. Boy'll need a mother and you won't lack for creature comforts.

GILTINAN: You understand there's no hope of any offspring. I made a fool of myself when young.

JONAH: I have my son.

GILTINAN: And I won't be marrying to stop from working—that's understood?

JONAH: Understood.

GILTINAN: Liar! You're counting on it.

JONAH: Mmm.

GILTINAN: Then I'll be serious too. From the day you took me on I've seen you like a sort of god who reached down, picked me up and showed me me talents were worth using. It ain't often God asks you to marry him, so I'll say yes. Want me to turn those headlights off?

JONAH: I'll do it.

As JONAH *crosses to the car, the* CHORUS *appears on high.*

CHORUS: [*sung*] Armies march in
      Armies march in
      Armies march in
      Boots!

JONAH: It's horses for courses, let's call a spade a spade
         When nations clash there's a lot of cash to be made
         You talk about the balance of forces
         Me? I'll think about the balance of trade!

CHORUS: 'Cause armies march in

JONAH: So stitch the thread and punch the holes

CHORUS: Armies march in

JONAH: So build the heels and shape the soles

CHORUS: Armies march in
         Armies march in
         Armies march in
         Bomp stomp bomp stomp

JONAH: *Boots!*

The car lights go out.

CHORUS: As for Jonah being out of the Bible
         You got the wrong man
         If you sought a tale from the Good Book
         Sorry to upset that plan
         Noah wouldn't park Jonah in his ark
         Born wrong side of the blanket
         The man of your nightmares is a creature of the dark
         From King of the Push
         To War Profiteer
         The papers'll trumpet it
         You first saw it here…

JONAH *has returned to* GILTINAN *and they embrace.*

         Who decides what's wrong?
         What decides who's right?
         Are we born to tango?
         Or bred to fight?
         Sydney 1914
         City of a million stories
         City of a million stories
         City of a million stories
         This one happened tonight!

THE END

Top End

Maggie Millar as Rosa and Peter Cummins as Dolly in the 1989
Melbourne Theatre Company production of *Top End*.

Top End was first produced by the Melbourne Theatre Company at Russell Street Theatre, Melbourne, on 30 September 1989, with the following cast:

JILL	Pamela Drysdale
DOLLY	Peter Cummins
ROSA	Maggie Millar
DIGHT	Cliff Ellen
NORMA	Bunney Brooke
MANNY / ROD / GREEN	Vince Colosimo
HARRY / FRANCISCO	Hao Zhou

Director, Paul Hampton
Set Designer, Judith Cobb

This version of the script is based on the MTC's premiere production. I am indebted to the MTC for their faith in the play. And to the Victorian Ministry of the Arts, for an Arts Fellowship, which allowed me to complete a script I began in 1975.

JR

CHARACTERS

JILL, a journalist in her mid 20s
DOLLY, a wharf labourer in his early 50s
ROSA, a nurse in her early 50s
MANNY, a wharf labourer, mid-20s, of Aboriginal-Greek parentage
DIGHT, a retired transport operator, early 60s
NORMA, his wife, early 60s
HARRY, a Darwin-born Chinese in his early 30s

Three other characters appear: FRANCISCO BORJA DA COSTA, a Timorese poet; ROD, a union organiser; and GREEN, a businessman. With some attention paid to costuming, make-up and lighting these roles can be doubled by the actors who play Harry and Manny. Indeed, the actor playing Manny could take on all these roles, including Harry.

SETTING

Top End is set in Darwin in December 1975, one year after Cyclone Tracy, during the 1975 election and the Indonesian invasion of East Timor. It principally spans five days in the lives of its characters.

The set envisaged is 'multi-locational', and the flow of scenes could be termed 'cinematic', but with a 'theatrical' amount of verbal and visual stylisation.

PART ONE

SCENE ONE

Darwin wharf, 12 December 1975. The sound of a tug's hooter. A Japanese freighter glides into view. DOLLY, *beside it, is dragging a line and yelling at a figure above.*

DOLLY: The Harbour Board? The chess board, the draught board, the Board of BHP—take me to any board you like! You pilot 'em in— down here's the wharf and what you say doesn't matter a dead dog's fart. 'Stow that line, my man!' Who you talking to, Thunderguts: the dirt between your toes? If you think I'm running this line across to there for some mug to break their neck tripping over it think again. [*To someone approaching*] Better watch your step, lady.

 JILL *has entered, looking up.* DOLLY *secures the line.*

Calls himself the Harbour Master. Wouldn't harbour a thought in his head. You couldn't berth a boat in a bath!

JILL: I'm after Brian Manning.

DOLLY: So are the bosses.

JILL: Any chance of seeing him?

DOLLY: How good's your eyesight?

JILL: Good.

DOLLY: Darwin to Sydney's two thousand miles.

JILL: Not that good.

DOLLY: Brian's down south on a wage case. You a friend?

JILL: A journalist.

DOLLY: Then you wouldn't be a friend. Who owns your soul? Murder, Packet of Lies, Unfair Facts or The Herald of Weekly Crimes? [*Shouting up*] 'Listen, mug, I'm moving as fast as I can.'

JILL: East Timor.

DOLLY: What about it?

JILL: The Waterside Workers Federation's got a ban on handling Indonesian shipping, and has had—

DOLLY: Since October twenty-first. Here's where it started. This wharf.

JILL: Why I'm here. How long can you keep the bans in place?

DOLLY: As long as a bunch of Javanese Nazis keep acting like a bunch of Javanese Nazis.

JILL: A quotable quote, can I quote you?

DOLLY: Yeah. Name's Oscar.

JILL: Oscar?

DOLLY: Wilde. Kid—

JILL: I'm not a kid.

DOLLY: At my age, anyone under fifty's a kid. I don't like Murdoch. I don't like Packer, Fairfax or—

JILL: The Herald and Weekly Times—I work freelance. I don't care who prints the Timor story, just wanta be sure someone does!

DOLLY: You with that 'Lean and Nosey Like a Ferret' rag?

JILL: When their cheques don't bounce.

DOLLY: Accounts for your underfed appearance.

>*The sound of a car horn.*

JILL: My taxi.

DOLLY: You want the drum on Timor? Fresh out of Dili, three days ago, what was left of the Portuguese administration pulled in here. See that corvette. I'd start there.

JILL: I arrived on that corvette.

DOLLY: Did you?

JILL: Been in Timor for the last nine months. If I can't see Brian Manning, who's worth talking to?

DOLLY: You are, by the sound of it. Try the Health and Safety Officer.

JILL: The Health and Safety Officer. Where's he?

DOLLY: In heat like this: the first-aid room. It's got a fan.

JILL: I'll pay the cab.

>*He shouts up, taking off his work gloves.*

DOLLY: All finished, all done, said your piece? Now hear mine: The Waterside Workers Federation of Australia, Darwin Branch, offers fraternal greetings to our brothers in the Seaman's Union of Japan— and welcomes the *Kota Baru*, out of Yokohama, to the Stokes Hill Jetty, Darwin, Australia. *Do-itashi-mashite.* If any of you Japanese wave-watchers speak English and can tell me how Karl Marx is faring in Tokyo I'll shout you a beer and a feed.

>*Crossfade to:*

SCENE TWO

The first-aid room. An overhead fan. MANNY *is extracting two cans of beer from the fridge as* DOLLY *enters.*

DOLLY: Caught—with your hand in the till.

MANNY: I owe you two bandaids, alright?

DOLLY: You're not gonna drink 'em.

MANNY: No. I'm gonna pour 'em out. I'm building a raft for the beer-can regatta and I'm short two tins.

DOLLY: Wharf's a bloody dangerous place. No-one works it boozed.

MANNY: Except Jack the Hat.

DOLLY: DTs?

MANNY: So it would seem.

DOLLY: If they're for him, okay. Wasn't always a lush, you know.

MANNY: No.

DOLLY: Didn't touch a drop till he was twenty-eight.

MANNY: Shonky equipment. A timber sling gets away from the crane. Several hundred super-feet of oregon make mincemeat of his best mate. I've heard it.

DOLLY: Happened in front of him; could have been him. Jack hit the bottle.

MANNY: Hasn't stopped. One of life's numberless tragedies.

DOLLY *fetches the occurrences book.*

DOLLY: It for sure is not all dancing and rooting and your muscles bulging outta your t-shirt. You get old. You get like Jack. You drag yourself to work. When that happens to you—as it happens to us all—I hope there's some young bucks on the wharf in your gang twenty years from now who'll carry, and cover, for you!

MANNY: I'm getting him his medicine, aren't I?

DOLLY: [*writing*] 'Friday December twelve, 1975, 1400 hours, self and Harbour Master disagree on correct procedures for berthing the *Kota Baru*.'

MANNY: Are you gonna put these [*the beers*] in the book?

DOLLY: I'm doing this first—the bandaids go in another book.

MANNY: You might mention this to Brian. One for the in-tray. Our gang's jack of covering for Jack.

DOLLY: He's not working, is he?

MANNY: No, but we are, one man short, and after a while, dot dot, join 'em.

DOLLY: What?

MANNY: The dots.

DOLLY: [*writing*] 'Harbour Master suggests I go to hell. I point out the inappropriate nature of this remark finding it prejudicial to the hitherto high regard generally accorded this well-liked Port of Darwin official.'

MANNY: Silly prick, he is.

DOLLY: The Harbour Master? A non-fucking-entity.

MANNY: I'm talking Fuckwit Jack! Pardon my French. And his.

    He's become aware JILL *has entered.*

JILL: Your French sounds like Greek-Australian to me.

MANNY: On the money. I'm Manny. Manoli.

DOLLY: Anastassiades.

JILL: Hi.

DOLLY: Apologies, didn't introduce ourselves properly before. Bill.

MANNY: Dolly—

DOLLY: But they call me Dolly.

MANNY: 'Cause he's an old woman.

JILL: I'm Jill.

MANNY: Gidday, Jill.

DOLLY: Dolly's from Dyer.

JILL: Irish?

MANNY: It's not Italian.

DOLLY: We Dyers came out with the First Fleet. Five generations later, down the holds of ships, there's Dyers still.

MANNY: You're making me weep. Plonk. That's the sound of me tears hitting the linoleum.

DOLLY: Be warned. Anything you say, do, imply or intimate, could be taken down and used against you.

MANNY: She a cop?

DOLLY: In print.

JILL: A journalist.

MANNY: Where's your pencil?

JILL: I sat on it—it broke.

MANNY: That's an idea I could run with.

DOLLY: Except someone's doing a Nelson Eddy. Two bandaids. Sign here. Jack the Hat's calling you-ooo-ooo-ooo.

MANNY: [*signing*] You doing anything tonight?

JILL: Helping to run a meeting, would you like to come?

She hands him and DOLLY *a leaflet.*

MANNY: Would I like to come?

DOLLY: Skedaddle.

MANNY: I drink at The Vic. What say I cop you later?

MANNY *exits.*

JILL: Manny's not the Health and Safety Officer?

DOLLY: No.

JILL: Phew. You are.

DOLLY: 'The War Next Door—Australia Must Act. Eight O'clock, Trades Hall.' You as parched as you look?

JILL: Any chance a water?

DOLLY: This is the waterfront. So what's your slant?

Reading the leaflet, he moves to fridge.

JILL: Filing copy from Timor for nine months meant getting to like the Timorese. Does 'human interest' cover it?

DOLLY: Where I come from journos don't go in for building support groups, meetings, doing the hard yards.

JILL: It's an industrial issue. Two months ago members of a Channel Nine newscrew, and a Channel Seven newscrew, murdered by Indonesian soldiers. Five Australian newsmen rubbed out. I'm a journalist. And getting killed for being one, I'm not in favour of.

DOLLY: Have a water, my friend.

JILL: Friend's better than kid.

He hands her a glass. She drinks.

DOLLY: Timor. Spare me the learned treatise, a stab'll do. Your take on what the Indons are playing at?

JILL: A foreign adventure to divert attention from the internal shortcomings of a corrupt military regime. Stab one.

DOLLY: Plausible.

JILL: Stab two: A case of doing what comes naturally to the Indonesian military. Quashing an independence movement in case other parts of the archipelago get secessionist ideas.

DOLLY: Stab three?

JILL: An opportunity grasped: let's resurrect an Indonesian empire that in the fourteenth century stretched from Sumatra to New Guinea.

DOLLY: Are they that un-modern?

JILL: No. Which leaves stab four, oil. The Timor Sea's rumoured to be full of it.

DOLLY: Oil's what's in it for Exxon and the Yanks.

JILL: Not if you understand the history of Pertamina and the Indonesian elite.

DOLLY: Go another H_2O?

JILL: Please. You weren't by any chance working the wharf 1946 to 1949?

DOLLY: You gonna ask me about 'the black armada'?

JILL: You know about the black armada?

DOLLY: If being part of it counts as knowledge.

He has taken her glass to fetch more water.

How the wheel turns. When the Japanese reach the East Indies in 1942, the rags and tatters that are the Dutch army, navy and air force fall back to regroup in Australia. 1945, come the surrender, when the Japs fall short of the finishing line, the Dutch stage a move back for more business as usual. WW2's over. The French, who are trying to outwit Ho Chi Minh in Vietnam, have reoccupied Cambodia. The Brits, who've never left India, are singing here we are again in Malaya, Singapore and Burma. The Dutch assume they'll resume the Dutch East Indies. But don't count on the Waterside Workers Federation of Australia saying: Did we fight World War Two so you animals could re-invent the 1930s? For two going on three years we refuse to load, supply, untie, maintain, aid or abet a single Dutch ship if it's gonna be used against Sukarno and the Indonesian nationalists. Thirty years ago, we black-ban Dutch shipping. Thirty years later we're banning Indonesian ships 'cause the imperialised have become the imperialisers. One step forward, one step back.

JILL: How was it for you?

DOLLY: A shit fight like all the others. Again, pardon my French.

MANNY enters.

MANNY: I need a bandaid pronto.

DOLLY: Another one?

MANNY: A bandaid bandaid. Cut myself opening a can for Jack. The tropics. This gets infected I could lose it. Then how could I go: 'Sit on this!' [*He goes to the first-aid cupboard.*] What's he on about?

JILL: The first time an Australian union actively supported a Third World independence movement.

DOLLY: You should listen up. You might learn something. Wasn't just wharfies in on that action.

JILL: That I'm hazy on.

DOLLY: Off the top of my head, the other unions involved were...

MANNY *cleans, dries and bandaids his finger.*

... the AEU, the ASE, the AFLE, the AMEU, the ARU, the Blacksmiths Society, the Boilermakers Society, the Breadcarters Union, the BWIU, the ETU, the Federated Clerks, the Federated Engine Drivers and Firemans Association, the Federated Ironworkers, Federated Ship Painters and Dockers, the FDA, the Hotel, Club and Restaurant Employees Union, Maritime Stewards, Merchant Services Guild, Miners Federation, Moulders Union, Operative Painters Union, Plumbers Union, Seamans Union, Sheet Metal Workers Union, Shipwrights Union, Storeman and Packers Union, TWU, VBU, West Australian DRHWU, WA Carpenters and Joiners. Name a trade union worth a bumper, it was for the Indonesians against the Dutch.

MANNY: Face like a horse's arse, the memory of an elephant.

DOLLY: '*Merdeka! Merdeka!*' we were shouting. 'Down with Dutch Imperialism!'

JILL: What price *merdeka* for the East Timorese?

DOLLY: What price independence for any of us?

JILL: Will you speak at our meeting?

DOLLY: Thought you'd never ask.

MANNY: Macassan fisherman told me an Indonesian joke the other day, you heard this one, Dolly...?

They freeze. Crossfade to:

SCENE THREE

A hotel bedroom. Twin beds. ROSA *nurses a whisky.* JILL, *fresh from the wharf, enters telling the joke.*

JILL: A crowded bus in Jakarta. You ask the old lady crammed against you: 'Your husband isn't in the army, is he?' No. 'Is your father a military man?' No. 'You got a son, grandson, uncle, brother in the armed forces?' No. 'Then would you lift your foot off my foot!' It's a joke doing the rounds in Darwin. Not your idea of funny? So you're sitting in the dark?

ROSA: The world is dark.

JILL: Not dark if you open the blinds.

> *She does. A slash of afternoon light.*

ROSA: Care for a drink?

JILL: Three in the p.m. you've put a three-in-the-morning-size dent in the whisky bottle? Tears?

ROSA: Whisky with a splash—weather like this, the eyeballs sweat.

JILL: Something's happened.

ROSA: Look on the bright side. Francisco Borja da Costa has happened, but Fretilin's transmitter's back in action.

> ROSA *passes* JILL *a transcript.*

While getting drunk I've been counting my blessings. Do I have leprosy? No. That's a plus. Do I have yaws? [*To herself*] If I did I'd give it right back. [*To* JILL] This morning was I bitten by a rabid dog? Negative. This afternoon did I have the wrong tooth pulled by an untrained dentist? No. And I'm not starving. My, how the pluses mount up.

JILL: [*the transcript*] When did this come?

ROSA: I repeat: I'm not starving. It arrived at my table in the motel dining room during luncheon. Precisely when? Before the peach melba, after the steak diane. I cancelled the peach melba. But what, me worry? I'm not being murdered on a Dili street. It isn't my body the Indonesians are mutilating while telling onlookers: 'This is what happens to communist scum!'

JILL: Francisco—

ROSA: Wasn't a communist? You know that and I know that but whatever he was—he's a corpse! And…

> *She sings.*

> 'My eyes are dim, I cannot see.
> I haven't brought my specs with me.
> I have not got my specs with me…'

My next drink's on the rocks. [*She makes her way to the bar fridge, closing the blind en route.*] All over the globe I've sung that jolly song, in the company of jolly doctors and jolly nurses, what a jolly life I've led!

JILL: When I close my eyes I see him.

ROSA: One more who's never going to be there, ever ever ever ever ever again!

JILL: I slept with him.

ROSA: Really? I only imagined doing so.

> *A ghost appears, strangely lit: the wounded and mutilated* FRANCISCO. *Music under.*

FRANCISCO: It's good the living remember the dead when the dead can't even remember living.

JILL: Silence my reason.

FRANCISCO: *Silenciaste minha razao.*

JILL: In the reason of your laws.

FRANCISCO: *Na razao das tuas leis.*

JILL: Suffocate my culture.

FRANCISCO: *Suffocaste minha cultura.*

JILL: In the culture of your culture.

FRANCISCO: *Na cultura da tua cultura.*

JILL: Smother my revolts.

FRANCISCO: *Abafaste minhas revoltas.*

JILL: With the point of your bayonet.

FRANCISCO: *Com a ponta da tuas baioneta.*

JILL: Torture my body/With the chains of your empire.

FRANCISCO: *Torturaste meu corpo/Nos grilhoes do teu imperio.*

JILL: Subjugate my soul/With the faith of your religion.

FRANCISCO: *Subjugaste minha alma/Na fe da tua religiao.*

JILL: Plunderers! Assassins! Murderers! Thieves!

FRANCISCO: *Saqueaste! Assasinaste! Massacraste! Philaste! Na ponta da baioneta.*

JILL: In the point of the bayonet.

FRANCISCO: *Assinalaste o rasto da tua passagem.*

JILL: Is carved the road of your coming.

FRANCISCO: *Na ponta da minha baioneta.*

JILL: In the point of my bayonet.

FRANCISCO: *Marcarei na historia a forma da minha Libertacao!*

JILL: Is carved the shape and the future of my Liberation!

> *The music ends. A gunshot.* FRANCISCO *slumps.* ROSA *passes* JILL *another transcript. She activates a standard lamp.* FRANCISCO *is sinking through a trap in the floor.*

ROSA: The next report's a mere PS. Tells us Francisco died with a poem on his lips. Bravo! God, I hate it!

JILL: It's what we do with our hate that matters.

ROSA: 'My eyes are dim, I cannot...' Can't! Am not gonna be able to... speak at your meeting.

JILL: Not speaking makes what kind of people of us?!

A Fretilin flag falls. Blackout.

SCENE FOUR

Stretched across the flag, a banner reads: 'The War Next Door—Australia Must Act'. A meeting. JILL *is seated,* ROSA *speaking.*

ROSA: As you can see from the sheet/leaflet, I'm a nurse who's been working in Timor with an International Red Cross health team for the last eighteen months. When I arrived in this small part of the once-extensive Portuguese Empire, there was, on salary, in the whole of the country, one doctor serving six hundred and fifty thousand people. An absurdity, an obscenity, and (an unpopular thought perhaps), it's hard to imagine the Indonesians doing worse. I'll mention one only additional statistic. Under-five infant mortality: forty-nine per cent. By five, a one-in-two chance of being dead? Hmm. The absence of medical services in the Timor I worked in made diseases such as malaria, leprosy, yaws, hepatitis and tuberculosis endemic. The inadequacy of the water supply and poor sanitary arrangements meant outbreaks of cholera and typhoid were frequent. A chancy form of subsistence agriculture ensured malnutrition-related disorders were the rule. Whose imperialism will prove better or worse, Portuguese or Indonesian? I say a plague on both their houses, but if the Indonesian invaders can't make a better fist of it than the Portuguese who had four hundred and fifty years of trying, God save the human race 'cause nothing else will...if you can pardon a phrase that springs to mind.

DOLLY *creeps in late. He shoots an apologetic look* JILL's *way, who nods a greeting. He sits.*

Hardly surprising, in eighteen months our team of six health workers did little to rectify the appalling health profile four plus centuries of European imperialism had visited on East Timor. And the little we did will now be as nothing in the eye of the storm. For me, on a personal note, with the Indonesian invasion has come the realisation that I have spent another eighteen months of my life patching people up, only to see another set of troops shoot them down. It's like building sandcastles below the tide line. A similar thing happened when I went nursing in Goa. Did happen when I was in Angola and Mozambique. And when I worked in Brazil. Now: Timor. *Sama sama.* It sounds ironic coming from a nurse, but this nurse is sick! Sick sick sick sick sick of this endless, stupid—stupid, this endless… I'll leave it there.

ROSA *exits.* JILL *indicates* DOLLY *should speak.*

DOLLY: Thirty years ago (some history) my union, the Waterside Workers Federation of Australia, put bans on Dutch shipping into and out of Australian ports, and I'm glad, as a trade unionist and an Australian, that we did that. Thirty years ago my union allied itself with the cause of Indonesian independence, and I'm glad, as a unionist, and an Australian, that we did that. And if today, thirty years after banning Dutch ships, my union has to ban Indonesian ships then so be it. I'm glad. Independence was the go then, is still the go now, and is still dear to the waterside workers of Australia. Could be you saw this in the papers. [*He holds up a clipping.*] Adam Malik: 'We praised Australian Labor for backing Indonesia's independence struggle during the revolution'. The man has a long memory—and I thank him on behalf of my union for the praise. But when the same man, Adam Malik, Indonesia's Foreign Minister, goes on to suggest my union 'should not be so easily influenced by incorrect information', what am I to think? I'm to him, probably to many here tonight, just a working stiff, but I can read, write and reason. And I say to you Adam Malik—if you want to give me access to correct information then maybe you can start by telling me why, as recent events have proven time and time again, official Indonesian press sources lie. And, if you value correct information so highly, why have Indonesian soldiers taken to murdering Australian journalists?!

This is JILL's *cue.* DOLLY *sits.*

JILL: Greg Shackleton. Gary Cunningham. Tony Stewart. Malcolm Rennie. Brian Peters. These are Australia's disappeared. Five names. The five Australian newsmen killed in Balibo. Mere days ago, but more than a month after the event, the Indonesian authorities delivered to the Australian Embassy in Jakarta what purportedly were the burnt remains of those newsmen. It's not been widely reported. The Australian Embassy held a brief interment ceremony and the card on the wreath staff laid read: 'They stayed because they saw the search for truth, and the need to report at first hand, as a necessary task'. I'm here tonight because I share that sense of a necessary task. As a journalist I have sought to report first hand the truth about East Timor. I saw those five newsmen going to Balibo. Our paths crossed when, fearing for my life, I was coming from Balibo back to Dili. I told them what they'd find: an undeclared war was being waged in that border town. I already had the story and needed to get it out. I hadn't stayed, but it chills me to think had I done so the fate those five Australian newsmen suffered would have been mine. To their five names I'd like to add a sixth. Rosa, the nurse you've heard from, and myself, this afternoon learned a good friend of ours has been killed in the recently-fought battle for Dili. He was captured, as a prisoner paraded, then shot in the street, and his body mutilated. Indonesian officers branded him a communist. He was not a com but he was a com-municator. Francisco Borja da Costa was the new Republic's first Minister For Culture and spearheaded Fretilin's literacy drive. A writer, a poet, when you hear the East Timorese National Anthem, his words are what you're hearing.

With the ghost of FRANCISCO *appearing beside her,* JILL *sings the anthem in Tetum.*

> *Eh! Foho Ramelau, Foho Ramelau eh!*
> *Sa be as liu o tutun.*
> *Sa be bein liu o lolon eh!*
> *Tan sa timur oan hakruk bei-beik?*
> *Tan sa timur oan atan bei-beik?*
> *Tan sa timur ulun sudur uai-uain?*
> *Tan sa timur oan ata uai-uain?*
> *Hader rai-hun mutin ona la!*
> *Hader loro foun sa'e ona la!*
> *Loke matan loro foun to'o iha o knuak.*
> *Loke matan loro foun iha ita rain.*
> *Hader kaer rasik kuda talin eh!*
> *Hader ukin rasik ita rain eh!*

Lights and music under crosscut to:

SCENE FIVE

The sounds of a hotel bar. ROSA *with a drink,* DOLLY *beside her.*

ROSA: A word in your ear. I've got a lot on my mind. As a result I'm un-pickupable!

DOLLY: Not trying to pick you up.

ROSA: But you did? Once upon a time? When we were gay, free and up for it?

DOLLY: That's my drift.

ROSA: Townsville?

DOLLY: Townsville. 1944.

ROSA: Yes, I was in Townsville in 1944, nursing.

DOLLY: I know, and I was with the Second AIF, there was a dance.

ROSA: Is that a jukebox?

DOLLY: It's a cigarette machine.

ROSA: Pity, if it was a jukebox I could buy a song and drown this conversation.

DOLLY: Seeing and hearing you, I didn't twig. But suddenly—

ROSA: It all comes back. I pay the line. A fifty-three-year-old woman's in a bar getting sloshed, you tell her she slept with you thirty years ago. She doesn't remember but you do.

DOLLY: Magnetic Island, 1944.

ROSA: And did the island move for you?!

DOLLY: It doesn't ring a bell?

ROSA: Perhaps I should and they'll take you away.

DOLLY: Not, I admit, a phenomenally memorable event.

ROSA: Us making love?

DOLLY: But one thing you said's stayed with me.

ROSA: That was?

DOLLY: 'If this's your idea of sex I suggest you take up stamp collecting.'

ROSA: How big's your collection now?

DOLLY: Ha ha.

ROSA: If it helps, it is in my repertoire, I have had cause to use that wounding remark several times since.

DOLLY: I'm right, aren't I? It is you? You said 'since'.

ROSA: 1944, like a lot of years 'since', is for me something of a blank. I do recall around about that time, that put-down was one a group of us nurses found amusing. I don't doubt someone said it to you.

Was I that someone? Or were you told it by someone else? On that the jury is out.

DOLLY: And this is a conversation going nowhere?

ROSA: 'Fraid so.

JILL: [*entering*] You were great tonight.

>   JILL *hugs* ROSA.

ROSA: I was awful. Strange how being part-way through a nervous breakdown makes you tongue-tied.

JILL: Names, addresses, pledges of support. Things are starting to move. We collected enough money—in Jack the Hat's hat—for a really big ad.

DOLLY: Glad to hear it.

JILL: She was great. You were great. I owe you a beer.

ROSA: You know this man?

JILL: No. I'm in the habit of spotting old blokes in pubs and offering to buy 'em a beer. He spoke at the meeting!

ROSA: You saw him there?

JILL: You didn't?

DOLLY: I was late. You left early.

ROSA: But did you see him in Townsville in 1944?

JILL: I wasn't born in 1944.

ROSA: And I wasn't born yesterday. This man's suggesting we met during World War Two. And slept together!

JILL: If old flames meet—wise friends retreat.

ROSA: I don't remember him from Adam.

DOLLY: It was William then.

ROSA: Piss off, William!

DOLLY: Bill these days.

ROSA: And take Bill with you.

DIGHT: [*entering*] Hello, Dolly!

ROSA: Dolly, Bill, William? More names than Mandrake's got disguises!

>   DIGHT *has joined them.*

DOLLY: Jill—Dight. Dight—Rosa.

DIGHT: How's it going? Oops. I never learn.

DOLLY: Kerr's doing the CIA's dirty work, Fraser's getting round in jack boots, Whitlam and Hawke have refused to call a general strike, there's an election being held tomorrow that shouldn't be happening, good day for it—the thirteenth—the population's pretending we live in a democracy, the Indonesians have just invaded Timor, and you ask me how it's going?

DIGHT: Just touching base. Needed elsewhere.

DOLLY: They haven't closed the kitchen, have they?

DIGHT: You've got half an hour. And I've got less. The Dragon'll knock me down.

ROSA: The Dragon?!

DOLLY: Dight's wife.

JILL: Where I come from we call that sexist shit.

DIGHT: You haven't met my wife—ba-boom!

JILL: Also sexist shit.

DIGHT: Ar, the young women of today. They're beyond a joke.

> DIGHT *leaves.*

DOLLY: You could do worse than have a yak with Dight. He was with Sparrow Force, fought in Timor.

JILL: He what? Excuse me! Hello…

> *She catches* DIGHT *up. They exit conversing.*

ROSA: You, sounding highly strung. Me, feeling strung out. I feel I've been less than civil. Any chance of starting again?

DOLLY: Try me.

ROSA: I've had a thought.

DOLLY: What's your thought?

ROSA: Was it the night Artie Shaw played Townsville? A huge dance. Big band.

DOLLY: You do remember?

ROSA: Don't count your chickens. I remember Artie Shaw.

DOLLY: On the topic of chickens, I'm about to order a feed, can I do the same for you?

ROSA: Anything you'd recommend?

DOLLY: The Vic's barramundi and chips is hard to beat.

> JILL *returns.*

JILL: Sheer coincidence! Fantastic. Fabulous. Thanks for the tip. He's agreed to an interview. Dight fought in Timor during the Second World War!

ROSA: Ar, that word again.

MANNY: Again again! That word again. Again again! We meet again.

JILL: It was in the stars.

ROSA: Men keep approaching. You know this one?

MANNY *has lobbed.*

MANNY: Mr Health and Safety, you sly dog.

ROSA: Bill, William, Dolly—add another name to the mix—Mr Health and Safety.

DOLLY: It's not a name, it's my job.

MANNY: Dyer, you've done it.

ROSA: Dyer. Add that.

MANNY: You've hooked a woman.

DOLLY: Rosa. Meet Manny. He works with me.

MANNY: And quite a looker.

ROSA: What can I say? May your good times be manny—may they never be with me?

MANNY: Okay, Awesome Foursome, this is your Captain speaking. Tonight. My first and final offer. Eleven fifty p.m., the Darwin Cinema. 'Election Eve Shock Stunner'. Two flicks for the price of one. In fact Price, the immortal Vincent P, is *The Incredible Two-Headed Transplant*! Preceded by *Cry of the Banshee*. I'll shout!

JILL: You just did.

MANNY: Have to. This joint's loud. What do you say?

ROSA: Nothing. In the end I feel a 'Piss Off' coming, but so far....

MANNY: Grafted to the body of a giant, two heads, two brains. One wants to kill. One wants to love. And *Cry of the Banshee* is wall-to-wall splatter.

JILL: I hate horror.

MANNY: I'll hold your hand. Cinema's just down the road.

ROSA: She'd go but her mother told her: Beware of Greeks.

MANNY: Bearing gifts?

ROSA: No. Just beware of Greeks.

Voice-over through the PA.

VOICE: Last meal orders! Last meals!

ROSA: Is that our cue?

DOLLY: It is.

MANNY: Wait, my second and final offer, designed to keep us a cosy foursome, the Parap Cinema, Sunday night, seven thirty on: Greek movies. That got rid of them. Alone at last. Hold still.

ROSA *and* DOLLY *have walked to the rear and are ordering food.*

JILL: Something in my hair? What?

MANNY: Turn around. Ooo, ooo yes. No. Nix.

JILL: Nits!

MANNY: A ruse. Starved of human contact I just had to get close to you, babe.

JILL: You're a fast worker.

MANNY: Not me. Fast workers die young.

JILL: Upfront, cards on the table, don't beat around the bush.

MANNY: I hate the bush. Give me big cities.

JILL: Like Darwin?

MANNY: When you beat around the bush Darwin is a big city.

He puts an arm around her which she removes.

Aw no, the brush off!

> MANNY *hits the deck clutching his heart and twitching.* DOLLY *and* ROSA *(after ordering) return, holding meal tickets.*

ROSA: Am I drunk or is the carpet moving?

DOLLY: The pub epileptic have a seizure? Management know what to do. The first hour's free, after that they start charging him rent.

ROSA: What happened?

JILL: He made a move on me—I knocked him back.

ROSA: He died of a broken heart? William tells me the what…?

DOLLY: Back Bar kicks on, but they lock The Cage in twenty.

ROSA: They sluice it out apparently. Just in case you wanted to know where I'd got to, we two are wining and dining out the back.

> *They exit.*

JILL: So how come you weren't at my meeting, Manny…?

MANNY: Greek school.

JILL: Sure.

MANNY: True. Every Friday night. Keep the language happening. Learn the dances. I lead a rich and rewarding multicultural existence. [*He has begun a Greek-style dance.*] And me. I'm not just Greek, right? Desert people call Arnhem Land people 'swamp rats'. My mum's a swamp rat, so with me double trouble's what you get.

> *He shakes a leg, Aboriginal-style.*

JILL: Two for the price of one! How can a girl not be impressed? Of Greek, but also Aboriginal extraction!?

MANNY: You're making me sound like a tooth. But that's the alternative suggestion: totally hot local black band playing the Back Bar, midnight on, three bucks a head, front bar prices, you and me could dance all night.

JILL: You'd fall over on me.

MANNY: Me?

He keels over again.

JILL: Will you stop doing that!

He scrambles lightly to his feet.

MANNY: My party trick. You want the serious me? WTC, babe.

JILL: WTC?

MANNY: What's The Chances?

JILL: Gosh, me and the Zorba of Darwin?

MANNY: Look around. You could do worse.

JILL: There's no-one left.

MANNY: There's your answer. Wanta be my date? Back Bar's a totally where-it's-at nightspot.

JILL: What if where I'm at is the going home end of the night?

MANNY: Rosa's not, she's up for a feed with Dolly, and they look in the mood for dancing.

JILL: I should really be keeping an eye on Rosa, shouldn't I, she's in a fraught and frazzled state.

MANNY: Same with me. Dolly's kinda my boss. Election Eve, if he mouths off he may need backup.

JILL: Gotta look after the elders.

MANNY: Animals if we don't.

JILL: I know! We could join forces!

MANNY: Great, isn't it, when great minds think alike?

JILL: What a smooth talker you are.

MANNY: She likes me, she likes me!

JILL: So answer the question: Why weren't you at the meeting, Manny?

Blackout.

SCENE SIX

Exterior. Dolly's place, the next morning. DOLLY *is in a yoga position.* ROSA *wears a bedsheet and is looking anywhere but his way.*

ROSA: I said something witty last night. I stopped drinking rum. Moved back on to whisky. You said I was crazy. I said I'll be fine. You said tell that to your hangover in the morning. I said I won't even be talking to my hangover in the morning. We laughed. I'm here to report I've stuck to my word. I'm not talking to my hangover. I am, however, hearing from it.

DOLLY: Hair of the dog in the fridge.

ROSA: No. Hair of the dog in my mouth. How'd I get here?

DOLLY: Taxi.

ROSA: Good. Taxi suggests delivered. Walked would suppose I chose this destination. Don't feel compelled to tell me what you're doing, but don't expect me to guess.

DOLLY: Saluting the sun.

ROSA: One less thing I have to do.

She dons sunglasses and peers his way.

DOLLY: I yoga twenty minutes a day. Otherwise I go to pieces.

ROSA: That's a place I've been, many times, and this is one of them. They should make a film here, where are we, the end of the world?

DOLLY: Nightcliffe.

ROSA: There would be a cliff in it—I suppose we're only feet from the edge?

DOLLY: It's a suburb—of Darwin.

ROSA: Oh well, that's alright then. I was born in a suburb. A house that's not really a house, just the stumps under what used to be a house. Canvas walls, a caravan, flywire panels? I went camping last night? You live here?

DOLLY: Cyclone Tracy cut a swathe through Nightcliffe last Christmas Eve. Wasn't much of my place left standing. When your first wife's left you for the second time, when your second wife's left you for the last time, when the kids are grown up, rebuilding in a hurry isn't high on a sane list of priorities.

She spots a deckchair and starts to set it up none too expertly.

ROSA: I said a second witty thing last night. Three in the morning. You'd put your arm around me. Made your move. 'Since ten o'clock, William Dyer, I've been on the tiles with you. Not a single amorous moment, not a single sexual overture, suddenly—three a.m.—bed beckons: bingo, you're all over me. Oh, what a marvellous thing is man. Mind informing me what took you so long?!' Did I care who heard me? No.

DOLLY: I don't remember you saying that.

ROSA: 'Course not. You'd fallen asleep on the bar stool, head in my lap. I asked the barman to ring a cab. It would seem the cabbie, knowing you, knew where to take you, us. Half the suburb's like your place, stumps roofed over, screened in. Hell, eh?

DOLLY: Last night?

ROSA: Cyclone Tracy, looks like it must have been.

DOLLY: I consider hell a Christian concept.

ROSA: And you're a heathen. What are you doing now?

DOLLY: Plank Pose.

ROSA: That makes what you're up to sound vaguely respectable.

DOLLY: Hell however gets close. Without the fire, the brimstone. Just you and a wind that's taking more of your house with it by the minute.

ROSA: Were there lulls?

DOLLY: None I noticed. No light, no power, no radio, no TV, no way of knowing what was going on. Twelve hours of that, come dawn, I walk into a flattened suburb. In the vicinity the sole structure left standing is a carport, and it's got a car on top of it. Streetlamps are down, steel streetlamps twisted into incredible shapes, one, a perfect corkscrew. I'm a Marxist, therefore a materialist, I look for rational explanations.

ROSA: You found one?

DOLLY: Hell, wasn't it. Hiroshima was. World War Three sprang to mind and I thought the Russians have tried to take Pine Gap out but undershot the mark and dumped on Darwin. Not a soul to be seen, no-one, nothing, just wall-to-wall wreckage.

ROSA: Everyone's worst nightmare.

DOLLY: You don't get killed in a nuclear war.

ROSA: You survive it.

DOLLY: My first recollection of something faintly real is a voice in my ear. 'A cyclone hit us during the night.' That was reassuring. A neighbour. She fills me in. I look down. Twelve hours have passed. I'm clutching still the Christmas turkey I'd been taking from the fridge to thaw when something huge picked Darwin up and shook it.

ROSA: This is awkward. A lot of last night's a missing chapter. I surfaced this morning with that Goldilocks feeling. You wake up, you can't help noticing you've fallen asleep in someone else's bed. Have you eaten their porridge? I realise a lady is meant to remember such things. These days people use the term work-out.

DOLLY: Work-out?

ROSA: Did we?

DOLLY: We tried to—

ROSA: It didn't work out? I didn't come?

DOLLY: Wasn't the problem.

ROSA: You didn't come?

DOLLY: More I didn't arrive.

ROSA: All I remember are the two witty things I said.

DOLLY: There was a third. On the subject of my erection, the lack of. 'You can lead a horse to water but a pencil's not always lead.'

ROSA: I hope I then told you how this has happened to me before.

DOLLY: You did.

ROSA: And we must neither of us feel bad about this.

DOLLY: Hasn't disturbed my equilibrium, I'm business as usual, doing my yoga then heading for my favourite Chinese restaurant. Yum cha to kick start the day.

ROSA: If I'm invited I should freshen up.

DOLLY: Town water's laid on. There is a shower.

ROSA: Good. Ow! What's biting my foot?

DOLLY: A motorcycle helmet.

ROSA: Do I pull out a raffle ticket?

DOLLY: No. But you will need it. It's the spare.

ROSA: You ride a motorcycle?

DOLLY: Hmm.

ROSA: Curiouser and curiouser, said Alice.

> *She exits to discover the bathroom.*

SCENE SEVEN

The motel foyer. DIGHT, *looking dapper, is on the telephone.* JILL, *in her motel room, is answering his call. She's wearing a bed sheet.*

JILL: Knock knock?

DIGHT: Knock knock.

JILL: Who is this?

DIGHT: You mean who's there? Knock knock.

JILL: Pardon?

DIGHT: Dight.

JILL: Dight Falls?

DIGHT: No.

JILL: Dight Eisenhower?

DIGHT: Eisenhower was a Dwight, not a Dight.

JILL: Oh, what a Dight it was, it really was.

DIGHT: You want to tell me about it?

JILL: Hello. It's six thirty in the morning, I've had insufficient horizontal
recovery and am not in operational mode. Go away.

DIGHT: This is the young lady who wanted to interview me?

JILL: Interview you? I don't even know who you are!

DIGHT: About Sparrow Force?

JILL: Where are you now?

DIGHT: The motel foyer. And it's eight o'clock not six thirty.

JILL: Give me five minutes, I really do need to shower.

> *She hangs up and* DIGHT *disappears from view. A lump stirs and
> groans in Rosa's bed. A head appears.*

What have you done with the woman who usually sleeps there?

MANNY: What have I done to myself?

JILL: I remember everything. You were great. You were fantastic. It was
marvellous. [*She blows him a kiss.*] Try not to be here when I get
back!

> MANNY *groans. He's draped in a sheet. He sits on the edge of the
> bed. Pause. Cut to:*

SCENE EIGHT

A Chinese restaurant. DOLLY *and* ROSA *enter, both carrying motorcycle
helmets.*

ROSA: Last night.

DOLLY: I thought we'd left that subject behind.

ROSA: Was I shrill, insistent, single-minded, husky-voiced?

DOLLY: All six.

ROSA: All four. There were two hyphens in there. And you?

DOLLY: As we know—out of practice. We've been over this ground. Let's
just say the forces of historical necessity threw us together.

ROSA: Only one bed?

DOLLY: Only one bed. As for the rest? It takes two to tango. It's a hassle
when one party doesn't know the steps.

ROSA: Was it your idea or mine?

DOLLY: The madness was mutual. What is it the Chinese use? As an aphrodisiac.

ROSA: Rhinoceros horn, snake's head wine, monkey glands.

DOLLY: Not likely items in this joint.

ROSA: Brains.

DOLLY: Monkey brains?

ROSA: Plain brains. Also a recommended antidote for impotence.

DOLLY: That they might have. I'll gorge myself on brains.

> HARRY *appears with chairs.*

HARRY: Good idea. He's got none of his own.

DOLLY: I eat here a lot—I'm a well-known customer.

HARRY: Seven dollars forty.

DOLLY: See what I mean, so well-known I don't even get to sit down before Harry hands me the bill.

HARRY: Wednesday night. You ate without paying. He was drunk.

ROSA: *Qiang dao.*

HARRY: *Da qiang dao.*

DOLLY: You speak Chinese?

HARRY: *Ni zai nar xue de zhong wen?*

ROSA: Macau.

DOLLY: Macau?

ROSA: He wants to know where I learnt Chinese. Macau.

HARRY: *Zhe ge can guan yi du gui yi ge ao man ren suo you shi wo fu qin zai yi cu du bui zhong shu gei ta de.*

ROSA: *Hou lai ta you ba can guan ta de.* [*To* DOLLY] His father lost the restaurant gambling with a man from Macau.

HARRY: She's wondering if he worked to get it back. *Mei you.*

ROSA: The answer's no.

HARRY: *Ta ba ta ying hui lai le.*

ROSA: He won it back.

HARRY: It took two years.

DOLLY: Rome wasn't built in a day.

> *They've seated themselves.*

HARRY: *Chai?*

ROSA: Please.

DOLLY: Ta.

HARRY: *Yum cha?*

ROSA: Yum cha.

DOLLY: Yum cha.

HARRY: I'll hang those up for you.

DOLLY: Yeah, put 'em with the smoked duck.

> HARRY *exits with the motorcycle helmets only to stick his head back through the curtain.*

HARRY: My father heard all that and wants to meet you.

ROSA: Oh, really.

HARRY: The last Chinese-speaking Australian he met was Morrison of Peking.

ROSA: Your father was in Peking?

HARRY: No, Morrison was in Australia.

DOLLY: Harry's father's Darwin born and bred.

ROSA: His father would like to meet us.

DOLLY: I understand the bits in English.

ROSA: *Wo men fei chang yuan yi jian ta.* [*To* DOLLY] Wouldn't we?

DOLLY: What?

ROSA: Love to.

DOLLY: I've met his father. Hundreds of times.

ROSA: I haven't.

DOLLY: This is my town. I live here.

ROSA: So: Dolly Dyer's Darwin—give me the guided tour!

DOLLY: Don't let on you're a nurse or the old boy'll show you his scars.

ROSA: Scars?

DOLLY: End of the war, Australian troops stationed here went on an anti-Asian rampage. Put all of Chinatown to the torch. Harry's father got badly singed trying to put his mother out. A skeleton in Darwin's closet.

> *They pass through the curtain.*

SCENE NINE

A polling booth. DIGHT *and* JILL *queue to get ballot papers, then proceed, side by side, to fill them in.*

DIGHT: You don't mind voting first? Wouldn't want to get yakking and forget our civic duty.

JILL: Lest we forget.

DIGHT: I went back in '73.

JILL: To Timor?

DIGHT: The wife was elsewhere, down south with her sister rings a bell. I was at a loose end. A Queensland property developer fella owned a boat going to the Philippines. Turned out to be Mr Big in a drug smuggling operation. Guns, drugs, a lot happens in these waters.

JILL: So I believe.

DIGHT: Anyway, I help crew his boat to the Philippines, and sail the good ship *Buddha Stick* back, as far as Timor. Pile out at Dili.

JILL: And?

DIGHT: Hire a young bloke with a Kwaka to take me inland. Want to look up my old friends to thank them.

JILL: It wasn't a happy reunion?

DIGHT: Wasn't a reunion. Found sons and daughters, grandchildren. Couldn't find a single one of the Timorese I'd known still alive. Learnt too, I'd never looked up the figures, how forty thousand faces went missing during the war. That's how many Timorese died supporting us in our hour of need.

JILL: How many of us will support them today in theirs?

DIGHT: Shocking. I'd left it too late. Flew back a deeply guilty, deeply disappointed man. Don't s'pose you can do that nowadays, fly out of Dili, the only planes'd be—

JILL: They are, yet again.

DIGHT: Warplanes. How's this? Size of the Senate ticket. Gotta have a laugh, like a bloody Chinese scroll! If voting wasn't compulsory I wouldn't do it.

JILL: Some say if voting could change things it wouldn't be compulsory. You fought in Timor how long?

DIGHT: The full eighteen months, 1942 into '43. We were in retreat to start with, but couldn't retreat as fast as the Japanese advanced. Four hundred of us trapped behind enemy lines. We're still on Timor the Japs are already in New Guinea, and of course by then they'd been bombing Darwin, Broome, the islands in the Strait on a fairly regular basis.

JILL: Why the nickname?

DIGHT: Sparrow Force?

JILL: Small but cheeky?

DIGHT: Small's right, four hundred, down to two hundred by the end. Cheeky's also right. Nothing like as important as Kokoda, but we staged a hit-and-run rearguard action tying down, at one particular time, fifteen thousand Japanese troops who otherwise would have been in the Battle for New Guinea.

JILL: And the Timorese?

DIGHT: Our ears, our eyes. Covered our tracks, led us past ambushes, got us food, got us drink, safe places to base ourselves. I wouldn't be here telling you what I'm telling you but for the Timorese. Saved my skin more often than I care to remember.

JILL: How's that make you feel, given what's happening up there now?

DIGHT: How d'you think I feel? I can tell you how it was, and how it was going back, but up there the past nine months, you can tell me how it is now.

JILL: You're interested?

DIGHT: Couldn't live with myself if I didn't get your thoughts on the matter.

JILL: Go, Gough.

DIGHT: Go, Malcolm.

> *They deposit their votes. Crossfade to:*

SCENE TEN

A betting shop. DOLLY *and* ROSA *enter with* HARRY *who gets straight into the business of organising his bets.* NORMA*'s already at work on hers.*

NORMA: God strewth! What have you done? A woman. He's no good to you, you know. Take him back to the shop. Can't get it up.

DOLLY: You're giving away me secrets, Norma.

NORMA: You should be ashamed of yourself leading a good-looking woman like her down the garden path. You get yourself a real man, Joyce.

ROSA: It's Rosa. Who's Joyce?

NORMA: Well, if you don't know her I don't either, so at least we've got that in common. Gidday, Harry!

HARRY: No time.

NORMA: I see, off to make a million—nice talking to you.

> HARRY *passes en route to pay in.*

ROSA: Those people walking up and down with chalk in their hands—

DOLLY: Are not teachers. They're putting up the odds.

ROSA: Jezebel, Grand Beauty.

DOLLY: And the name of every nag running this Saturday anywhere in Australia. You name it, we'll bet on it. The Darwin Betting Shop, the working class's answer to the stock exchange.

NORMA: If you run into mine round the traps, Dyer, tell him he's a wanted man.

DOLLY: What's the reward, Norma?

NORMA: Like him: no prize.

DOLLY: The window she's headed for is where they look after your money.

NORMA: Before giving it back.

ROSA: Doubled.

DOLLY: At least, if not.

NORMA: Quadrella-ed—they're a very benevolent outfit, this mob.

DOLLY: Wanta put money on it, Norma: Whitlam by three seats?

NORMA: Who?!

DOLLY: Whitlam!

NORMA: Didn't hear you.

DOLLY: Norma can't bring herself to mention his name. Spits, great gobs of it, at the television when Whitlam's on.

NORMA: Satan done up as a six foot seven smoothie.

DOLLY: That's right, Norma, you fill her in.

ROSA: I've been out of the country a good while.

NORMA: Ain't been too good while you been gone. No good while his mob's been in power. Fraser'll romp home.

DOLLY: Who?

NORMA: Go, Malcolm!

DOLLY: Never heard of him.

NORMA: Knock the country back into shape and not before time.

DOLLY: Norma has a blown-up picture of Sir John Kerr on her front door.

NORMA: Saved Australia from rack and ruin.

DOLLY: Surrounded by Christmas lights.

NORMA: Christmas is coming, so's the end for your mob of blood suckers.

DOLLY: When the equal pay for Aboriginal stockmen case went to Arbitration—

NORMA: Don't start me on coons in front of strangers.

DOLLY: Who argued against? Kerr. Judas in a golliwog wig.

NORMA: St George slaying the socialist dragon.

DOLLY: Whitlam isn't a socialist, Norma.

NORMA: Who?

DOLLY: While we're at it, who jailed Clarrie O'Shea?

NORMA: Who let him out's a better question.

DOLLY: John Kerr's always been a boss's man. Links with the CIA, links with the DLP, links with Australian intelligence.

NORMA: According to you there isn't one. Okay, smartie. If Kerr's a can of worms, who gave Kerr the job? Who appointed him? Got you there.

MANNY *enters.*

Have a hard night, did we?

MANNY: How now, brown cow.

NORMA: Who are you calling a cow? Or brown for that matter.

MANNY: Just seeing if I could still talk. Stand aside, Norma, you're looking at a man who's got a hot tip.

NORMA: Territory humour.

ROSA: Pretty basic.

NORMA: Basic doesn't get close. Your money where your mouth is, Dyer? Fifty bucks says Fraser by ten seats.

DOLLY: Done.

NORMA: Who'll hold the stakes? [*To* ROSA] You can. Manny?

MANNY: Politics? That's like backing snails up walls.

NORMA: What about you, Harry? You like a bet.

HARRY: Whitlam a shoo-in.

NORMA: Fifty bucks says otherwise.

HARRY: Make it a hundred. He recognised China.

NORMA: I'll take it.

ROSA *suddenly holds stake money aplenty.*

ROSA: Next stop Rio de Janeiro!

NORMA: Is that running today, what race's that in, that's a good nag.

Lights crossfade to:

SCENE ELEVEN

JILL *and* DIGHT *walk on the spot along a pier.*

DIGHT: [*reciting from 'The Man From Snowy River' by Banjo Paterson*]
There was Harrison, who made his pile when Pardon won the Cup,

The old man with his hair as white as snow;
Few could ride beside him when his blood was fairly up—
He would go wherever horse and man could go.
And Clancy of the Overflow came down to lend a hand,
No better horseman ever held the reins;
For never horse could throw him while the saddle-girths would
stand,
He learnt to ride while droving on the plains.
And one there was a stripling on a small and weedy beast
He was something like a racehorse undersized,
With a touch of Timor pony...
See, a touch of Timor pony, that's when I first heard the word Timor,
as a kid, learning that poem. Never thought I'd see action there, but
did. Bit of a walk I'm afraid: there she lies!

JILL: You said a yacht.

DIGHT: I call it my yacht.

JILL: It's a fishing boat.

DIGHT: I lease it to fishermen. In transport before I retired. This is an
investment come hobby. Ordinarily, after the prawns in the Gulf,
she'd go south for the tuna. This year we're using the wet to careen
her and do a long overdue refit. Don't suppose you had breakfast—
up for some bacon and eggs?

JILL: The eggs yes, the bacon no.

DIGHT: Jewish?

JILL: Vegetarian.

DIGHT: It takes all sorts. So have Fretilin got a show or what?

JILL: They've got more than a show.

They exit to Dight's boat. Reveal:

SCENE TWELVE

DOLLY *and* ROSA *ride a suspended motorcycle. As the pillion passenger,*
ROSA *nurses a slab of cans. Music under. It's like they're flying.*

DOLLY: A misunderstood part of the Australian Dream, the Australian
backyard.

ROSA: Aw, yeah?

DOLLY: Hire a plane, fly across a suburb, any suburb, any day of the
week. Behold, below, in one backyard someone's fixing a car. Next

door a neighbour's at work on a pushbike or pruning their fruit trees. Two doors up someone else in a flowerbed. Place beyond that who is it tending a vegie patch? Circle back. How many households keep fowls, pigeons, rabbits, ducks, here a goat, there a dog, a cat, a guinea pig? Ooops.

He swerves. A car horn is heard.

Sorry about that.

ROSA: What, me worry? I didn't see the car either. Then again I don't have to. I'm not driving this thing.

DOLLY: For kids the Australian backyard is…?

ROSA: A dawn-to-dusk learning experience?

DOLLY: Look there! Sporting homemade wings, seven-year-old John and eight-year-old Betty leap from the roof of the carport.

ROSA: The airline pilots of tomorrow, born in the backyard of today.

DOLLY: There someone's building a caravan, a boat, a barbecue. Everywhere citizens at work, hammering, nailing, sawing, draping, tending, mending, wherever you look endless, ceaseless, multifarious human activity. But does the infant science of Economics measure all this output? Record it as part of the Gross Domestic Product? No. And yet Backyard Incorporated is probably the biggest factory in the whole of Australia! More intriguing still: Who is boss of it all? Answer? No, boss. Us, free human beings freely engaging in what we choose to be engaged in. When you have fully penetrated the Australian backyard then can you say: I have seen the future and it works.

The music under ends. They 'land' in Dolly's backyard and get off the bike.

ROSA: So Saturdays, yum cha at Harry's, bets on, highlight of the day is ending up here?

DOLLY: Where I am king of my domain.

ROSA: Your chunk of the Australian Dream, your own backyard.

DOLLY: Affirmative.

ROSA: That's the swimming pool you promised me? Five bathtubs?

DOLLY: Courtesy of Cyclone Tracy.

ROSA: Tracy dumped five bathtubs in your backyard?

DOLLY: Three. The other two I found half a mile up the road, both trying to get into the same phone box. Four constitute my above-ground swimming complex, the one in the middle with the lid I call my esky, in which there oughta be a mound of ice.

ROSA: Ice?

DOLLY: A mate works at the refrigerating works and Sat'day mornings a stash falls off the back of a truck into there, I know not how nor do I ask, I merely give thanks for the black economy. Keeps the weekend slab cold.

ROSA: You have a number of mates, don't you? The mate who shoots buffalo.

DOLLY: Yeah.

ROSA: Hence I shared the bathroom this morning with a slab of meat.

DOLLY: Shoots buff—can't hang the stuff.

ROSA: You can.

DOLLY: Got taught how.

ROSA: By a mate who's a slaughterman.

DOLLY: Recognised it was buff? I'm impressed. Telling buff from beef, or beef from goat.

ROSA: I'm trained in nutrition. Have had to be. Worked in a lot of eat-anything parts of the world. Only two questions: It moves, can it be eaten? If it can be eaten, can it be caught?

DOLLY: I've got some swimmers inside'll probably fit you.

ROSA: Courtesy of Cyclone Tracy?

DOLLY: Left by wife number two when she left for the last time.

ROSA: And never came back.

DOLLY: And never came back.

> *They move into 'the house' at the rear.*

SCENE THIRTEEN

The interior of Dight's boat. JILL *and* DIGHT *are descending stairs from the hatchway above.*

JILL: Fretilin's got two thousand five hundred fully trained regulars.

DIGHT: Trained by?

JILL: The Portuguese. Seven thousand reserves. On top of that, another ten thousand Timorese have undergone military training on a crash course basis since Indonesia started rattling the sabre six months ago. An army twenty thousand strong. You know the terrain up there.

DIGHT: If four hundred of us could lead the Japanese a song and dance in '42–'43, and we weren't even locals, it'll be the way it was in

Vietnam. Indonesians will pretend to be in control saying there's a few naughty boys in the mountains.

JILL: Twenty thousand is a lot of naughty boys. And Timor's got a lot of mountains. Plus—

DIGHT: There's more?

JILL: When the Portuguese pulled out they'd recently replenished their arsenal. They left the toys behind. Fretilin has at its disposal, and knows how to use, a wide range of modern NATO-type light weaponry.

DIGHT: That's what I wanted to know. Your tip is a resistance to be reckoned with?

JILL: My tip is it won't be long before a lot of Indonesians make it back to Java in body bags. The Timorese have a saying.

DIGHT: The invaders will never govern us—they'll only rule our bones.

JILL: You've heard it?

DIGHT: Did hear it. Bit of a tactless question, given what we're talking about, but how do you have your eggs?

JILL: Poached.

DIGHT: Galley's through here.

JILL: This is a boat and a half.

DIGHT: I call it my home away from home.

He leads her out.

SCENE FOURTEEN

Dolly's backyard. The five bathtubs. ROSA *and* DOLLY *enter in swimwear and hats. He carries the slab.*

ROSA: What do I do?

DOLLY: Take the waters, when I've done the necessary and opened the floodgates. [*He deposits the slab and turns on the taps.*] That coil of black poly pipe up top…

ROSA: Absorbing the sun's rays.

DOLLY: I call it the 'rainbow serpent dreaming'. Storage tank. Gravity feed to here.

ROSA: This really is hot.

DOLLY: Yeah. That's a hot, this a cold, one with the lid's the esky, another cold, another hot. Actually in temperatures like ours even the cold gets hot, but if you hop in the hot, when you hop in the cold the cold feels cold, even though it's hot.

ROSA: You go from hot to cold?

DOLLY: If that's your wish. Sort of a poor man's solar sauna's the concept.

ROSA: Swedish, you could say?

DOLLY: Someone did. Ex-com second-hand car salesman mate: Not as elegant, Dolly, but as ingenious as the Volvo.

ROSA: A communist second-hand car salesman is a mate?

DOLLY: You interested in a car?

ROSA: If I was he could arrange for one to fall off the back of a truck! Do I kiss this frog and something nice happens?

She hurls it from the tub and steps into it.

DOLLY: Nutted the system out with the Professor of Civil Engineering at the Darwin College of the Advanced and Educated, of whom I think the country is decidedly short.

ROSA: You haven't lived in Brazil.

DOLLY: But as Plato said to Aristotle: You don't have to be a chicken to know what an egg is.

ROSA: So—word me up.

He's loading beers into the esky.

DOLLY: About?

ROSA: Whitlam. Fraser. This election. I've been a long time out of the country.

DOLLY: 'On Our Election'. This election is a classic. It's about an elected government being forced to the polls three times in as many years. It's about the way the coalition parties stopped the elected government's means of governing by blocking supply over a Labor senator's dead body. What it's about is the right of Mr and Mrs Average to elect a reformist government without it being overturned by Big Business and the forces of Conservatism. It is about: A Vicious Rape of Democracy— One Vote, One Value—Medibank—Education—Pensions. A better way of life—about a new Australia setting sail in a changing world looking to the future with confidence. [*He starts turning off the water supply to the tubs.*] To assert, as the conservatives do, that a couple of extra dollars in the pay packet will win the election for the Liberal and Country Parties is to greatly underestimate the Intelligence of the Australian Voter.

ROSA: You sound like a Letter to the Editor.

DOLLY: I am a Letter to the Editor. I appeared last Monday.

He gets into a tub himself.

ROSA: And you remember it word for word?

DOLLY: Documents, minutes, standing orders. Remembering reams of stuff, I'm good at. Probably should have been an actor. Anyway, the editor replied to the Letter to the Editor, that is himself, by placing it alongside an editorial penned by himself, entitled: 'Why Labor Must Go'. This razor-sharp, unbiased, objective, highly intelligent individual had penned an earlier editorial just prior to the events of November eleven: Let The People Decide. You know you live in strange times when the Tories are crying: 'Let the people decide'. Like the boy who cried wolf they'll cry let the people decide once too often. The people will. And that'll be the end of the Capitalism those shit sacks know and love.

ROSA: The original Letter to the Editor accords with your sentiments?

DOLLY: Are my sentiments, written under a *nom de plume*, but I agree with the shit sacks: it's a pay-packet election. Most are.

ROSA: Greed is all.

DOLLY: All could, perhaps should, be construed as greed.

Adjusting her hat, ROSA *settles back in her tub.* DOLLY *draws a can of beer from the esky beside him.*

Where the Tories lose me is they don't have an adequate working definition of, nor an adequate appreciation of, how profound and widespread greed is. Wanting food on the table, shoes on your children's feet, a living wage, a roof over your head—call it greed. But how greedy does one have the right to be? What occurs, in the bourgeois mind, is the profoundly human desire to lead a rich and rewarding existence gets transformed into an urge to accumulate. But accumulate what? Bits of paper. Money. Deeds of title. Stocks, shares, bonds, this is the stuff of the bourgeois imagination. Interest bearing debentures! Can you get interested in a debenture? I can't. Time I came in from the cold. [*He steps into the hot tub one along.*] Me, and millions like me, are not strangers to this urge to accumulate, but with us it's the urge to accumulate a few fun times before that slot in the ground looms large! You live once, and you're a long time in the underground motel.

He lowers himself a second time into the hot tub. NORMA *has entered, looking on.*

What today's conservatives will live to rue is that using a relic of the Monarchy in their greed to seize power will leave most sane Australians greedy, alright, greedy for a Republic!

NORMA: Name twenty. Happened to be in the vicinity.

ROSA*'s hat slips off. She sits up.*

ROSA: I dozed off.

NORMA: And I woke you?

ROSA: You must have.

NORMA: No prize for guessing who put you to sleep. Eek, a nearly naked man. Have you seen mine?

DOLLY: Your what?

NORMA: Man!

DOLLY: Whenever the nearest and dearest slopes off for a few drinks, Norma suspects an affair.

NORMA: I'll give him on the nest—

DOLLY: Once—

NORMA: I'll murder him. And whoever he's with—I'm past caring!

DOLLY: Once—

NORMA: He's gonna tell you how I stormed into an innocent couple's hotel bedroom.

DOLLY: With a machete.

NORMA: There was no machete.

DOLLY: Legend has it there was a machete.

NORMA: Legend has it a lot of things.

DOLLY: Hubby was home in bed—but had Norma, juiced on rumour, fuelled by jealous rage, looked for him there?

NORMA: There's been a sighting.

DOLLY: Dight chasing fanny?

NORMA: At the Fannie Bay polling booth.

DOLLY: Caught in a leg-over situation?

NORMA: No! But seen voting, and leaving together, him and this piece, heading God knows where. If he shows here let him know I'm at home cleaning the twenty-two. And there a bullet waits, with his name on it. I'll take him out first, then go looking for the floozy.

DOLLY: Norma's a tragically typical leap before you look Territorian. Drives a four-wheel drive Toyota. Has a carcass crate welded to the roof. A pig dog welded to the side. She mouths ratbag racist slogans that even Goebbels would hesitate to utter. And gets round shooting road signs, pub walls, anything that moves.

NORMA: We tolerate him because he keeps us amused. He's referring to the fact that I'm a crack shot. Especially good at bringing down bores, Dyer! Brought you some prawns from me freezer. Has to be watched, well-known for forgetting to feed his ugly dial.

DOLLY: Meals on Wheels, I call her. It's nice to know you care.

NORMA: It's not you I loathe and detest—it's your politics. Be good if a good sort were to sort him out, he'd probably scrub up okay. Abyssinia.

She exits, having parked the prawns in 'the esky'. They relax in their tubs.

DOLLY: Forty-three years married and still besotted by her bloke.

ROSA: The course it runs ever astounds, ever astonishes.

DOLLY: Yes. It does. What?

ROSA: True Love.

DOLLY: Is that the young Goethe?

ROSA: No. My ageing mother on the hold over his female admirers exercised by Liberace. Do you have a clock?

DOLLY: I should set the alarm. If I fell asleep in the goddam tub and forgot to vote, my credibility would be shot.

ROSA: I'll make a point of getting you to the polling booth on time! She wouldn't really neck her husband, would she?

DOLLY: I doubt it—but I wouldn't want to be 'the other woman'.

A half curtain (the Timorese flag) falls, masking them.

We hear a 1975 polling day radio newscast which fades out.

END PART ONE

PART TWO

SCENE ONE

Dusk. The grounds of the Darwin Sailing Club.

DOLLY: This—an idea cooked up by a committee—is a gas barbecue. They overruled my suggestion of an electric one. [*He sniffs.*] Okay! Which mug left the gas turned on! At work I'm the Health and Safety Officer. I lob here for a feed, I'm still on deck! Someone's turned that on, realised they haven't got any matches, gone to get some, and forgotten all about it. Health and safety, there aren't enough hours in the day.

ROSA: Shall I turn it off while you're gone?

DOLLY: Does the Health and Safety officer have to do everything?

ROSA: Is a light all you need?

> *She hands him some matches.*

I want you to know I appreciate what you're doing.

DOLLY: What am I doing?

ROSA: Dolly Dyer's Darwin: showing me round. It's doing me good.

> DOLLY *lights a match, thrusts it into the barbecue, and there's a dull roar. He rolls forward, acrobatically landing on his feet.*

DOLLY: And the right wing reckons human beings can be trusted to run nuclear power plants!

> NORMA *enters with a tray of barbecue goodies.*

NORMA: No uranium out of Darwin Harbour, is that what he's bending your ear about? Do you ever give politics a rest, Dyer? Where were we?

ROSA: I was asking you—

NORMA: About Darwin. It's a town like Alice: lots of his sort, Men Without Women, where The Man Who Has a Woman is a Prince, though of course in my book any man who is a prince will always have a woman.

DOLLY: You're sounding deep, Norma.

NORMA: Just an avid reader of Mills and Boon. Ar, there it goes. That's what we've been waiting for. The sun going down. Makes my day.

DOLLY: Usually ends everyone else's.

A sunset passes into darkness.

ROSA: That's it? People come to the Darwin Sailing Club to watch that?

NORMA: Tropical sunsets are a swift and sudden affair. We say we're here for the sunset. Really we're here for the beer.

ROSA: Lightning! What chance rain?

DOLLY: None.

NORMA: How's your handle?

DOLLY: I'll go a second… [*drinking*] soon.

NORMA: Waiting for the Wet to break. Nice time of year she picked to look us over. Lots of Darwin Ugly. Madness and mayhem. We call it the suicide season.

ROSA: Because people—

NORMA: Yeah, kill 'emselves, and each other. November, December, the suicide rate rises. Homicide rate rises. Number of divorces skyrockets. Baby bashing—

DOLLY: Goes through the roof.

NORMA: You got the barbie going.

ROSA: We did.

NORMA: I'll see to the rest while I'm getting the refills. [ROSA*'s drink*] You sitting on that?

ROSA: I'm fine.

As NORMA *is taking* DOLLY*'s empty mug from him, there's a second barbecue explosion—off.*

NORMA: Holy hell!

DOLLY: Night of the exploding barbecues. That barbie's the north end of the clubhouse. My hunch: a practical joke of a very warped sort is afoot.

NORMA: Exactly the anti-social mental instability I speak of. Waiting for the Wet to break brings it on.

She exits. ROSA *watches her go.*

ROSA: Today's been a kind of therapy for me. And Norma's—

DOLLY: A tonic?

ROSA: Someone in whom the life force runs deep, as they say.

DOLLY: And we all wish they wouldn't. How about some illumination this end of the ship!

Fairy lights snap up and JILL, *at a distance, sights* ROSA. JILL *moves to join her.*

JILL: Located at last.

DOLLY: If it isn't the mad scribbler.

ROSA: Correction. A kind of therapy until now, given until now I haven't thought once about what I'm trying not to think about.

JILL: Two old flames meet, is there still a fire burning down below?

ROSA: If you mean have we got the barbecue going, yes we have.

JILL: Am I looking at the reason your bed wasn't slept in last night?

DOLLY: It's not how you think—

JILL: I know, it's how you act.

DOLLY: Perhaps, at your age.

ROSA: But at ours.

JILL: No sex please, we're geriatrics. You can tell me, I'm your friend and confidante, not your parole officer.

ROSA: Mr Dyer and I have arrived at a cosier arrangement. More brother and sister.

JILL: So why aren't you fighting?

DOLLY: More tourist and guide.

JILL: Whatever you say.

ROSA: Shelter from the storm, heard of it?

JILL: Is it raining?

ROSA: In my life right now it is.

JILL: Not so in mine. Today I unearthed a hero.

ROSA: How deep was he buried, are there any left, can I borrow the spade?

JILL: One of the Australians left stranded on Timor when the Japanese overran the island. In his words: Saved from the Imperial Japanese Army by the Timorese in 1942 more often than he cares to remember.

DOLLY: You of course can't understand anyone wanting to forget.

ROSA: [*her drink*] Ooo, look, I'm empty. So are you.

JILL: I'll do it.

ROSA: Let me.

She takes JILL'*s glass.*

Dolly?

DOLLY: Norma's getting me a beer.

ROSA: Right. This is?

JILL: A G and T.

ROSA: A gin sounds a nice change. If I'm not back within five minutes it's because I'll have walked into the sea.

JILL: What would be—

ROSA: The point of that? None. That's the point. There is no point.

   ROSA *exits.*

DOLLY: We've been watching the sunset.

JILL: And?

DOLLY: It sat.

JILL: Is it my breath or my body odour? I'm starting to feel about as welcome round here as a bad smell.

DOLLY: The bad smell's probably the gas. She's at the end of her tether—

JILL: I haven't noticed the rope? And it'd help if I didn't mention a certain island three hundred miles to our north? I see: We eat, we drink, the world's problems go away.

DOLLY: Wrong. We eat, we drink, we do what we can—sometimes it isn't much and sometimes some us need some time on the bench. You've got a good political imagination.

JILL: Thank you.

DOLLY: Unfortunately it's the only kind of imagination you've got.

JILL: Not a bundle of sensitivity? Is that the charge?

DOLLY: Myself, I often find little difference between reds and rednecks.

JILL: Fuck you! But there I go. Getting loud. It isn't done. People will look.

   NORMA *returns with a second tray.*

NORMA: Only a few. And, believe me, in this part of the world they've heard worse. Salads. I put the works on every plate and if someone doesn't want what they've got, too bad, their complaints'll be falling on deaf ears if they fall on mine. It's a gold nugget spread. As in Welcome Stranger. Stick around. There's heaps and more's coming.

DOLLY: Where's my beer?

NORMA: Rosa's getting it. I had my hands full.

JILL: Rosa's a mess, I'm a mess, it's a mess, we all fall down what good's that? It's not how you feel it's how you answer the question: What is to be done? Right?

DOLLY: How do you want your steak?

NORMA: She'll have it cooked and well-cooked which is why an expert's required.

   NORMA *is at the barbecue.*

JILL: I don't eat steak.

NORMA: Don't blame you. Cook it and cook it, it's still old boots. Pig's the best flesh you can get, followed closely by snake, speaking of which—

JILL: What?

NORMA: Snakes.

JILL: I don't eat any sort of flesh.

NORMA: Snake isn't any sort of flesh—the snake I'm married to's been off all day with some Trixie.

DOLLY: Bar talk, Norma.

JILL: I'm Jill.

NORMA: Gidday—Norma.

JILL: I'm vegetarian.

NORMA: And I'm Ned Kelly. Half the town's talking about it.

DOLLY: Half the town's pulling your leg.

JILL: It's true—

NORMA: See. Even she's heard it!

JILL: I don't think I'm being listened to. It's true I'm a vegetarian.

NORMA: But you'll have a piece of grilled barramundi?

JILL: No meat, no fish.

NORMA: Not even barramundi?

DOLLY: It gets worse, Norma. She's a newspaper writer.

NORMA: I see. One of his commo mates?

DOLLY: In Norma's scheme of things Joh Bjelke Petersen is a rabid left-winger.

DIGHT *appears at a distance.*

DIGHT: Jill!

NORMA: That who I think it is, Dyer?

DIGHT: I won't be a jiff, I'm in the middle of a fishing story!

JILL: Fine by me!

NORMA: So. Mystery solved. The Trixie he's been holed up with all day is you? Don't go away. I'll deal with him first. Then you. And his story had better be about more than fishing! Where'd he go?

ROSA: Who?

NORMA, *exiting with barbecue fork, encounters* ROSA, *returning with two gins and a beer.*

NORMA: A twerp—so high in a hat. He's been shagging that floozy friend of yours.

ROSA: Jill? I counsel looking before you leap, and I'd believe me if I was you, I used to be a nurse.

NORMA: Before you became a drunk?

ROSA: In vino, much veritas.

NORMA: I'll kill him.

ROSA: Norma—

> NORMA's *gone.* ROSA, *to follow* NORMA, *retraces her steps. Meanwhile, at the barbecue:*

DOLLY: First Rosa—now Norma, you're top of the pops. Have you really spent the day with Dight?

JILL: She doesn't think…?

DOLLY: Not logically.

JILL: Ridiculous.

DOLLY: Reality usually is.

JILL: He's old enough to be my grandfather.

DOLLY: In her eyes—twenty-four forever.

JILL: Who said romance was dead—it's alive, well and living in Darwin. Should I leave town?

DOLLY: That, or buy a gun. How'd you say you'll have the barramundi?

JILL: I didn't. No fish.

DOLLY: No fish.

JILL: No meat, no flesh of any kind.

ROSA: [*returning*] I'm back! And I brought Norma with me.

> *She steps aside to reveal* NORMA.

NORMA: Salt, mustard, tom sauce, pepper, bread.

DOLLY: Go on.

NORMA: Bread.

DOLLY: Apologise.

NORMA: You coulda said you'd been interviewing him. Though how you can spend all day doing it, I do not know. I can talk to the old fart from dawn to dusk and not get two words out of him.

ROSA: There's an African saying about an old fart.

JILL: It's Chinese.

ROSA: No. Heard it in Africa, but from, admittedly, a Chinese person.

DOLLY: The night Norma accused Dight of having a fling with a vegetarian newspaper writer. This'll take some living down.

NORMA: Not if you don't bring it up. You're from down south, I s'pose? A Mexican.

JILL: Up north. Timor.

NORMA: That's been in the news.

DOLLY: Where's my beer?

ROSA: Norma gave it to me. I gave it to Dight. Forgot to get another.

DIGHT: Here I am, Treasure.

DOLLY: Drinking my beer!

NORMA: Don't Treasure me, you *bêche-de-mer*! Things of this sort have happened once too often to be funny.

ROSA: I've remembered it. The saying. An old fart is easier to live with than a more recent one.

JILL: Lightning!

ROSA: But will it rain?

NORMA: No. There'll be a few more stinking days and nights like this before we're put out of our misery.

DIGHT: Are you gonna tell me or not?

NORMA: Tell you what?

ROSA: A tropical night sky. A barbecue by the water's edge. A married couple—

DIGHT: What the crime I've committed is?

ROSA: In the middle of a domestic. I feel like I'm in an ad for gin.

DOLLY: Jesus, the things a man has to do to get a drink round here!

JILL: What's he in an ad for?

ROSA: Beer perhaps?

JILL: Or grumpiness.

As DOLLY *exits,* MANNY *enters, Zorba-fashion.*

MANNY: Big world, babe—

JILL: Small Darwin. And a small announcement. Last night Manoli here proposed to me. Admittedly he was in his cups. I said yes and I want you all to know: day the Wet breaks, he and I are gonna be married.

MANNY's *danced entry becomes an exit.*

Is he gone?

NORMA: Like a dwarf shot out of cannon.

JILL: To be kind sometimes a girl must be cruel.

NORMA: I brought you a double serve of chips.

JILL: Be Kind to Vegetarians Week has started!

Blackout.

SCENE TWO

Dight's boat. DIGHT, DOLLY and ROSA *enter above.*

DOLLY: How'd you vote, Dight?

DIGHT: You know how I voted.

DOLLY: Not today. In 1951. The Communist Party Dissolution Referendum.

DIGHT: I didn't know you then.

DOLLY: How many coms did you know? None. But you voted to put me and my kind on the chopping block. This when you'd not long finished fighting a war against fascism for ideals like free speech, freedom of association and assembly, et cetera.

DIGHT: 1951 was the Cold War.

DOLLY: You voted for the party of lies then and you did it again today, am I right?

DIGHT: How I voted, then, and today, is my business.

DOLLY: Politics shouldn't come between friends?

DIGHT: You think it should: feel free to leave my boat.

DOLLY: Just arrived and you're tossing me off?

DIGHT: No. It'd give you too much pleasure.

DOLLY: You see what a gentleman he is.

ROSA: Not quite, but that's only because it's dark.

A light goes on below.

NORMA: You can stay the night, you lot. Heaps of bunks. They come outta the walls.

JILL: Cunningly designed, Dight showed me how they work.

NORMA: He showed you?

DIGHT *climbs down with* ROSA *and* DOLLY.

You showed Jill how the bunks work during your long chat on the good ship *Talk A Lot*?

DIGHT: Stop picking on me or I'll get in a huff.

JILL: I should wait up top for Manny.

DOLLY: Manny's coming?

JILL: I invited him. Felt I'd been too harsh.

DOLLY: Has your blessing, does it, Norma?

NORMA: I see nothing wrong with an Australian girl getting interested in a Greek.

DOLLY: Manny's only half Greek. He's also half Aboriginal.

NORMA: When he's on this boat he's Greek.

DOLLY: Given that whenever you see him you call him a half-caste lay-about, no doubt he's thinking twice about fronting the do. [*To* ROSA] Do you wanta go through with this?

ROSA: Election night drinks?

DOLLY: Yeah. With Dight and Norma, two of this town's far-right, red-neck, fascist racist twerps.

DIGHT: Hasn't stopped us being friends before, don't see why it should now.

ROSA: Does the boat have a name?

JILL: [*exiting*] The *C'est La Vie*.

NORMA: French for 'Such Is Life'.

DOLLY: Dight's dead to the idea of keeping the French out of the Pacific.

NORMA: I'll organise the drinks. [*To* DIGHT] You find the cards. That's if you aren't already past the point of usefulness.

DIGHT: My vote's Pontoon.

NORMA: Coon-Can's better.

DIGHT: But harder to explain.

> DIGHT *hunts up a pack of cards. They stow drinks, eats, stuff they've carried on board, and arrange themselves for a card game.*

ROSA: Does it have trumps?

DOLLY: It's nothing like Gin Rummy, Five Hundred or Euchre. Starts with a two-card draw.

ROSA: I've got a pair.

NORMA: And you don't tell people what you've got, but—

DIGHT: A pair you can split like this and play both hands. Hit me—

NORMA: I'd love to.

DIGHT: —is what you say, when you buy a card.

DOLLY: Or buy, buy for one, two, three, that way you're raising the stakes.

DIGHT: It's you against the dealer.

DOLLY: Called—

DIGHT: In this game: The Bank.

NORMA: Flip.

ROSA: Flip?

NORMA: Flip's another word that's used.

DOLLY: That's getting a card for free face upward, you say flip.

ROSA: Should I buy, split or flip?

NORMA: With that pair I'd sit.

ROSA: I'm sitting.

DIGHT: To warrant a flip you have to hold cards in your hand with a numeric value of twelve or more—say you sat after flipping a seven—bank would know the odds—you'd drawn two cards for a twelve plus seven: nineteen; thirteen plus seven, or fourteen plus seven: twenty or twenty-one.

DOLLY: It's twenty-one or nearest.

DIGHT: Over twenty-one's out.

NORMA: The word used is 'busted'.

ROSA: So it's like Blackjack?

NORMA: It is Blackjack, only they call it Pontoon, and I reckon they make the rules up as they go along.

DIGHT: A natural's any picture card with an ace. Bank pays a natural double and short of drawing a natural stops being the Bank.

ROSA: I love your boat.

NORMA: We do what we can about the smell of fish.

DOLLY: Hit me.

> *Up above,* JILL *is listening to the election broadcast on a transistor radio through headphones as she waits for* MANNY. *Below, the card game's underway.*

NORMA: Suppose somebody was dying.

DOLLY: Shouldn't be hard, there isn't a minute of the day when somebody isn't.

NORMA: Suppose this person knew they were dying, but couldn't bring themselves to tell anyone they were dying 'cause they wanted to keep it a secret from their nearest and dearest. Ever hear of a case like that?

DIGHT: Forgot to tell you Bank also pays five under double. Five under's drawing and buying two twos, a three, a four and a seven for example.

NORMA: What would you suggest in a case like that, professionally speaking?

ROSA: As a nurse?

NORMA: As a nurse.

DOLLY: Hit me again.

DIGHT: Is he going for a five under? So far he's drawn a four-card hand. My palms are getting sweaty. Who's this?

NORMA: Dad. Mum being a case in point. Leukaemia. But she wouldn't tell my father. Had this idea it might be the death of him.

ROSA: All the while knowing it would be the death of her.

DOLLY: Sit.

DIGHT: Or he could be busted and not telling the Bank.

NORMA: Dad had a weak heart but Mum dying didn't kill him.

DIGHT: Lived to be ninety-two. In fact married again.

DOLLY: It was years before these two got their mitts on any of his money.

NORMA: Buy for one.

DIGHT: It was kidneys, not heart.

NORMA: Kidney failure carried him off but his weak heart had Mum concerned. Buy again. Dight has a weak heart, don't you, dear? Buy again.

DIGHT: You're not five under? She probably isn't. Probably busted but wants to keep me in suspense.

NORMA: Sit.

DIGHT: Wants me to have a heart attack so she can inherit all me goods and chattels.

NORMA: I said sit.

DIGHT: I'm pointing out that there's an element of bluff in the game. Now the Bank plays its cards.

ROSA: Not telling the truth seldom achieves much.

DIGHT: Pay eighteen and over.

ROSA: Pay me.

DOLLY: Pay me.

NORMA: Pay me double.

DIGHT: What is this, a run on the Bank?

NORMA: Five under, see.

DIGHT: Lucky that was a practice round.

> MANNY, *slickly attired, whistles.* JILL *takes her headphones off.* MANNY *comes aboard. They embrace. Down below,* DIGHT *shuffles the cards.*

ROSA: If he'd been as fragile as she supposed, your father would have died of shock when your mother died.

DIGHT: But he didn't.

ROSA: So he could have coped. If she'd told him he could have helped her through her dying.

NORMA: She didn't know whether to or not, and in the end she didn't.

> DIGHT *has dealt a new hand.*

DIGHT: Buy?

DOLLY: Sitting.
DIGHT: Her first.
ROSA: Buy for one.
NORMA: I'm sitting.
DIGHT: She isn't finished.
NORMA: Keep your hair on.
ROSA: Pass.
DIGHT: You mean sit.
ROSA: Sit.
NORMA: Ditto.
DIGHT: It's his turn.
DOLLY: Sit.

> *Up top,* JILL*'s attention has shifted from embracing* MANNY *to sharing the radio's headphones with him.*

NORMA: She was very brave about it.
ROSA: Did she tell anyone?
NORMA: In the end she told us girls, but swore us to secrecy—imagine carrying that at our age, the burden of that.
ROSA: How old were you?
NORMA: I'm sitting.
DIGHT: Thank you, the Bank can now proceed.
NORMA: I was sixteen, my sister eighteen.
DIGHT: Nineteen.
NORMA: Eighteen when Mum died.
DIGHT: Pay nineteen.
DOLLY: Eighteen.
ROSA: Eighteen.
NORMA: Eighteen.
DIGHT: Are we playing cards?
NORMA: No, we're attending an auction of elephant tusks. I just bought three, would you like to sit on one! So really you don't know what you'd recommend.
ROSA: I'd have to know the people concerned.

> JILL *partly climbs down through the hatchway.* MANNY *stays above with the radio.*

JILL: Malcolm Mackerras is talking a landslide.
DOLLY: Which way?
JILL: Which way do you think?

DIGHT: Who's winning?

NORMA: Who's being buried alive? I've got money riding on this.

JILL: Early figures.

DOLLY: But?

JILL: Predicting the first time in living memory the primary vote for Labor will be lower than forty per cent. A wipe-out's the tip.

DOLLY: Sounds like 'It's Time' alright. Time to pack up and set sail for Paraguay, found the New Australia. Feel like a long voyage, Dight?

ROSA: I've been to Paraguay.

DOLLY: And you wouldn't bother?

ROSA: And given what cooks in Argentina...

DOLLY: I need some air.

NORMA: Upset about the fifty bucks, are you, Doll?

DOLLY: I've lost more than fifty bucks, Norma. I've lost a place I felt good about living in. Radio up there?

> JILL *nods.* DOLLY *exits up to the deck.*

NORMA: How can people get so worked up over an election?

JILL: A colonial relic turns the elected government of the day into the opposition and the people give their shenanigans the good-housekeeping seal of approval. I can see how someone could get upset about that.

NORMA: Whatever way you vote, nine times out of ten you're voting in a man.

DIGHT: Should I—

NORMA: The man wants a bit of time to himself.

JILL: Won't get much. Manny's up there.

NORMA: He'd like a drink, I s'pose.

JILL: We both would.

DIGHT: I'll get it.

JILL: I'll help.

NORMA: I'll show Rosa the *mandi.* You look like a cool-off wouldn't go astray? I know I could use one.

> *Up top,* DOLLY *has joined* MANNY *who offers him the headphones.*

DOLLY: No. Forget it. Turn the fucker off!

> *The low-level audio of the election broadcast ends.* MANNY *sets the radio down.*

Weak, mate, we are deadset, piss-fucking weak!

MANNY: Sure, we should be out there getting shot at.

DOLLY: We shoulda been on the streets in our thousands every day since November eleven. A general strike shoulda been called. We should be burning rich people's houses, panelbeating Rolls Royces, sabotaging assembly lines, destroying Capital 'cause Capital is fucking destroying us!

MANNY: We should be getting round with baton creases in our skulls.

DOLLY: If you don't fight, you lose. Eat or get eaten. Beat or get beaten. One law.

MANNY: Law of the jungle!

JILL and DIGHT *enter, to hand out drinks.*

DIGHT: Catching the sea breeze?

DOLLY: Straining my ears for the sound of troop movements.

MANNY: With the crazy grazier in charge, Dolly's thinking here today, Belsen tomorrow.

DIGHT: My bet's business as usual.

DOLLY: And business as usual is what, Dight? Some are born to rule. Most are born to suffer! A million, five million, ten million men and women wondering where the rent's coming from—worried sick about how to meet the mortgage or this month's never-never. Got a house, got a car, gotta keep the head down, gotta work a job and a half to keep the show on the road!

DIGHT: Life wasn't meant to be easy.

DOLLY: Was it meant to be this hard! The illiterates of tomorrow being bred in the crowded classrooms of today? A generation of kids for whom the word work'll only ever be a word! Thousands of sick, thousands of injured, the old but poor, unable to pay the scheduled fee let alone what those money-grubbing sawbones are asking. Guess what party the AMA backed?! Doctors don't have a licence to heal—they've been given a licence to kill!

JILL: The Fabian Socialist George Bernard Shaw could not have said it better. In fact I think he said it in exactly those words.

DIGHT: When Dolly's had a few he operates in quotation mode.

MANNY: What union's the AMA?

DOLLY: Isn't a union—it's 'a professional association'.

DIGHT: I won't argue politics with you.

DOLLY: You couldn't, mate, you couldn't.

An uneasy silence between them. Cut to below:

SCENE THREE

The boat. NORMA, *wearing a sarong, is using a scoop to douse* ROSA *from a* mandi. *The amplified sound of sloshing water.*

ROSA: The person in your story is not really your mother.

NORMA: No. It's the Queen of England.

ROSA: It's you.

NORMA: It's a brain tumour. Doctors can't say what brought it on. Coulda been wearing myself to a frazzle those months after Tracy trying to get the town back on its feet. Ella picked it.

ROSA: Ella?

NORMA: Stack. She's the mayor. Also a quack. I been going to her for years. Put me in for tests. They wanted to operate there and then. I insisted on being sent to Brisbane. Told his nibs I was going south to stay with my sister. A well-deserved holiday he called it. They operated soon as I got there. I came good. Right as rain the last ten months, the last few days its come back on me. Funny sort of a thing. I wake up and the words for what's around me—shower, wall, carpet—I've lost them.

ROSA: Eyesight?

NORMA: Like the words, comes and goes.

ROSA: But going?

NORMA: Of course it's going!

ROSA: I can see you're gonna be great to nurse.

The scooping finished, NORMA *drapes* ROSA *in a sarong.*

NORMA: Sorry, it's the booze talking.

ROSA: Why wouldn't you be upset? I would be. From what I know of brain tumours, this time they won't be able to operate, is that what you've been told?

NORMA: That's the long, short, fat and wide of it. Together over forty years. And he's already had one stroke.

ROSA: And you can't bring yourself to tell him?

NORMA: Hearing my bill of health might kill him.

ROSA: That's your fear? They carve roads through mountains, lay waste to forests, blast holes through mountains, rain bombs from the sky, plant landmines. They torture each other, we make ourselves sick worrying how strong our men are.

NORMA: Funny sort of a setup, eh? I know you think I should tell him.

ROSA: I do.

NORMA: And maybe I will. But I don't want you letting on, is that a deal? You ever married?

ROSA: Once.

NORMA: Divorced?

ROSA: Separated. My husband was taken from me.

NORMA: By another woman?

ROSA: By Salazar's goon squad.

NORMA: Salazar? If that's a country I've never heard of it.

ROSA: A la Franco, in Spain, Salazar's the military dictator who led Portugal out of the twentieth century back into the Middle Ages. My husband was Portuguese.

NORMA: You met him in Portugal?

ROSA: In Macau. I was on leave. Nursing with the Occupation Forces in Japan.

NORMA: In Macau for a holiday you met Mr Right.

ROSA: Pure chance—at the gaming table, as it were.

NORMA: He was a gambler?

ROSA: He worked in a casino there.

NORMA: The nurse and the croupier, I've read a Mills and Boon just like it.

ROSA: We married. I stopped nursing.

NORMA: Children?

ROSA: A series of miscarriages.

NORMA: Happened to me and Dight. I think they're putting something in the water.

ROSA: Except for that, blissful years. Then in late 1956 we got a telegram from Portugal. Death in the family. Till then I hadn't met his parents.

NORMA: They weren't with him in Macau?

ROSA: No. We went 'home' for his father's funeral. My husband was a *deportado* but hadn't told me.

NORMA: A *deportado*?

ROSA: A political exile. Were met at the airport. Not by the family, by the police. He was arrested. It was six months before they'd let me see him.

NORMA: And?

ROSA: Six months solitary confinement changes people. Hardly recognisable. I petitioned the Australian Embassy, the British, the American, any embassy that would listen, all to no avail. Some months later I got an official letter. My husband had died.

NORMA: In jail?

ROSA: Wounds inflicted by other prisoners.

NORMA: You'd think they'd have enough guards to prevent that kind of thing.

ROSA: The guards did it!

NORMA: Killed your husband?

ROSA: This is the twentieth century, there's a lot of it about.

NORMA: We're a strange breed.

ROSA: All we ever want's a nice place to lay us down.

NORMA: All we get's a bed of nettles.

ROSA: Or a bed of nails.

>   *Lights widen for:*

SCENE FOUR

Dight's boat. DOLLY, JILL, DIGHT *and* MANNY *on deck.* ROSA *and* NORMA *enter in their sarongs.*

NORMA: Conceded defeat, have you, Dyer?

DOLLY: What do you think, Mata Hari?

NORMA: And I don't s'pose Harry'll have any objections?

ROSA: I now hand the stake money to the winning party.

NORMA: Manny, you're a witness. Note it well, Dight, while you've spent all day chewing the fat with a certain young lady, I've been earning our keep.

MANNY: Hey, Norma. Thanks for the invite.

NORMA: Think nothing of it.

MANNY: How do I look? A good Greek boy? Shoes even.

NORMA: What a witty young man you've got there, Jill. Well, Dight dear—I'd say for us 'it's time' to go to bed. Bunks aplenty on the hulk. Will the last to leave 'turn out the lights' or should we be 'liberal' with the electricity?

DIGHT: I was about to fix more drinks.

>   NORMA *exits.* DIGHT *takes the hint.*

Goodnight, all. Drinks on the house. Tucker, ditto. Thanks for today, I enjoyed it.

He kisses JILL *on the cheek and goes.*

MANNY: The old fart's got the hots for you.

JILL: Come on, he's old enough to—

MANNY: What?

JILL: Know better.

ROSA *and* DOLLY *head for the other end of the boat.*

SCENE FIVE

In the bow of the boat are ROSA *and* DOLLY, MANNY *and* JILL *to the stern,* DIGHT *and* NORMA *below decks.*

ROSA: A Marxist and therefore a materialist?

DOLLY: Guilty.

ROSA: Matter is the heart of the matter?

DOLLY: The material world is the world that matters.

ROSA: What isn't matter?

DOLLY: Doesn't matter.

ROSA: Is hand on hand material?

DOLLY: You know it is.

ROSA: Is lip brushing lip?

DOLLY: Lip brushing lip is—

ROSA: Extra—

DOLLY: Material.

They kiss. MANNY *and* JILL *end an embrace.*

MANNY: What bugs me, really bugs me?

JILL: Mmmm.

MANNY: You're saddled with a Greek name, people think 'dumb wog'. But I'm smart, don't worry, I'm smart.

JILL: Being part Aboriginal isn't a hassle, being part Greek is?

MANNY: Part Aboriginal, mate, is fashionable, the wog thing's the downside.

He keels over. Rolls on his back.

JILL: I thought I asked you to stop doing that?

MANNY: What?

She mimics his fall. Lands beside him.

JILL: That.

They lie there staring up.

MANNY: That's what bugs me, what bugs you?

JILL: Being scared.

MANNY: Of?

JILL: The world.

MANNY: The world's nothing. Check out the stars. What's to be scared of?

JILL: The people in it.

MANNY: They're, most of 'em, alright.

JILL: I worry about what's inside 'em. Us. The species. And what's not. Me? I'm not sure when, how, why, but I've lost a lot of my nerve this year.

MANNY: Being in Timor?

JILL: How much nerve do you get served? How much can you lose and still do your job?

MANNY: Hey, Dolly!

DOLLY: What?

MANNY: Clock this. I got someone here, it's the weekend, and she's talking about work.

ROSA: We can't hear you.

A light snaps on in the cabin below. DIGHT *and* NORMA *are in bed, she's wearing eyeshades.*

DIGHT: They're fucking.

NORMA: What?

DIGHT: Listen to it—they're fucking.

NORMA: What do you want me to do about it, Dight? Shout: Stop fucking, you're rocking the boat! Turn on the light.

DIGHT: Take your eyeshades off. The light's on.

NORMA: I still can't—

DIGHT: What?

NORMA: Nothing. [*To herself*] See.

DIGHT: There's bunks, you know!

DOLLY: We'll deck it, Dight!

ROSA: Shudup below!

MANNY: Wanta hit the toe?

JILL: Your place—

MANNY: Or mine?

JILL: Mine. Being this close to sex after fifty, it's so…

MANNY: I know, a gross-out.

They exit. DIGHT *turns out the light below.*

ROSA: You mean by 'deck it', sleep out?

DOLLY: Yeah.

ROSA: Here?

DOLLY: Not your idea of the way to go?

ROSA: On the contrary.

DOLLY: A tropical night sky.

ROSA: Romantic, how—

DOLLY: Magnetic Island, 1944?

They kiss again, stretching out.

ROSA: Young once.

DOLLY: Young once.

ROSA: Old now.

DOLLY: Old now.

ROSA: Say I said I need you.

DOLLY: I'd say I need you.

ROSA: Say I said I want you.

DOLLY: I'd say I want you.

ROSA: Should this be happening?

DOLLY: Is that question material? It is. I'm glad. You like that?

ROSA: Murder.

DOLLY: I thought I was giving pleasure, if it's murder—

ROSA: It's murder.

DOLLY: I'll stop.

ROSA: Don't stop.

As they embrace, the lights fade to black.

SCENE SIX

Three days later. The wharf. MANNY *is speaking.* DOLLY *and* JILL *are present.*

MANNY: Mr Smooth Talker's done it again. Okay, okay. Great feeling, eh, being putty in someone's hands—try being a head the wrong end of a baton. I'm for this ban, alright! But I'm for it in circumstances. I'm for it if, when, and in sufficient numbers, other unions are backing us.

DOLLY: There are other unions backing us!

MANNY: I'm for it if we've got the blessing of the ACTU.

DOLLY: We have.

MANNY: 'Cause if we're one-out, forget it, if we're isolated—

DOLLY: We are not isolated!

MANNY: Will you let me finish. Who's this 'we' Dolly's talking about? Thirty years ago, the time he's referred to, when this union black-banned those Dutch ships, there were a hundred thousand blokes on the wharves. Ten years ago it was down to fifty thousand. Today, Australia-wide, this union's got ten thousand blokes working the wharves, and getting fewer by the fortnight. Containerised cargo, conveyors, bulk loaders, automation, bulk-handling equipment—we used to be an army—make that a division—oops, we're a battalion. The old guard, blokes like Dolly talk it up, give this union a lot of bark—but get real, where's our bite? Ten thousand of us, we stick our necks out, it's not a lot of heads to bash down.

DOLLY: Anyone else wanta speak against the motion?

MANNY: I'm not speaking against. I'm saying you can't throw weight around when in the weight department we're nothing to write home about. There's more secretaries in Australia than there are wharf labourers, get them dark on Indonesia, get them dark on what's happening in East Timor, get the teachers, get the nurses, the draughtsmen, the airline pilots, then we might be getting somewhere.

DOLLY: Shall I read the motion again?

MANNY: We know the motion.

DOLLY: So I'll put it to the vote. Carried. The ban on Indonesian shipping remains in place and the Waterside Workers Federation, Darwin Branch, renews its condemnation of the Indonesian invasion of East Timor.

> MANNY *walks off.* JILL *approaches* DOLLY.

JILL: Thanks for making sure that motion got up.

DOLLY: Thanks for what, doing the right thing?

JILL: The right thing isn't always easy.

DOLLY: No, people don't always do the right thing, do they? Listen, kid, there's a lot of powerful people around who want this union smashed. My union's on the line. Always has been. Always will be.

> *They've walked towards the first-aid room.* DOLLY *enters and* JILL *follows.*

Your boyfriend.

JILL: Not my boyfriend.

DOLLY: Alright, your squeeze got it right out there, waterside workers aren't the force we once were. Last thing we need—

JILL: I've done something to offend?

DOLLY: Offend? Monday night you went through the bar of The Vic asking every Tom, Dick and Harry what they know about gun running in and out of Darwin. Who smuggles arms, who owns boats, who would, and for what fee would they take a trip to a certain island three hundred miles north of here!

JILL: How'd you hear?

DOLLY: A little bird.

JILL: Manny?

> MANNY *enters to get two cans.*

MANNY: Get off her back. She was drunk.

DOLLY: Aw, lucky for the Russian Revolution Lenin wasn't always into a bottle of red.

MANNY: She shot off her mouth.

DOLLY: Loose lips sink ships.

JILL: If I was drunk you weren't much better. I'm surprised you remembered a thing I said.

MANNY: You too—

JILL: Me too what?

MANNY: Is she shitty 'cause I spoke against the motion? I didn't speak against the motion, I said get smart or get hit.

DOLLY: Darwin's a small town but I's got big ears.

JILL: And Noddy?

DOLLY: And Mr Plod—you want the Special Branch down on you, terrific, this union doesn't. Are they for Jack the Hat?

MANNY: I've had an idea—let's roster Jack off on wages.

DOLLY: This is a clean wharf, a straight union, there's no phantoms on our books.

MANNY: Then ask Jack to retire and pull the pension.

DOLLY: He'd drink it in four days.

MANNY: Meanwhile nine of us do the work of ten, what are we running here, the welfare state?

DOLLY: The Waterside Workers Friendly Society and don't ever forget it. One day—

MANNY: Don't tell me—I too will grow old.

DOLLY: Sign the book.

JILL: Point taken. It was not very cool of me.

DOLLY: No it was not. So when are you leaving us?

JILL: Tomorrow.

MANNY: What!

JILL: I was gonna ring you.

MANNY: Oh, yeah?

JILL: Explain.

> *The phone rings.* MANNY *answers it.*

I'm addressing a meeting in Mt Isa Friday. On to Townsville, then down to Brisbane.

MANNY: [*to* DOLLY] It's for you. [*To* JILL] Then coming back?

> DOLLY *moves to take the phone from* MANNY.

JILL: Going further south. Sydney, Canberra, Adelaide, Melbourne.

MANNY: So what'll we do tonight?

JILL: I don't think going out's a good idea.

MANNY: Nor me, let's stay in and do filthy things to each other in the privacy of your motel room.

JILL: I'll be washing my hair.

MANNY: This is shaping up as the brush-off. Ships that pass in the night? *C'est La Vie.*

JILL: A girl has to do what a girl has to do.

MANNY: Love 'em and leave 'em. Well, has it been good or has it been good?

JILL: It's been good.

MANNY: Yeah. Life's a game, right, but play it for keeps—

JILL: Otherwise it plays you for a sucker.

MANNY: She's leaving me!

> MANNY *keels over.*

DOLLY: Check you later, something's come up.

> DOLLY *hangs up.*

MANNY: I'll come round tonight anyway.

JILL: I said—

> MANNY *has gone.*

JILL: My mother was right. Beware of Greeks. Was that her?

DOLLY: Your mother?

JILL: Who do you think? *Habeus corpus*. Where is she? She who checked out of our motel room Sunday.

DOLLY: Rosa's in Mataranka Springs with Norma.

JILL: That's what she said in the note she left for me, only in Mataranka Springs they've never heard of her. Say I want to write to you, where do I write?

DOLLY: Care of the wharf'll find me.

JILL: You're not gonna give me your home address? I think I can put two and two together.

DOLLY: She doesn't want to see you.

JILL: I'd like to hear that from her, thanks all the same.

   She exits. The lights fade around DOLLY.

SCENE SEVEN

Dolly's place. ROSA *is working a bowl of flour dough.* JILL *enters.*

JILL: What is that, don't tell me, a football.

ROSA: Bread, in its second rising. I punch it down. Then knead it some more, but briefly.

JILL: Nobody needs it—joke. I'm impressed you seem to know what you're doing.

ROSA: How'd you find me?

JILL: The electoral roll.

ROSA: I'm not on it.

JILL: He is. What next, wedding bells?

ROSA: Me contemplating shacking up with someone your business is it?

JILL: I didn't spend half the day finding this place to be shocked, horrified and rendered distraught.

ROSA: Well, I hope you didn't find it in order to render me distraught, horrified and shocked. I haven't read a newspaper for days, haven't heard a news report, and don't want to know how everything's going, I'm finding no news is good news.

JILL: This isn't news. It's an agreed upon arrangement. About going south. To address meetings.

ROSA: And meetings do what?

JILL: Disseminate information, raise money.

ROSA: For more meetings?

JILL: They aid the cause.

ROSA: If I never side with another cause…

JILL: Plus, we had a pact.

ROSA: I'm not the person who made it.

JILL: I'm not talking to someone who's just been working twelve-hour days for eighteen months caring for the Timorese?

ROSA: It's needlework.

JILL: Needlework?

> JILL *is looking at a piece of fabric.*

ROSA: It relaxes me. The writing's Chinese.

JILL: I picked it wasn't Arabic.

ROSA: I started it in Luanda.

JILL: That's going back.

ROSA: A brief fling with a Chinese diplomat. You know the sort of thing. You meet in broom cupboards. Very hush-hush. 'Dare To Struggle Dare To Win'. I sew little mirrors on to the characters. I'm working on the 'To Win' bit.

JILL: The 'to win' bit you've stopped working on.

ROSA: Have it your way! On three, make that four continents—

JILL: I seem to have hit a nerve at last.

ROSA: —I have dared to struggle, I haven't won. I'm fifty-three. I'm washed-up. I want to be hung out to dry.

JILL: To die.

ROSA: Or die. Left—

JILL: Alone, with what? Your memories?

ROSA: With a bit of time to acquire some new ones.

JILL: Will Francisco Borja da Costa be included? What have I walked into? Embroidery, making bread. Is this the Nightcliffe sheltered workshop?

ROSA: Could be.

JILL: At long last Mr Right?

ROSA: Stranger things have happened.

JILL: Happy ever after in this, what, humpy?

ROSA: It isn't the Taj Mahal. He's got plans.

JILL: What happens round here when it rains?

DOLLY: [*entering*] Same as Bangladesh, that's when we have running water.

DOLLY *has a motorcycle helmet.* ROSA *and* DOLLY *embrace.*

Hello, you.

ROSA: Hello, you. Excuse us. [*To* DOLLY] A radio transmitter came for you today.

DOLLY: Dunno what you're talking about.

ROSA: A radio transmitter.

DOLLY: You dunno what you're talking about either.

ROSA: I get the picture. A radio transmitter didn't come for you today. Who doesn't it belong to?

DOLLY: How long's it here for?

ROSA: Overnight. Maybe longer. Is it—?

DOLLY: The less you know, the better off you are. I should have warned you.

ROSA: That Jill was coming?

DOLLY: No. That the transmitter might be. Did you follow me home?

JILL: I've been here a while.

DOLLY: You can send her packing.

ROSA: I know. We're just discussing our differences.

DOLLY: I'll shave.

DOLLY *exits.* ROSA *rejoins* JILL.

ROSA: He shaves after work. He does it for me. Says if he did it in the morning he'd be doing it for the Harbour Master.

JILL: And he's not in love with the Harbour Master.

ROD: Gidday.

ROD *appears outside the flywire screen.*

ROSA: It's a man.

JILL: Too big to be a moth even if he is beating at the flywire.

ROD: I'm Rod.

ROSA: That isn't the door.

ROD: Dolly's expecting me. I'm a diver.

JILL: Which is why you're not so good on the land.

ROD: Sorry?

JILL: The business about the flywire not being a door.

ROD: Oh right, and me being a diver, gotcha, joke, the door's…?

ROSA *indicates a direction.* ROD *exits.* DOLLY *enters with shaving cream on his face.*

DOLLY: There's another thing, I've invited someone round tonight.

ROSA: I know.

JILL: We know.

ROD *reappears at the flywire.*

ROD: You're Dolly?

DOLLY: You're Rod? [*Exiting*] He's a diver.

JILL: We know that too.

ROSA: Dolly's coming out, we don't want a diver drowning in the outdoor above-ground swimming complex.

ROD: The what?

ROSA: The backyard—

ROD: Oh right, five bathtubs.

DOLLY *reaches* ROD.

DOLLY: It's my swimming pool.

ROD: Looks the go.

DOLLY: Have a squiz.

DOLLY *leads* ROD *from view.*

ROSA: You're angry.

JILL: Am I?

ROSA: Angry because you're young and when young what's hard to stomach is human weakness.

JILL: Weakness is on the money. Mine. I need you to come south.

ROSA: Which I don't need to do.

JILL: You've got a tale to tell, tell it.

ROSA: I came, I saw, they conquered. It's told. Look at me. This happens. You get old. You run out of steam. All you want is to be—

JILL: Left alone.

DOLLY *and* ROD *enter.*

ROD: I won't be boring you stupid, will I? Most people think of diving as fun. But for some people diving's work.

DOLLY: Rod's here to establish a branch of the Divers Union in Darwin.

ROD: Currently the divers of Darwin are paid under an AWU award. Peanuts compared to what we've won by organising federally and bargaining in our own right.

DOLLY: He's been ten months signing up Queensland. Now he's shifted his attention to the Territory.

ROD: Dolly invited me round for a yak vis-à-vis the local situation. You must be Rosa.

JILL: And I must fly. I'm Jill.

ROD: Rod.

JILL: I wish you well.

ROD: Thanks.

DOLLY: Got something that'll interest you, Rod, ten years of rank-and-file newsletters. Not even Cyclone Tracy could part me from these.

He leads ROD *to where they are.*

JILL: So it's *sayonara.*

ROSA: Here's looking at you, kid.

JILL: You too.

ROSA: Am I forgiven?

JILL: Only if you're both very happy and I get an invite to the wedding.

DOLLY: What wedding?

ROSA: Jill's assumed we're contemplating marriage.

ROD: Really. Congratulations.

DOLLY: Thanks. [*To* JILL] I'll have to get a divorce first, but you'll get an invite. Best finish shaving.

JILL: Ring in the morning.

ROSA: I will.

JILL: Better still, come and see me off.

ROSA: One or the other.

JILL: [*to* ROD] It's a pretty crazy house but don't let it fool you. Coming in, I spotted a fridge.

ROD: Where?

DOLLY: Left and left again, follow her.

DOLLY has returned. ROSA *watches* JILL *go with* ROD, *clutching bottles, in tow.* DOLLY *and* ROSA *are alone.*

You had a simple marriage ceremony in mind?

ROSA: I thought at the wharf.

DOLLY: The Harbour Master officiating?

ROSA: On one side a row of wharf labourers. On the other—

ROD: I seem to have done it again.

ROSA: A row of divers?

ROD *is outside again.* DOLLY *indicates the way.*

DOLLY: If he's a bother…

ROSA: A candlelit dinner for two can easily become a candlelit dinner for three.

> *She takes focus. Music under with* ROD *and* DOLLY *half-lit in the background.*

I served dinner. Coffee. Cake.

DOLLY: You made this cake?

ROSA: I cleared the dishes.

ROD: That's the first home-cooked meal I've had in months. My wife and kids have forgotten what I look like.

ROSA: Washed the dishes.

DOLLY: I know the feeling.

ROSA: They were still talking.

DOLLY: More port?

ROSA: I showered.

DOLLY: I won't be long.

ROSA: Went to bed.

ROD: I should be going.

DOLLY: Knock that back.

ROSA: Half slept, half woke. Dolly!

DOLLY: Still here.

ROD: This spot, we're guarding it.

ROSA: I thought it won't get worse, but this is how it'll be. If not tomorrow, the day after. He'll bring someone home from work, or bring work home from work, or have to see someone after work. Outside would always be breaking in. You don't escape, I kept thinking. There is no escape.

> NORMA *appears.* DOLLY *picks up the phone.*

NORMA: Which is when I rang.

DOLLY: It's Norma. For you. Didn't say what about.

ROSA: Which is when you rang.

NORMA: With the really good news.

ROD: Great to meet you.

DOLLY: I'll see you out.

> DOLLY *exits with* ROD. ROSA *and* NORMA *are left on phones. The scene transforms to:*

SCENE EIGHT

Day. NORMA *and* ROSA *are outside the motel.*

NORMA: There's a patch of country we'll be going through I first saw as a young woman. Just married. Travelling in a truck. He'd set up in business. A fleet of one—the truck we were in—and one employee, himself. Me? I was the silent partner. We were gonna make a pile.

ROSA: And did you?

NORMA: Sure, means nothing now I'm at the end of the road, but back then, chasing dollars drove us. I'd nodded off in the cabin. When I woke we were trucking through an endless plain, flat as, far as the eye could see, left right forwards backwards, a white endless plain, just it and the dust we were making. Wasn't till well into the day we saw anything else and all we saw then was two distant black dots. When we finally got close enough turned out to be two emus—out there in the middle of nowhere—having a feed. Birds of a feather, the same thought hit Dight and me. He stopped the truck. We looked at each other. Human beings, what are we, animals, only a different sort. Got out of the cabin. Just married. Climbed on top of the load. Like being on a cloud. That plain everywhere you looked. And we made love, as in we fucked. He came, I came, the first time we'd managed to come together. It'll do me good to pass through that bit of country again.

JILL: Car's ready.

NORMA: Where?

JILL: Dight's putting your suitcase in the boot, I'm fetching mine.

NORMA: Right you are.

ROSA: The eyesight's not good?

NORMA: Shithouse.

DIGHT: Stroke of luck, Norma being able to hitch a lift with you two. She has a fear of flying.

NORMA: I don't trust planes. And I don't trust you either, fart face. No wine, women and song while I'm gone.

DIGHT: Who me?

NORMA: Wipe that grin off your chops. And say goodbye like it might be goodbye.

They embrace. JILL *appears with her case.*

JILL: How is she?

ROSA: Sssh.

JILL: Doesn't he know?

ROSA: She hasn't told him.

NORMA: Can't hang about, let's go.

ROSA: Will you be seeing Dolly, Dight?

DIGHT: Normally not till Friday, but it happens I've teed up a meet.

ROSA: Will you give him this?

She hands DIGHT *a letter.*

JILL: You haven't told your bloke either.

ROSA: The car's the other way.

NORMA: Well, take my fucking arm, for Chrissake. Steer me!

ROSA steers NORMA off.

DIGHT: You'll be sadly missed.

JILL: By?

DIGHT: Me for one.

MANNY: Me for another. I assume this is going with you?

JILL: How could I forget old faithful.

MANNY *hands* JILL *her portable typewriter and picks up her case. They exit. The sound of a car starting up.* DIGHT *is there alone, waving.*

SCENE NINE

The Hotel Darwin foyer bar. DOLLY, *wearing a shirt and tie, joins* DIGHT. *Musak under.*

DOLLY: What couldn't you tell me over the phone?

DIGHT: Idea I've had.

DOLLY: Make it quick. I want out of this tie, and the bastard on the door nearly didn't pass me sandals, plus Rosa's waiting for me—she's playing house, for how long for I dunno, but it's okay with me if it's okay with her. And I'm certainly not gonna blow it by getting on the tiles with you.

DIGHT: Rosa's not waiting for you.

DOLLY: What?

DIGHT: She's on the track with Jill. [*Handing* DOLLY *the letter*] Said to give you this. Norma's with 'em. Going to stay with her sister in Brisbane. Jill's hired a car. Some meeting in Mt Isa.

As DOLLY *reads her letter,* ROSA *appears.* DIGHT, *sipping his beer, talks but* DOLLY *is barely hearing him.*

ROSA: Patterns. There are several patterns in my life, and this is one of them.

DIGHT: I've thought this through. Points in favour. One: I've got a boat.

ROSA: It's as though the way my first marriage ended was so traumatic for me that ever since all I've been able to do is flirt with the idea of settling down.

DIGHT: Two: Norma's away for a while. Plenty of time.

ROSA: In relationships since—and I've done it more times than enough—it's always me who gets cold feet. Here I am again, doing a runner.

DIGHT: So it makes sense.

DOLLY: What does?

DIGHT: Me idea.

ROSA: I suppose what they mean by 'been there, done that' is what I'm feeling. Norma's with us. I'm travelling with her to Brisbane. Don't tell Dight but she's very ill.

DIGHT: The idea I'm telling you about.

DOLLY: Dight, I'm trying to read a letter.

ROSA: It's like I don't trust myself to love.

DIGHT: You, me, and whoever else'll be in it, for a crew.

ROSA: I'm unwilling to risk myself emotionally.

DIGHT: We load the *C'est La Vie* with medical supplies.

ROSA: Instead I go back to what I know.

DIGHT: Medical only.

ROSA: I can nurse, so I nurse.

DIGHT: We do a drop for Fretilin on the south coast somewhere.

DOLLY: You know what you're saying?

DIGHT: Betano, say, Beaco—I was there, I know the places.

ROSA: Right now nursing Norma seems as much as I can commit to.

DIGHT: We do something practical, for Fretilin.

DOLLY: Will you lower it to a roar?

DIGHT: Good idea. In case we're overheard. But what do you reckon?

DOLLY: Dight! I need a minute to think a few things through!

DIGHT: I'll hustle up two more beers.

DOLLY: Make mine a brandy, a big, big brandy.

DIGHT: You're upset.

DOLLY: Am I?

DIGHT: About Rosa leaving?

DOLLY: What do you know! A political animal with feelings!

ROSA: I'll write. [*To herself*] How often have I said that before?

DIGHT: You know, don't you, as far as I'm concerned I owe the Timorese?

ROSA: I say I'll write, but this, I guess, really is goodbye.

> ROSA *turns away.* DOLLY *sets the letter down.*

DOLLY: What the fuck are you saying? Your boat? Have you read the papers? Half the Indonesian Navy's in Dili Harbour. Other half, you better believe it, is patrolling the coast, north and south. We front with medical supplies for a bunch of guerrillas?

DIGHT: Not a good idea?

DOLLY: All over, red rover. They'd blast us back to the Stone Age. You're serious?

DIGHT: It's a debt of honour. But for the Timorese I wouldn't be here.

DOLLY: Then listen up. I've got a mate. In the PMG. He's parked a radio transmitter, my place. Idea is drive into the sticks. Use a certain frequency. With luck make radio contact with Fretilin. Do him and me, do it on my Kawasaki? Or you, me and him, use your Toyota?

DIGHT: I'll be in that.

DOLLY: So fetch me the brandy. Best letter anyone's ever written me and I want to savour all over again the way it breaks my heart.

> DIGHT *exits to the bar.* DOLLY *starts to re-read Rosa's letter.* GREEN, *another patron, in passing spots him.*

GREEN: Don't see much of you in here, do we, Dyer?

DOLLY: No. The Hotel Darwin is a slops trough frequented by ruling-class swine, I tend to give it a wide berth.

GREEN: Collar and tie?

DOLLY: Keep one in my locker at work in case I have to attend a funeral. I'm looking forward, one day, to attending yours.

GREEN: Get you a drink?

DOLLY: Couldn't get it past my lips.

GREEN: On the subject of funerals, didn't your side get trounced last Saturday?

DOLLY: Been good for shares, hasn't it?

GREEN: We'll get yellowcake shipped out of the Territory, but I suppose you know that.

DOLLY: Over my dead body.

GREEN: I hardly think that'll be necessary, do you?

GREEN *leaves.* DOLLY *reads. Slow fade to blackout.*

SCENE TEN

FRANCISCO *is singing 'Eh Foho Ramelau', the Fretilin flag his backdrop. The slogan seen at the Darwin meeting. A hall in Mt Isa where* JILL *is speaking.*

JILL: The song you're hearing is the anthem of the East Timorese people. It was written by a friend of mine who nine days ago was shot on the streets of Dili. Not by a long shot is he the only friend I've lost in Timor. I've just arrived here in Mt Isa to learn, via a radio message monitored in Darwin, of other deaths, the fate of other friends. 'Led by Fernando Carmo, a small Fretilin contingent tried to reach Roger East. They ran into an Indonesian unit. After bitter fighting, they were themselves wiped out. Shooting was soon heard from the Hotel Turismo, where East was a guest. It's not thought he survived.' Prior to this despatch we knew Roger East was missing. Now we must suppose him dead, a supposition more or less confirmed by a second report, again monitored some hours ago in Darwin: 'A Chinese witness claims to have seen a European, whose description resembled that of East, being dragged to the wharf by three Indonesian soldiers, his hands bound with wire. He was ordered to face the sea. He turned to face his captors. And shouted: "I am an Australian". The firing squad fired. His body fell from the wharf into the sea.' Greg Shackleton, Gary Cunningham, Tony Stewart, Malcolm Rennie, Brian Peters. Now Roger East. How many more journalists will be silenced? Why, in what we're told is fast becoming an information-based society, do so many who would inform, suffer such abrupt ends? As for, the Timorese people, the people whose story we as journalists try to tell, I… I'm sorry… sometimes… the words, to do their struggle justice… elude me.

Musical discord. Blackout.

THE END

Lost Weekend

A SURREAL AND GOTHIC WESTERN
DISTRICT TALE

Michele Fawdon as Zelda, Daphne Grey as Margie and Claire Jones as Therese in the 1989 State Theatre Company of South Australia production of *Lost Weekend*. (Photo: David Wilson)

Lost Weekend was first produced by the State Theatre Company of South Australia at The Space Theatre, Adelaide Festival Centre, Adelaide, on 12 August 1989 with the following cast:

ERIC	Denis Moore
ZELDA	Michele Fawdon
MARGIE	Daphne Grey
CHARLES	John Gaden
THERESE	Claire Jones

Co-directors, John Gaden, Ian Watson
Designer, Mary Moore
Lighting Designer, John Comeadow
Original song and incidental music, Alan John

This version of the play is based on the draft performed for the 1989 premiere season. It was condensed and slightly rewritten at the behest of Queensland Theatre Company for their subsequent production. I am indebted to the support of both companies.

JR

CHARACTERS

ERIC, ex-unionist recuperating from a stroke, late 40s

ZELDA, physiotherapist, late 30s, migrant parents, would-be divorcée

MARGIE, early 50s, private school background, enamoured of Xanadu

CHARLES, late 50s, ex-Korean War veteran, reluctant farmer

THERESE, in her 20s, bright, energetic, competent at her job

SETTING

The action spans a day and a night on a Saturday.

The stage space is multi-locational, combining interiors and exteriors.

The weather: idyllic, late summer, early autumn.

The play can be performed without an interval. If an interval is preferred, it should take place at the end of Scene Thirteen.

SCENE ONE

Introduction to the theme tune ('Lost Weekend') plays under. Lights up on ZELDA *and* ERIC. *They 'hang' (vertically) in bed sheets, covering their (we assume) nakedness. They have just woken and he's kissing her bare arm.*

ZELDA: To think: Dame Nellie Melba once slept in this bed.

ERIC: Have they changed the sheets since?

ZELDA: They'll have to when we leave!

ERIC: Gravity-defying, yes?

ZELDA: Nothing defies gravity.

ERIC: We do. Low-grade ore sample and femme fatale stage sex romp in Western District mansion!

ZELDA: You're no low-grade ore sample.

ERIC: You are a femme fatale. Pinch me, I'm dreaming.

ZELDA: I don't see why not kiss you.

They kiss. In half-light CHARLES, *with four whiskies on a tray, enters to flank them on one side. On the other, a piano slides into view,* MARGIE *seated at it, playing.* ZELDA *and* ERIC *sing a duet.*

ZELDA & ERIC: [*sung*]
    A lost weekend
    A lost weekend
    Not your place
    Not mine
    A case of us taking time
    In the country
    The city behind us we're hoping to find
    In fresh air, fine food, good wine—
    Bliss of a kind—on a
    Lost weekend
    This lost weekend.

The music continues as a gentle underscore.

ZELDA: How did you find our hosts?

ERIC: Last night? Spooky.

ZELDA: 'Sorry we're late—'

ERIC: 'The traffic out of Melbourne—a nightmare.'

MARGIE: But I like sitting up, tinkling the ivories.

CHARLES: It's the closest Margaret gets to a vice.

ZELDA: I kept thinking *Rocky Horror Show*—we're in it!

MARGIE: Will you join us in a nightcap? In the early 1900s grandfather drank with the gifted poet Christopher Brennan in Sydney. When in Victoria, the gifted poet.

CHARLES: Drank himself pie-eyed here at Xanadu. Have a Brennan.

ERIC: 'A Brennan'?

CHARLES: A neat Scots Malt. Drunk thus:

> CHARLES *downs a whisky.*

ZELDA: 'Eric's not totally teetotal but is on short rations.'

ERIC: 'Health reasons.'

MARGIE: And it is late, Charles.

CHARLES: Right—I'll get rid of these glasses and turn in.

> *He starts to exit, passing behind the suspended sheets. As the piano revolves to mask* MARGIE *still playing,* CHARLES *re-appears with tray, all glasses drained. He passes the piano to exit and it (with* MARGIE *still playing) rolls out with him. From the PA or wings the music continues.*

ZELDA: Spooky's the word.

ERIC: I kept thinking 'a pair of characters'.

ZELDA: But in whose story?

> *They embrace again and sing a second time.*

ZELDA & ERIC: [*sung*]
>> We're Adam, we're Eve
>> With our hearts on our sleeve
>> We leave a sweet whisper of love in every word said
>> Waves of desire climb higher around us
>> Raise and amaze us
>> Astound and surround us
>> Like two drunken seafarers we sail Melba's fair bed
>> May our lost weekend
>> This lost weekend
>> Not end!

> *Silence. The lovers in a tableau. A voice heard.*

THERESE: [*offstage*] Knock—knock—coming ready or not.

ERIC: Ooops.

ZELDA: Ooops.

ERIC: Hang on!

ZELDA: We're coming!

Sliding to the floor, each ends up wrapped in a sheet. The trapeze that's been supporting them acquires the look of a bed end.

Morning light widens, revealing THERESE *at a trolley. The faint underscore resumes.*

THERESE: Breakfast comes with a story attached. Margie, I mean Mrs Risdon-Allyn, Xanadu being a sheep property, has made a feature of the fact, and to this end has mastered lamb and mutton recipes from around the globe, including some from the Middle East, adapted from the goat. You slept well?

ZELDA: Like logs.

ERIC: But don't toss us on the fire.

ZELDA: Eric's a wag.

THERESE: So I gather. Been to England?

ZELDA: Yes—

ERIC: No.

THERESE: If you have, and even if you haven't, it's very English.

ERIC: England—?

THERESE: This dish. Devilled lambs' kidneys. You like…?

ZELDA: Love—

THERESE: Kidneys? You came to the right place.

ZELDA: Offal of any sort—I'm a fan, and they smell to die for.

THERESE: Margie, I mean Mrs Risdon-Allyn's, secret's the sauce. Boiled eggs here if you'd rather. Porridge and/or muesli for a starter, fresh milk's in the jug. Tea, and/or coffee. This: a mound of linen-wrapped fresh-baked bread. Excellent with your choice of three homemade marmalades: Cumquat, Poor Man's Orange, and Navel hyphen Grapefruit—not to mention (my fav) our justly famed Quince Jelly. Xanadu has a stand of quince—and a citrus grove. The homestead orchard's in no end of gardening books, the story attached there is Baron von Mueller designed the grounds, and selected the species.

ERIC: Do you also come with a story attached?

THERESE: As much round here does, yes: I'm the hired help, anything I can help you with, just ask.

ZELDA: I'm Zelda—this is Eric.

THERESE: Therese, but I answer to Tess. In or out?

ERIC: Pardon?

THERESE: View of Mt Difficult's a stunner. And likewise the Grampians. French doors give on to the verandah. We recommend guests take breakfast there. Trolley's on wheels.

> THERESE *exits and the underscore ends. They approach the trolley.*

ERIC: So, Miss Pritikin, what chance the kidneys?

ZELDA: They're cooked in butter.

ERIC: And in order to pig out at dinner this evening I better graze lightly today?

ZELDA: The porridge looks filling.

ERIC: Was a time I would have huffed, puffed and wolfed those kidneys down.

ZELDA: Would have been when you had two of your own.

ERIC: A kidney's gone AWOL—stroke's left my body a joke.

ZELDA: I adore your body, and said so.

ERIC: Said, last night, being a physiotherapist has taught you to appreciate bodies of all shapes and sizes.

ZELDA: The memory of an elephant.

ERIC: Walk of an orangutan—right hand's a parrot's claw—what's a dish like you see in me?

ZELDA: The sleep apnoea may prove a sore point.

ERIC: The what?

ZELDA: You snore!

ERIC: People learn to live beside railway lines!

> *A voice reaches them from off.*

CHARLES: [*offstage*] I can't stand strangers in the house!

ERIC: Should we have heard that?

ZELDA: I think not, therefore we didn't. The verandah?

ERIC: Drink in the view?

ZELDA: This famished is something I haven't felt in yonks. Sex leaves me feeling starved.

ERIC: Is that a compliment?

ZELDA: My way of saying our shenanigans last night left me ravenous.

ERIC: Wanting more?

ZELDA: Wanting breakfast! Bread's still warm: you can feel it through the linen.

ERIC: Does it beat feeling butt through cotton?

ZELDA: Food first.

ERIC: Then what?

ZELDA: I'll haul you back to bed.

> *As the trapeze that suspended them flies out,* ZELDA *and* ERIC *exit to the rear with the trolley.*

SCENE TWO

A kitchen bench slides into view, MARGIE *seated at it jotting a list.* CHARLES *enters, nursing a coffee.*

CHARLES: Do you hear me?

MARGIE: I heard you, Charles.

CHARLES: I hate strangers in the house.

MARGIE: I heard you. So did, no doubt, our guests, not to mention the ewes in the lambing paddock. They most likely heard you in Hall's Gap—in fact right now half Ararat probably has its hands to its ears.

CHARLES: I hate—

MARGIE: Hate, you might—get used to it, you must. As last weekend it was others, so next weekend it will be others still. And the weekend after that, yet more. The sooner you adapt, the better off we'll be. I'm running a business here.

CHARLES: Two guests!

MARGIE: All businesses take time to establish.

> *Eye to a recipe book, she keeps listing items.*

CHARLES: Your girl—

MARGIE: Yes?

CHARLES: —came late this morning.

MARGIE: I'm aware of that. And she told me why.

CHARLES: Out whoring all night?

MARGIE: She's lost her licence. I'm sympathetic. I recall the years I was dependent on others for my transport. Her beau was late picking her up.

CHARLES: Young whores, the lot of them—girls you get working here.

MARGIE: You'd know, would you, Charles? Or shall we not talk about it for fear of where that may lead?

> THERESE *has entered and paused. They sight her.*

THERESE: Am I—?

CHARLES: Intruding? How could you be? Xanadu Homestay Homestead, where all sorts are made to feel at home.

THERESE: Breakfast's delivered. Got the hamper on standby, and made a start on the next batch of bread, just waiting for the dough to rise. Am I doing something I shouldn't, or not doing something I should?

MARGIE: Here's a list of what I'll need from the garden.

THERESE: Right you are.

> THERESE *exits with Margie's list.*

CHARLES: What would your father make of the likes of her?

MARGIE: Back from the dead, she'd be a welcome sight. He'd see in her face the face of her dad, a shearer who, man and boy, father employed for over five decades. What he wouldn't welcome is the state Xanadu is in.

CHARLES: The price of wool my doing?

MARGIE: All I know is if we don't do something to repair our fortunes this place'll sink like a stone.

> CHARLES *sets his cup down with exaggerated care.*

CHARLES: If needed, I'll be in the workshop.

MARGIE: Where I trust you'll lower it to a roar.

> CHARLES *exits one way,* MARGIE, *with the cup he's left, another. The bench too slides from view with* ERIC *coming forward to the stage edge.*

SCENE THREE

Exterior light. Casually attired and taking in the scene, ERIC *is buttoning a batik shirt one-handed, this evidence of his having suffered from a stroke.* ZELDA *will appear in a blouse and Country Road-style skirt.*

ERIC: A magpie.

ZELDA: [*offstage*] What?

ERIC: You asked what's going on out here—late-breaking news is a magpie has landed on the croquet lawn. There's a cypress-lined gravel road leading up to the house. No-one on it. Elsewhere a swag of

gums—rooted to the spot. A swathe of dry-looking paddocks. Empty.
On the further horizon a distant bunch of mountains squat.

ZELDA: [*offstage*] The Grampians.

ERIC: Could be, they're not wearing a neon sign.

ZELDA: And you're wearing [*entering*] what? My God, a vision splendid—

ERIC: The shirt? Physio I know bought it for me.

ZELDA: Did I really?

ERIC: Just back from a holiday in Bali, you wanted to reward me for the
progress I'd made in your absence.

ZELDA: What was I thinking?

ERIC: I wondered that at the time, but if the shirt fits...

ZELDA: Wear it? You sound—edgy.

ERIC: Edgy is what real Australians get when the nearest milk bar's seventeen kilometres away. Hello: There was movement at the station.

CHARLES: [*offstage*] Get in the back!

ERIC: He means the dog—not us.

CHARLES: [*entering backwards, to the dog*] Sketch a rabbit.

ZELDA: Sketch a rabbit?

ERIC: It's little known, but most kelpies are artists.

ZELDA: Beautiful day.

CHARLES: Is it?

ZELDA: Made even better by the kidneys I ate—out of this world.

CHARLES: Not so—out of the two sheep I slaughtered yesterday.

ERIC: [*indicating a fence post*] Alright if I use that post over there?

CHARLES: Be my guest.

ZELDA: Eric's a stroke victim—there's certain functions he has to
reconstruct.

ERIC: Just making sure it doesn't belong to the dog.

CHARLES: What's he reconstructing?

ZELDA: His sense of humour? He's on an exercise program.

CHARLES: Well, if he's hoping to push that over [*the post*] he won't—it's
buried three foot deep—every post on the place is. Dates from an
earlier age, when labour was cheap as chinks.

ZELDA: You mean chips?

CHARLES: I think you heard what I said.

  ERIC *has begun a sequence of isometric presses against the post.*

ZELDA: By night impressive, but this morning the homestead is...

CHARLES: Yes?

ZELDA: So…

CHARLES: Rural?

ZELDA: Charming.

CHARLES: Not too rambling for you?

ZELDA: You and your wife must be very happy here.

CHARLES: Must we? Happens, I'm under instructions from the wife to make guests feel welcome to Xanadu. Happens, I don't feel good about guests staying here, period.

ZELDA: Thank you.

CHARLES: For?

ZELDA: Frankness is something I prize.

CHARLES: Then you won't be too sur-prised if I run into you both as little as possible during the rest of the day. Damn dog. [*To the offstage dog*] C'mere!

> CHARLES *starts to exit as* MARGIE *enters.*

MARGIE: Bravo, Charles. Making conversation. And what have you found out about our guests?

> CHARLES *has stopped. His eyeline goes to* ERIC *and* MARGIE *follows his gaze.*

CHARLES: He's on an exercise program.

ZELDA: Eric's had a stroke but on the road to recovery.

MARGIE: Glad to hear it.

ZELDA: Remarkable really, he's making every—

CHARLES: Post?

ZELDA: —a winner.

MARGIE: By way of conversation, anything you'd care to add, Charles?

CHARLES: Me? [*To* ZELDA] You're a psychiatrist, I'm told.

ERIC: If she is, I'm in trouble.

ZELDA: Actually I know as much about Freud as I do about sheep, and all I know about sheep is they make good jumpers.

> *Their joint eyeline shifts at the sound of sheep offstage.*

MARGIE: Should the dog be amongst the rams?

CHARLES: Get out of it!

MARGIE: When you rang your booking through you mentioned your occupation. I jotted down physiotherapist. Charles most likely mis-read my note. Hence psychiatrist.

CHARLES: Very Freudian of me, I'm sure.

ERIC: Zelda's my physio. I became a vegetable, we became a team.

ZELDA: It's how we met.

ERIC: On the massage table.

ZELDA: In a swimming pool actually.

CHARLES: So you're recently married?

ZELDA: Married? [*With a look to* ERIC] Yes—

ERIC: Very—

ZELDA: Recently.

CHARLES: But married's the main thing, we're witnessing the destruction of the family unit as we know it, don't you think?

ERIC: We don't have to.

ZELDA: We know it.

The sound of poultry in a state of alarm.

MARGIE: First the sheep. Now the chooks.

ZELDA: [*looking at the dog*] Nice-looking animal.

MARGIE: Charles doesn't like people saying so in front of the dog.

ZELDA: Doesn't want it to get a swelled head?

MARGIE: Goes manic when let off the chain.

ERIC: Well-bred beast, by the look.

CHARLES: You know a thing or two about dogs?

ERIC: I was a postman. Only joking. Hey—

The dog is nipping at ERIC*'s leg.*

Ooops. Aw. Sorry. Here, boy. Or is he a one-person dog?

CHARLES: 'He' is a she, 'boy' is a girl.

ERIC: A little. I know a little about dogs.

In unison, heads circle as the dog hares off.

MARGIE: Next stop the azaleas—which reminds me. I'm on a mission. We've got a wedding in the district. The Niesches eldest daughter is tying the knot.

CHARLES: The Niesches are a Kraut—

MARGIE: German family up the road.

CHARLES: Blow-ins.

MARGIE: Who settled here a hundred plus years ago.

CHARLES: [*to the dog*] Stay!

MARGIE: I'm expected to help out in the flower department. You're welcome to accompany me, I can point out some of the property's features.

ZELDA: I'm for that. What about you, Eric?

ERIC: Should finish my workout first, don't want my physio getting cranky.

MARGIE: You could catch us up. Or Charles might take you in hand— show Eric round the farm while Zelda and I gather some blooms?

CHARLES: I'm en route to the workshop.

MARGIE: Charles keeps a bottle of Scotch in the workshop.

CHARLES: I don't, but if I did it would be nobody's business but mine.

MARGIE: Light banter, Charles.

CHARLES: Not a gentle reminder?

MARGIE: Meant as a joke. He rarely picks up on my subtlety.

CHARLES: Whereas you pick up so readily on mine.

ZELDA: I trust it is a joke. Eric, by and large, has to steer clear of the bottle.

ERIC: Hard not to pick up on the subtlety of that, Princess Pritikin.

MARGIE: Pritikin? A nickname? Charles has one for me. Mouse. Perhaps one day I'll roar.

The women exit. ERIC *resumes a press.*

ERIC: Do you?

CHARLES: What?

ERIC: Keep a stash of Scotch in the workshop?

CHARLES: What lies behind the wife's remark is she once walked in on me having a mid-morning tipple in the machinery shed, since when she suspects me—

ERIC: Of always having one at eleven? It's a tad past ten.

CHARLES: And I'm workshop bound—

ERIC: But not for 'a Brennan'?

CHARLES: To do a bit, because if somebody doesn't attend to the work round here the place'll tumble round our ears.

To ERIC's *dismay the post collapses.*

Has Xanadu seen better days? Yes.

ERIC: Will I—?

CHARLES: What?

ERIC: Dig a new hole and so on.

CHARLES: And give yourself another stroke? I'll sort it later.

ERIC: I might stick my head in—

CHARLES: The hole?

ERIC: The workshop. Tools, machinery…

CHARLES: Your line?

ERIC: I'm a tradesman, a die-maker, a mere cog but in a big wheel. In the vehicle trade—General Motors Dandenong.

CHARLES: You make cars?

ERIC: As fast as people can break them. Or did until the stroke laid me low.

CHARLES: Au fait with agricultural machinery by any chance?

ERIC: Is it a tractor?

CHARLES: No.

ERIC: As long as it's not a tractor. Do I have a tractor story...

CHARLES: There's many a man who's found the tractor the bane of his existence. I fancy I'm one of them. Workshop's that-a-way. [*To the dog*] C'mere! Goddamn bitch of a thing.

ERIC: [*to himself*] And I'm the one with the stress problem?

With CHARLES *exiting,* ERIC, *yoga fashion, breathes in, aiming to spread his arms in a circle above his head. One arm's fine, the other isn't. Exhaling, he lowers his hands. He stands on one leg, one foot tucked into his knee. The sound of a magpie. He casts a wary eye skywards.*

SCENE FOUR

A corrugated iron door slides open. MARGIE *and* ZELDA *step into a shearing shed's light-dappled interior.*

MARGIE: Charles has his hidey-hole. This is mine.

ZELDA: The Xanadu shearing shed.

MARGIE: As a child, the cathedral I worshipped at. The shearing was always the best, maddest, wildest time of the year.

ZELDA: That smell?

MARGIE: Sheep dung.

ZELDA: No no, something else.

MARGIE: Lanolin perhaps?

ZELDA: Of course, I work with it daily.

MARGIE: Comes off the fleeces—eight, ten, in the really good seasons twelve thousand or more sheep being thrust up and down these chutes, bumping against the timbers. Leaves the wood smooth to the hand. Billy-boy, tar-boy, picker-up... wasn't much I didn't try. Even got my ticket as a wool classer.

ZELDA: Really?

MARGIE: Really. I keep a fleece here to show guests I haven't lost the knack.

She throws a fleece across the sorting table. ZELDA *feels and smells the wool.*

ZELDA: So fine, and yes, lanolin.

MARGIE: Tasmania's the only state grows it finer.

ZELDA: Did you shear?

MARGIE: Learnt to—and did—till Father decided it was eroding my social standing. More likely the shearers told him his daughter didn't have a ticket. As for social standing—not much of that comes our way these days.

ZELDA: That I don't believe.

MARGIE: Pity you're not our bank manager. A Ferrier.

ZELDA: Pardon?

MARGIE: The bale press you're looking at. Pressed its first bales in 1888 and still going strong. Not that our clip's been much to speak of.

ZELDA: This year's drought?

MARGIE: And a decade-long fall in the price of wool. If turning the place into a tourist attraction's to be my lot, so be it. Not something I can walk away from. Xanadu's been home to my family for a hundred and forty-seven years. But this isn't getting flowers picked, is it?

ZELDA: Mush-mush.

They exit, MARGIE *sliding the door shut.*

SCENE FIVE

Exterior. ERIC *leans against a stretch of corrugated iron shedding, staring skyward. The sound of steel on steel.*

CHARLES: [*offstage*] You bitch-faced arse of a thing!

ERIC: [*to the dog*] It's alright, girl, he doesn't mean you.

The hammering has stopped and the distant sound of a jet overhead can be heard. Engineer's hammer in hand, CHARLES *walks out of the shed also staring skyward.*

Aeroplane?

CHARLES: Or just the noise of one, depending on your eyesight. I can never pinpoint where the sound's coming from. We're directly under the Melbourne-Adelaide flight path.

ERIC: So it's not Alan Bond, Kerry Packer and Rupert Murdoch jetting in to stay the weekend?

CHARLES: The wife would like it, but they're yet to honour the establishment.

ERIC: They're yet to honour the establishment is the way I'd put it. [*Indicating*] In there's where it's all happening?

CHARLES: Or not happening as the case may be.

They exit into the workshop.

SCENE SIX

The tour continued, MARGIE *and* ZELDA *come forward.*

ZELDA: This scatter of bricks was a church?

MARGIE: Timber construction. Got transported to the showgrounds in 1915 on two bullock drays. Seeing the need, grandfather volunteered it as a drill hall. Maids, gardeners, station hands, upwards of twenty families living here one time, a village you could say. Had a school, a church. The bricks are what's left of the chapel's foundations. This, of course, remains.

ZELDA: Nobody I know has a cemetery as part of their front yard.

MARGIE: For me—one of Xanadu's enduring charms.

ZELDA: No lack of Risdon gravestones.

MARGIE: Big breeders, in both the animal and human department. The round mound of rocks?

ZELDA: A capped well?

MARGIE: A Chinese fencer's grave.

ZELDA: Really?

MARGIE: Travelling gangs of Chinamen built dry-stone walls, five shillings a chain, one of them died and was buried on the job. Not the first Chinaman laid to rest here, however. Lei Feng holds that distinction, Xanadu's first Chinese gardener, and beside him—

ZELDA: Sha…?

MARGIE: Yexin. Our second Chinese gardener. Both converts to Christianity.

ZELDA: Hence the crosses.

MARGIE: [*indicating another gravestone*] This man didn't convert.

ZELDA: [*reading*] Ibrihim Ali Rendra.

MARGIE: One of our shepherds. Great Aunt Dorothea—in her cups—
would speak of Ibrihim Ali. Fondly.

ZELDA: A Muslim, but he got a cross anyway?

MARGIE: I don't think anyone knew what else to give him, but certainly
Great Aunt Dorothea wanted him remembered.

ZELDA: Do I detect a whiff of scandal?

MARGIE: Shake any family tree—

ZELDA: Watch out for falling branches.

MARGIE: I shouldn't pry, I know—

ZELDA: But you will. No, please. Pry.

MARGIE: You're not married, am I right?

ZELDA: Wrong—am married.

MARGIE: But not to Eric?

ZELDA: Correct.

MARGIE: I sensed as much.

ZELDA: Is that a problem?

MARGIE: For me—no.

ZELDA: Because were it a problem I'd have to consider checking out. It
wouldn't be personal, just Eric's condition makes unnecessary stress
unhelpful.

MARGIE: Please, I'm running a business and you being single, married or
divorced is no concern of mine.

ZELDA: But it could irk Charles?

MARGIE: My husband holds somewhat old-fashioned views. With that go
the old-fashioned courtesies and your marital status is not something
he'll raise with you, but with me.

ZELDA: He may?

MARGIE: It could prove a bone of contention—should he find out.

ZELDA: Clearly he shouldn't, and need not. I'll forewarn Eric. The full
story—

MARGIE: I don't need to hear it.

ZELDA: I don't mind, in fact talking about it helps. This weekend away's
for Eric and me, an experiment, a more than welcome thing, but one
I'm trepidatious about.

MARGIE: On his account?

ZELDA: On mine. A case of the fewer people who know about Eric
and me the better. Yes, physiotherapists dating their patients is not,
professionally speaking, kosher, but I'm in the middle of a long

drawn-out divorce. Were my estranged husband to discover I had a lover I could find myself on tricky ground.

MARGIE: The divorce is proving a trial?

ZELDA: Several trials. Not for my husband a wham-bam thank-you-mam visit to the Family Law Court. This is divorce with the works: property, custody, you name it, kidnapping.

MARGIE: He kidnapped you?

ZELDA: Our children. He flew them to Greece. Parked them with his mother. I've been a year trying to right that wrong but proceedings have ground to a halt.

MARGIE: Sounds—

ZELDA: Mad? Is mad, but because leaving him's the sanest thing I've ever done, anyone, your husband included, who thinks I should still be with that man can, to not mince matters: Go to the back of the bus.

MARGIE: Spoken with an admirable degree of grim determination.

ZELDA: Hard-won, but only recently acquired.

MARGIE: So a weekend away from it all makes perfect sense?

ZELDA: And last night with Eric made perfect sense. What—in sickness or in health—makes no sense is why I fell for my ratbag of a husband in the first place!

MARGIE: If all who married, married wisely—the wedding!

ZELDA: The flowers!

MARGIE: Flowers! Flowers. I must think flowers…

They move away. Hammering is heard.

SCENE SEVEN

The workshop. A shower of sparks. ERIC *watches* CHARLES *wield an angle grinder on a farm implement. Then take to it with the hammer again.*

ERIC: So your family property wasn't far from here?

CHARLES: Nothing as grand, and way poorer ground, but—

ERIC: Wild horses wouldn't keep you down on the farm?

CHARLES: Farming I could have stood, but second fiddle to the old man for twenty or thirty more years wasn't an option. Had a bit of schooling down in Melbourne behind me.

ERIC: Private school?

CHARLES: Is there another sort? Then came the army.

ERIC: The army?

CHARLES: Elder brother Alec and I joined the forces.

ERIC: And saw the world?

CHARLES: If Korea's the world we saw it.

ERIC: I see.

CHARLES: Some time in Malaya followed.

ERIC: Before it was Malaysia.

CHARLES: They can't run their own affairs, people like that.

ERIC: Need us to do it for them.

CHARLES: Shit a brick! This's gonna snap, right?

ERIC: Shows every sign of doing so.

CHARLES: Fuck fuck fuck fuck fuck it!

ERIC: [*to the dog*] Now he'll have to do what he shoulda done in the first place, eh girl—unbolt it and take it to the bench where he can work on it properly.

CHARLES: How would you do a job like this? Unbolt it.

ERIC: And take it to the bench, yes.

> But CHARLES *is bringing up a welder.*

CHARLES: Bugger that. I'll call that done and lay a weld along it.

ERIC: Top and bottom.

CHARLES: Whatcha mean?

ERIC: Both sides would be the go. Doing the top weld is easy enough, but coming at it from below…? You gonna show me how good you are on an up-and-under weld—overhead stuff's a bit of an art.

CHARLES: I'll top weld the shitbag of a thing and take my chances.

ERIC: You're the boss… but I wouldn't do that if I were you.

CHARLES: What?

ERIC: Or you really will be taking your chances. You haven't earthed the welder.

> CHARLES, *about to turn the welder on, sees his mistake. He attaches an earthing clamp to the job.*

I was an apprentice when I saw someone die that way. Gave new meaning to the term 'smoko'. [*To the dog*] Dear oh dear, cockies, eh girl? This bloke lives up to their she'll-be-right reputation.

CHARLES: You have your stroke on the job?

ERIC: Mmm.

CHARLES *is fitting a rod into the handpiece.*

CHARLES: Into your employer for a heap of money?

ERIC: Have a Work Care case in the works.

CHARLES: Got a union behind you, I expect? I'm not big on unions.

ERIC: If this had happened— [*gesturing with his crook arm*] and I didn't have a union behind me—I'd be on the scrap heap. Then again, if safety hadn't been drummed into me by my union I wouldn't have spotted you about to turn that welder on without earthing it, and you'd most likely be scrap heap material yourself.

CHARLES: Where'd I leave—?

ERIC: This what you're looking for? [*Holding out a welding helmet*] Not as well-trained as I thought.

CHARLES: Who?

ERIC: The dog. My mutt rounds up spanners. I get a puncture.

CHARLES: Dog brings you the jack?

ERIC: In his mouth.

Hold on their tight-lipped grins. As CHARLES *dons the helmet, the scene darkens.*

SCENE EIGHT

Return of the kitchen bench. THERESE *is at work preparing a tray of goodies.* ZELDA, *an armload of flowers, enters.*

THERESE: Anzacs and cordial or teacake and tea?

ZELDA: Anzacs and cordial is what the doctor ordered.

THERESE: Warm out there, eh?

MARGIE *enters, also bearing flowers.*

MARGIE: On the bench'll do for these, for now. The men not in the market for morning tea?

THERESE: Have asked. Busy-busy down the shed.

MARGIE: Their loss.

THERESE: Name your poison. Rosehip or lemon?

MARGIE: Both homemade.

ZELDA: Rosehip cordial I've never had.

MARGIE: And I'll go the lemon.

THERESE: I've packed a hamper for you and your bloke—

ZELDA: A hamper?

MARGIE: You did tick the box 'Xanadu hamper' as opposed to the box 'luncheon in the Xanadu gazebo under the Xanadu Canary Island Palm'?

ZELDA: Oh right, the options boxes.

THERESE: Phew. Hell round here when we get our wires crossed.

MARGIE: Cheers.

ZELDA: Cheers.

THERESE: Flowers look a picture.

MARGIE: Think there's enough?

THERESE: Eileen'll be over the moon.

MARGIE: She better be. We were discussing marriage, Mrs Engleman and I. How not all unions are made in heaven.

THERESE: Tell me about it.

MARGIE: Oh—the course of true love not running smoothly?

THERESE: Not running.

MARGIE: But Andrew's such a nice boy.

THERESE: Nice and mad. I've dropped him.

MARGIE: You haven't.

THERESE: I have.

MARGIE: He bought you here this morning.

THERESE: In the circumstances the least he could do, given it's my car he's pranged. Fact is, I'm considering scrubbing males from the agenda once and for all. How come every bloke I step out with ends up trouble from A to Z?

MARGIE: [to ZELDA] If we wait, all will be revealed.

THERESE: Thursday night at The Royal? Andrew, two pots and he's anyone's—on reflection that's probably how I ended up with him. Thursday night, punches out a complete stranger who he reckons is eyeing me off. Gets hauled to the lockup.

MARGIE: Andrew?

THERESE: Well, they wouldn't clink the stranger for doing nothing. Bloke he floored's bringing charges. Witnesses and everything. Talk about embarrassing. Not to mention b-o-r boring. Didn't leave the cop shop till six in the morning. Hard to believe, eh? They couldn't locate the magistrate.

MARGIE: No mystery there. In Ballarat with his mistress.

ZELDA: Fights in pubs, a wedding in the district, magistrates with mistresses.

MARGIE: Not quite Sleepy Hollow round here.

THERESE: Has the magistrate really got a mistress?

MARGIE: You did not hear that from me.

> CHARLES *enters.*

CHARLES: Hear what?

MARGIE: Women's talk.

CHARLES: And so much palaver the phone ringing's escaped your notice? I'll go.

> *A phone is sounding.* CHARLES *exits to it.*

MARGIE: Thank you, dear.

> *The phone stops as* CHARLES *answers it offstage.*

Take your cordial and the biscuits with you. I promised Zelda you'd show her the pantry and still room.

THERESE: The preserves in there are like a dream.

MARGIE: I'll ferry the flowers to the church.

ZELDA: I've been told to expect a library of marmalades.

THERESE: Bottled apricots, peaches, chutneys. Like a coloured page in a pop-up cookbook.

> *As they exit* CHARLES *pops his head through a serving hatch, hand over phone.* MARGIE *is twining the flowers.*

CHARLES: You seen him?

MARGIE: Who?

CHARLES: Engleman.

MARGIE: Not with you?

CHARLES: Wandered off.

MARGIE: Take a message.

CHARLES: You and I must have a serious talk about all this.

MARGIE: Can it wait? I'm trying to get to the church on time!

CHARLES: Alright, let it wait!

> MARGIE *exits.* CHARLES *remains framed in the serving hatch.*

[*Into the phone*] He's nowhere to be found… Uh-uh. [*He writes.*] Say the name of the union again. [*He writes more.*] Sure—I'll get him to call you. [*He hangs up.*] Like bloody hell I will.

> CHARLES *puts down the phone and tears up the note. He slides the hatch shut. Cut to:*

SCENE NINE

A croquet lawn. A ball rolls into view and stops. ERIC *enters, with a croquet mallet. He lines up his next shot,* ZELDA *entering to him.*

ZELDA: I imagine Nellie Melba striding across this lawn, parasol in hand, an aria from some opera on her lips, croquet hammer in hand. What are you aiming at?

ERIC: The far hoop.

> *He plays the stroke.*

ZELDA: You know the rules?

ERIC: Haven't a clue. Gathering flowers was…?

ZELDA: Fun.

ERIC: And Mrs Allyn?

ZELDA: Mrs Risdon-Allyn. Interesting. Energetic. And Mr Allyn?

ERIC: No Risdon?

ZELDA: She's the Risdon, he's the Allyn.

ERIC: A lunatic. Ex the services. Officer class. Served in Korea. Then Malaya. Rabid anti-communist.

ZELDA: You didn't engage in political debate?

ERIC: One lunatic in the workshop was ample, ask the dog. I spent quite a bit of time talking to the dog. Found she made more sense than her owner. He I merely congratulated.

ZELDA: On?

ERIC: Holding back the red tide, keeping the yellow peril at bay, thus making our country the comfortable (prosperous, safe, stable) entity it is today.

> *He is fetching two more croquet balls and preparing to play more shots.*

ZELDA: There was a rotunda but—

ERIC: The white ants got it?

ZELDA: How'd you know?

ERIC: Just a guess.

ZELDA: And a privet maze!

ERIC: A-mazing.

ZELDA: Had a Norman Lindsay sculpture in the centre which they donated to the Ararat Gallery.

ERIC: A tax dodge?

ZELDA: Don't be cynical.

ERIC: Graduates of the school of hard knocks get that way.

ZELDA: The plinth remains.

ERIC: The plinth?

ZELDA: Has a sundial on it now.

> ERIC *plays a shot and watches the result.*

Seems the crows at sunset put on a show. While heading wherever for the night they land in one of the home paddock gums. We can watch them coming in, and taking off.

ERIC: Will they be wearing hobnail boots? [*He plays a second shot.*] And how many hours of not much doing before that highlight keeps us spellbound?

ZELDA: You're bored?

ERIC: Croquet. What a game!

ZELDA: You know what I feel like?

ERIC: Shoot.

ZELDA: In the middle of a paddock.

ERIC: In the middle of a paddock.

ZELDA: Lunch.

ERIC: Not quite what I had in mind in the middle of a paddock, but maybe our plans can overlap.

ZELDA: Strange, thinking lunch when I've only just finished morning tea. Must be the country air.

ERIC: Making you ravenous, perchance?

> *They embrace and kiss. A wolf whistle is heard and* THERESE *enters.*

THERESE: Sorry. Couldn't resist. One hamper coming your way. Service with a toothy grin's my motto.

> THERESE *smiles and sets the hamper down.*

ZELDA: Our Xanadu hamper.

THERESE: Margie, I mean Mrs Risdon-Allyn (I'm supposed to say Mrs Risdon-Allyn in front of the guests) calls it the Xanadu Ploughman's Lunch. There's—

ERIC: A story attached?

THERESE: The picnic basket itself's a family heirloom. Dates from 1861 and made its first appearance at Flemington the year Carbine won the Melbourne Cup.

ZELDA: Any suggestions where we should go to eat it?

ERIC: The picnic basket? It's an heirloom, surely Mrs R hyphen A will want it back.

THERESE: The spot'd be 'the spot'. Creek—more a trickle than a torrent— goes round like so, curves back on itself, then wanders on. In there's where the old people used to gather for their dos.

ERIC: Their don'ts they had elsewhere.

ZELDA: You keep trying.

THERESE: Doesn't he? Toothy grin after toothy grin, my jaws are aching. On the subject of Aboriginals, not far from here there's a lake. You can still see some of the fish traps they built. Margie—

ERIC: Mrs Risdon-Allyn to you.

THERESE: —is thinking of making a trip there an attraction. One more reason to remember a visit to Xanadu. Head screwed on, that woman. Thinks things through. If you're interested, I happen to be, Bunjil's Cave's a bit of a drive—well worth a look.

ERIC: Who's Bunjil?

THERESE: Say you spot a wedge-tailed eagle, that's Bunjil coming back to check everything's alright. According to Aboriginal mythology he made all we see round here.

ERIC: Say you spot two wedge-tails—they can't both be Bunjil.

THERESE: Bunjil's got plenty friends.

ERIC: Is that in the Xanadu brochure?

THERESE: Nah, it's what we used to say at school.

ZELDA: They must be the twin fir trees, Eric.

ERIC: I see the firs. What's the story?

THERESE: Planted when the twins Amelia and Adelaide were born.

ZELDA: Amelia got sick.

THERESE: Adelaide.

ZELDA: Adelaide? Got sick—

THERESE: Glandular fever.

ZELDA: Why's one tree smaller than the other?

THERESE: Adelaide's tree stopped growing and only when she fully recovered—

ZELDA: It was a long illness.

THERESE: —did it start growing again, hence the difference in their sizes.

ERIC: Couldn't just be that one tree gets more sun than the other?

THERESE: That's what I said when I first saw 'em.

ERIC: If you ask me that's the story that oughta be attached.

ZELDA: But as a story, not half as interesting.

THERESE: A good moral, though. Stand in the shadow of something too long and you end up decidedly bonsai. Aw, well. Can't stand round yakking, better get on with it—go feed the yabs.

THERESE *has gone to one side for a bucket and is coming back.*

ZELDA: Yabs?

THERESE: Yabbies.

ERIC: For dinner tonight?

THERESE: For lunch tomorrow. Margie catches 'em Friday, keeps 'em in a tank for a day or two, on an oatmeal diet.

ERIC: Porridge-fed yabbies.

THERESE: She's a bit of a gourmet.

ZELDA: Eric had porridge for breakfast.

ERIC: Something of a yabbie [*clawing the air*] myself.

THERESE: It cleans their digestive tracts.

ERIC: Sunday lunch, you say?

ZELDA: Eric's interested 'cause he's semi-fasting today—means he can binge tonight and tomorrow.

THERESE: Word is, every second restaurant in Melbourne's doing something with yabbies. The brain's trust figured she'd do ditto here. Sees it as a haves and have nots market—the smart thing being to work the haves end of it. You two'd be earning a quid.

ZELDA: Not really.

THERESE: You must, to even be here.

ZELDA: It's a special occasion. In reality Eric's on sickness benefit.

ERIC: Got a Work Care case on the go.

THERESE: Compo? Put me on ten per cent.

ZELDA: And I'm a humble physiotherapist, not a lucrative calling.

THERESE: But a professional. I admire professionals. They know how to bleed the country dry.

ZELDA: You'd be surprised how little I take home.

THERESE: Not as surprised as you'd be if you found out what us bushies earn.

THERESE *has gone.*

ERIC: There goes a breath of fresh air.

ZELDA: Isn't she? But you're not a happy camper.

ERIC: Says…?

ZELDA: I can read between the lines—I didn't consult. And should have. Is that it? I've sprung this weekend on you—bundled you into a car, not a word as to where we were going, wonder I didn't blindfold you.

ERIC: Didn't have to—it was dark.

ZELDA: First date. My treat. Make it a surprise. Ooops.

ERIC: Gridlock on the Westgate.

ZELDA: Roadworks from Ballan to Ballarat.

ERIC: What, me worry?

ZELDA: Add a jackknifed semi the Melbourne side of Colac and I've turned a two-and-a-half-hour sprint away from it all into the East-West crossing.

ERIC: 'Hi, I'm Zelda, welcome to Disaster Tours.' You were funny.

ZELDA: Not so funny the morning after?

ERIC: Where's that thought coming from?

ZELDA: Where d'you think? It's a long time between drinks, Eric, for me, this sort of thing, and I know I can be over-over-hyphen something. I over-… stay my welcome, or something, my own worst enemy. And I'm—pushy—you can say it: 'Stop being pushy'.

ERIC: Aw, for Chrissake.

ZELDA: It is me, right?

ERIC: You? Can you begin to credit what a weekend with you means to me? This whole, this— [*dangling his crook arm*] seven-month nightmare: quit the smokes, get off the booze, count the calories, exercises without end—this stay calm do yoga—this [*slurring*] 'My speech'll come back—don't you w-w-w-worry about that'. If to meet you I had to go through it over again…

ZELDA: What?

ERIC: I would.

ZELDA: To meet me? Bullshit.

ERIC: You know what I'm saying.

ZELDA: Something resembling the nicest thing anyone's ever said to me.

ERIC: How insecure are you?

ZELDA: You know—kind of a basket case.

ERIC: But so good at hiding it! You, Zel Pal, are the best thing in my life and if I appear on edge, rest assured it's not your doing.

ZELDA: We don't send the ploughman's lunch back and check out?

ERIC: We plough on and the ploughman's lunch it is.

She picks up the hamper and starts out in the lead. He comes behind using the mallet as a plough. She stops sensing she's being got at. He veers off to stash the mallet to one side then rejoins her.

ZELDA: Is it what you said this morning—this far off the bitumen you're out of your element? A city slicker, born and bred.

ERIC: Part of it, but city slicker no. Born the backblocks of Gippsland, you're looking at a hayseed who, aged fourteen, kissed the bush goodbye, reached the big smoke, and stayed put.

ZELDA: Until this weekend?

They start to walk on the spot.

ERIC: Until this weekend I have not again set foot on a farm.

ZELDA: That's how much you hated the bush?

ERIC: You think that strange?

She stops.

ZELDA: Did Tess actually point to 'the spot'?

ERIC: Made a few marks on the ground. Want a bush kid's advice? Find the creek. Follow it. We'll end up somewhere.

They set off walking on the spot, but in a new direction.

ZELDA: Is that all there is to it?

ERIC: You arrive a place like this: 'the air, the birds, the trees'. For me it's a lot of what I got shot of. Doesn't stop there. What am I? My trade?

ZELDA: A metalworker.

ERIC: Yeah, but dig deeper—at twenty-eight became a shop steward, then an organiser, and with all that come the eyes I see things through. You spot a run of post-and-rail fencing, you're thinking—

ZELDA: Olde worlde.

ERIC: I'm seeing every adze mark. Vast flock numbers? I'm thinking convict shepherds working for rations. Charles asks do I want a peek at the shearing shed? No thanks. My first thought will be how many backs got busted making you fat cats fat? Grounds like these people have you don't get unless blokes work for decades, like Chinamen.

ZELDA: There were Chinese here, two gardeners and a cook.

ERIC: There you go.

ZELDA: It's a class thing?

ERIC: It's the folly of thinking we're born equal, not noticing how some inherit a swag more than the rest. Why do fewer than six per cent of the Australian population live out here? 'Cause a life on the land's hunky-dory? Every move made's a winner? It is, and has been, a soft cop for few, a cruel grind for many.

ZELDA: Funny. I nearly chose the coast. Would have been smarter, a coastal resort.

ERIC: A surfing carnival for the disabled? The leg, Snow, the arm—[*miming being a disabled surfer*] what happened? 'Shark attack at Gunnamatta but nothing's gonna stop Eric The Red shooting these Bell's Beach tubes!'

> *She aims the picnic rug that came with the hamper his way. He stops to roll it up, then places it under his bad arm. Unbeknownst to one another, each secretly smiles. The lights fade down as they set out again.*

SCENE TEN

An ABC radio program is heard. ('Ockham's Razor', first broadcast 3 April 1988.) During the broadcast we become aware of CHARLES *cleaning his service revolver in the shuttered gloom of his bedroom. Other items of military paraphernalia are evident.*

RADIO VOICE: We spend virtually nothing on soil improvement or stabilisation. In fact, by our cash priority system we actually destroy our soil as one means for our nation to get rich. An example of that is the fact that for every ton of wheat we sell to earn foreign currency, we are losing from three to sixteen tons of topsoil for which no-one pays, and for which no-one is held to account. Let me say right here that I have no criticism whatsoever of farmers for this. In fact, they are doing an incredible job even maintaining production under the prevailing circumstances. No. Soil degradation and the enormous problems it creates for us now and in the future is a matter for the whole society to face up to. How did we ever get in this mess? What happened to us as we moved towards this last eighth of the twentieth century? Perhaps one factor is the increasing alienation between man and the land… as our farming shed its labour force those that were left, have by circumstance, and mechanisation, distanced themselves from the soil—

CHARLES *turns the radio off. Loads the service revolver. One bullet.*
He spins the chamber and Russian roulette-style aims the gun to
his head. Fires. Click. He stands motionless. A blowfly starts up.
The blowfly stops. CHARLES *aims. Click. Blackout.*

SCENE ELEVEN

THERESE *is crouching at a dam, a bucket beside her. A small stage floor*
trap is open and she's sprinkling oatmeal into it. She reaches into the
space below, lifts and looks at a yabby. ERIC *and* ZELDA *appear on the*
dam bank behind her. She senses their presence.

THERESE: Gidday again.
ERIC: That the holding tank?
THERESE: Yep.
ERIC: How many you got?
THERESE: A hundred or so. Idea is luncheon with an all-red theme.
ERIC: Red wine?
THERESE: Laid on.
ERIC: Yum yum.
THERESE: Soup of the day: tomato, the stock made outta this mob's
    shells, with a fresh basil garnish. For mains: sun-dried tomato-
    flecked pasta—we'll be knocking that up this arvo—with yabs in
    a tomato, garlic and red chilli sauce, totally delish. A rocket and
    beet leaf salad, cherry tomatoes in that. For the antipasto: fat red
    capsicums—I'll be skinning them when I get back—baby beetroots,
    blood sausage—a German recipe—and kind of a burgundy salami—
    there's a Swiss-Italian family near here supply us with that. A
    big round of Chester cheese. Kalamata olives—that not black,
    but reddish colour. As for the dessert: scoops of red currant and
    raspberry sorbet nestling up to some quinces poached in muscat.
ZELDA: They turn pink, don't they, quinces, when you cook them?
THERESE: Yep.
ZELDA: [*looking into the tank*] Do they bite?
THERESE: These? Not if you've got the knack.

   Throughout, THERESE *has continued to feed the yabbies.*

ZELDA: We on track for 'the spot'?
THERESE: When you hit the red gums, follow them. No mistaking the
    spot when you get there.

ERIC: Hard to credit, cordon bleu yabbies. Public enemy number one when I was a kid. Burrowed holes in our dam walls. Broke our hearts, the number of dams they trashed.

THERESE: You a country boy?

ERIC: Yep. But bid the bush bye-bye as soon soon as I could could.

They continue to watch THERESE *at work. Then move off.*

THERESE: Have a good one.

ZELDA: Will do. Well, I will. Eric's finding being back in the scrub a bit of a trial.

THERESE: Appreciate where he's coming from. Can be a good place to get out of.

They exit. THERESE *finishes. Puts the tank top back. Grabs her bucket and heads for Xanadu.*

SCENE TWELVE

Charles' bedroom. The sound of a blowfly. It lands. CHARLES *again aims the revolver.* MARGIE *enters.*

MARGIE: Shooting blowflies?

CHARLES: Yes.

MARGIE: Is it loaded?

CHARLES: One bullet only and…

A click. The blowfly takes off.

… that wasn't it. Not amused, Mouse? But isn't it a Xanadu legend that your own father used to shoot the pegs out of the maids' hands as they hung out the wash?

MARGIE: Not loaded. But you are?

CHARLES: Am yet to touch a drop—will soon make a start. Wasn't there a time when Saturday afternoons were my own?

MARGIE: Shall I call you for afternoon tea?

CHARLES: No need.

MARGIE: And I needn't remind you we'll be dressing for dinner?

CHARLES: Well aware we'll be dressing for dinner.

MARGIE: This word you wanted…?

CHARLES: It can wait. I'm busy.

MARGIE: Doing?

CHARLES: Listening.

MARGIE: To?

CHARLES: The radio.

MARGIE: Not on.

CHARLES: Is now.

> *He activates the radio. The musical intro to 'Lost Weekend' is playing.*

MARGIE: Excellent. No afternoon tea. And given our guests won't be back for it either, I'll dispense with making the pumpkin scones, one less thing to worry about. You did have lunch?

CHARLES: Your girl came with a bite—to my room.

> *He holds a plate out for her. She takes it and exits. He spins the revolver chamber. Crossfade music under to:*

SCENE THIRTEEN

'The spot'. The basket's there. The picnic rug's spread. ERIC *and* ZELDA *are in a mellow mood, him twitching flies.*

ZELDA: You ate sparingly.

ERIC: Saving myself for the Xanadu Banquet.

ZELDA: Just these to go.

ERIC: Ar, the Invalid's after-dinner mints. Thank you, nurse.

> *She's placed some pills on the basket top.*

ZELDA: A blue, a red and a white.

ERIC: The tricolour. Liberty, Equality…

> *She blows him a kiss.*

ZELDA: Fraternity.

ERIC: Is fraternity all we're experiencing?

ZELDA: Whatever it is, let's agree to not rush it.

ERIC: Something the physically impaired get used to hearing—don't rush—but coming from you, music to my ears.

> *He is taking his after-meal medication. A beat.*

ZELDA: Did you hear a splash?

ERIC: A trout? A yellow belly? Not sure. Do know the ant on your leg's from the species called bull.

Leaning toward her, he twitches it away.

They tickle trout, you know.

ZELDA: This trout you can tickle only if you use the other hand.

ERIC: You know I can't.

ZELDA: Call it professional dedication.

ERIC: Even make going the grope a form of physiotherapy?

He trails his other hand along her leg.

What thinking?

ZELDA: How hot and bothered it used to make me.

ERIC: What?

ZELDA: Upstairs outside—downstairs outside—a hand round my pants,
I still love all that. For me boy's zips were a source of endless
fascination. I'd slowly, slowly ease them down.

ERIC: The zips?

ZELDA: Tooth by tooth—then up again, then down—and up.

ERIC: Perfecting the art of the tease?

ZELDA: No—learning to accept the tease was what I got off on—Y-
fronts—my, my, parting the folds, so much to explore—heart beating,
hormones racing. Outside rear wall of a dance hall. Will a parent
unexpectedly appear? All that furtive electric rubbing up against each
other. Sex without clothes when I first had it was to me a shocking
let-down. Shall I make myself, and you, a little more comfortable?

ERIC: I'm partially disabled—hard-pressed to stop you.

*She sits herself upon him, staring down, flaring and settling her
skirt across him.*

I can see the country boy in you.

ERIC: Sticky-up hair, the sad-sack look, pinched face.

ZELDA: The God-awful grind of so much milking—morning and evening?
Did all those udders turn the boy into a tit man?

ERIC: The reverse.

ZELDA: My breasts of no interest?

ERIC: Your breasts of supreme interest—my life and times as Slave Boy
to a Jersey herd is what I'd rather not think about.

ZELDA: Something else then. The bush—you remember it how?

ERIC: Empty.

ZELDA: Empty?

ERIC: Lonely.

ZELDA: Lonely.

ERIC: Boring.

ZELDA: Wasn't an idyllic place to come of age?

ERIC: More like hitting yourself with a crowbar—

ZELDA: Good when it stopped.

ERIC: But would it ever stop?

ZELDA: Tell me one extraordinary thing—

ERIC: That happened to me before I hightailed it to Melbourne.

ZELDA: There must have been something.

ERIC: A highlight? Church—the morning service been and gone. Sunday lunch—had. A hot afternoon stretching out before me and as usual nobody to spend it with.

ZELDA: No brothers, no sisters?

ERIC: Four sisters but—

ZELDA: Girls.

ERIC: Girls are another breed. Tennis court's a mere four miles away. I ride there. Pass no-one on the road. And no-one's at the tennis court when I arrive. Stillness is all.

ZELDA: Total?

ERIC: Total.

> *They freeze, listening. Nothing. They resume the gentle grind of fondling each other that's underway.*

It's been suggested I work on my serve. I own—precious possessions—five near-bald tennis balls. Five serves. Hup hup hup hup hup. And again.

ZELDA: Silence.

ERIC: I traipse to the other end of the court, gather the five balls and serve them back the other way. Hup hup hup…

ZELDA: Hup hup. And…?

ERIC: Silence reigning still. I do this from end to end to end for an hour, then stop. Tennis court's cut into a hill. Looking out, I can see across the valley and again nothing's stirring.

ZELDA: Nothing?

ERIC: Not even smoke coming out a chimney.

ZELDA: And not—

ERIC: Not many chimneys.

ZELDA: Your theme. Little to do and no-one to do it with.

ERIC: I realise I have not spoken to or seen another human being since leaving home and a thought starts to grow inside my teenage brain: Could it be the world has ended and I'm the only person left alive? I serve. Hup. Thinking yourself utterly alone can be a frightening prospect. Hup. Out of nowhere a kookaburra swoops low across the net, intersecting with the tennis ball I've struck. Thunk.

ZELDA: Down it goes?

ERIC: A stray breast feather floating after it. And did a single other human being see this miraculous moment, this mystic event? No. I'm clearly—silence, the stillness is all—the sole witness.

ZELDA: Was it dead?

ERIC: The kookaburra picked itself up seconds later and flew off. And would anyone believe me when I told 'em? I was having them on.

ZELDA: And that you rate the most extraordinary thing to happen to you till you were fourteen?

ERIC: That is growing up in the country for you, in a nutshell. Everything's nothing. Even something's nothing. Events that could and should astonish: who sees them? The country, that's the country. Three balls to go, I continue working on my serve.

ZELDA: End to end.

ERIC: End to end.

ZELDA: Like me with boy's zips.

She guides his hand under her skirt.

Want to know another country you can become a citizen in?

ERIC: Are you the Border Guard?

ZELDA: I'm the butch Customs Official.

ERIC: Any strange customs I need to know about?

ZELDA: Lots. And I'll have to search your baggage, sir. Have I permission to unzip you?

She rises a tad, making room enough to get her hand in there. They smile. And hold, lights fading gently down around them and their love-making.

When heard, a song will come from THERESE *singing live.*

And at some point, ERIC *and* ZELDA *will stand and go off. At another,* CHARLES, *nursing a Scotch, will stare into the gloaming before disappearing into the darkness of the house. By the light of an open oven door,* MARGIE *will be glimpsed in her kitchen checking the progress of a dish. Xanadu, at day's end, will be becoming Xanadu by night.*

THERESE: [*sung*]
    A lost weekend
    A lost weekend
    There's me and there's you
    There's the booking for two
    There's the light that reached through to the end of our bed
    The mountains before us
    Are lying there for us
    The birds rising chorus climbs like wine to the head
    Waves of desire astound us
    They gently surround us
    The mound where we'll moulder's a book left unread
    A thought perhaps but
    That lost weekend
    Our lost weekend… a thought never said
    Instead:
    We praise the day's gentle fading
    Raise again the glass of its moments which we've
    Drained like champagne
    Should the bliss of all this like a morning mist rise
    Should the moon we'll soon greet
    Mask an unwelcome surprise
    Should the fruit of the orchard by night prove a dark feast
    The day's harvest at least's been
    A feast for the eyes
    A lost weekend
    This lost weekend
    May our lost weekend
    Not end.

Sunset has faded into dusk, then complete shadow. At song's end, THERESE *is lit checking cutlery, setting candles in holders.*

SCENE FOURTEEN

The guest bedroom. ERIC, *in white dress-shirt and underwear, holds a dinner suit against himself. He is watched by* ZELDA, *in a swish gown of eastern inspiration.*

ERIC: At Xanadu we dress for dinner.

ZELDA: At Xanadu—a charming custom—we dress for dinner.

ERIC: And if I don't dress for dinner, the ultimate form of blackmail.

ZELDA: You starve.

ERIC: I'm seriously expected to make like a penguin? I've never worn a suit like this in my life! And for the record I'd rather be caught jogging!

ZELDA: The day you're caught jogging you really will have come back from the grave.

ERIC: If you'd tipped me off in advance.

ZELDA: Why—when I planned this whole thing as a surprise.

ERIC: That it's proving to be.

She pops the top on a small gift box.

ZELDA: Cufflinks. They go with the shirt.

ERIC: For me?

ZELDA: Mmmm.

ERIC: You shouldn't have.

ZELDA: Silly me. I thought I'd mark the occasion.

She takes out a dress-suit coathanger. Separates the trousers. Hands them to him. Hangs the jacket. Helps him dress.

ERIC: Was this clobber his?

ZELDA: No. My husband lives for one thing: to leave me with nothing. No house, no children, no money, and certainly no dinner suit.

ERIC: I draw the line at wearing something that animal wore.

ZELDA: That excuse is out. Hired. Like the car. I'll be returning it Monday morning.

ERIC: Trousers fit. How'd you know my size?

ZELDA: Is that question for real? For seven months I've had ample access to your medical records. For seven months I've towed you round a swimming pool. For seven months I've watched you progress from a Zimmer frame to a stick to walking unaided. For Chrissake, I know your body about as well as I know my own! May I?

She kneels to do up the zip.

ERIC: Your dress.

ZELDA: Thank you, I know.

ERIC: Is wow.

ZELDA: While I'm here, the shoes. Don't scuff them—they're also a Monday morning return.

ERIC: Black slip-ons. How'd you know—I won't ask.

ZELDA: Don't. 'Cause I don't believe this! Here I am having a shit fight over a dinner suit! [*She stands.*] Next, the cufflinks. I once made a vow never to sleep with a patient. Having met you, having decided to break with that vow, I thought I'd do it in style, a faint hint of class. Talk about style, talk about class!

ERIC: You sure I can't interest you in one of my stress pills?

ZELDA: The ground rules. We don't talk about children.

She eases him into the jacket.

ERIC: Especially yours.

ZELDA: I might get teary. And divorce.

ERIC: Especially yours.

ZELDA: Also is a no-no. Margaret thinks if he finds out we aren't married—

ERIC: It might shake his faith in the fundamental health of Western civilisation?

ZELDA: Or something. Or he'll beat her up. Things in the marriage aren't tiptop.

ERIC: I see. And the John Cleese of Faulty Acres will be wearing…?

ZELDA: Same as you.

ERIC: Comforting. Being a penguin's no picnic—being a solitary penguin's a pitiful fate.

ZELDA: Are you so out of your comfort zone?

ERIC: It's different for you. You're the daughter of a doctor.

ZELDA: I'm the daughter of an Eastern Suburbs wog.

ERIC: But a doctor—

ZELDA: Still a wog.

ERIC: You can use thirty-seven different kinds of cutlery.

ZELDA: Can I? I'm not here because I'm used to it, or because these are my sort of people. Want to know the difference between you and me? I'm the one with a sense of adventure!

ERIC: It's happening. Knew it would. I'm starting to feel like Sir John Kerr.

He's walking stiffly around.

ZELDA: Can I ask something?

ERIC: Kind of penguin I am, always entertaining the other fellow's point of view.

ZELDA: You're telling me you've never worn a suit like that? Not even when you got married?

ERIC: Not even when my eldest girl got married. To, of all things, a corporate lawyer. It makes for interesting Christmases.

ZELDA: At her wedding you wore what?

ERIC: Something blue, blue? I remember now: blue boilersuit by Yakka! Christ, you look edible.

ZELDA: Stop confusing me with food.

ERIC: Stop looking delicious.

ZELDA: Ogle, but don't touch.

   Blackout.

SCENE FIFTEEN

Margie's bedroom. MARGIE *is seated at the mirror in evening gown. She has a drink and is finalising her make-up.*

MARGIE: A Saturday night silver service dinner party much as it would have been in my grandparents' time is part of what guests pay for at Xanadu.

CHARLES: I don't believe I'm hearing this.

   CHARLES *has appeared in the doorway of the bathroom linking their rooms. His face is lathered for shaving. He wears the bottom half of a dinner suit and an unbuttoned dress-shirt.*

MARGIE: If helping supply this service irks you, Charles, I suggest you forgo dinner.

CHARLES: That's your answer?

MARGIE: Are we sober enough to remain civil?

CHARLES: Should I walk a line?

   He comes forward then retreats back into the bathroom, shutting the door.

MARGIE: Would you say you've been drinking heavily, moderately or not at all? I shall assume moderately, suspect heavily, and not at all is clearly out of the question.

CHARLES: [*offstage*] The man's a red!

MARGIE: This you know how? Did he call you comrade, Charles? It's a long time since anyone's been even half-friendly to you let alone called you comrade. How novel.

The bathroom door opens to reveal a KOREAN GUARD *who shouts a command.* MARGIE *does not see or hear him. The door closes then flies open again,* CHARLES *re-entering.*

CHARLES: A telephone call came for him.

MARGIE: 'It's the Kremlin—Gorbachev speaking.'

CHARLES *walks towards her again.*

CHARLES: The caller introduced himself as a trade union official.

The KOREAN GUARD *is glimpsed elsewhere.* CHARLES *'sees' him, she doesn't.*

The man's patently—

MARGIE: Patently—what?

CHARLES: Patently—

MARGIE: The man's patently recovering from a stroke. It happened at work. His union is trying to ensure he receives adequate compensation. Why wouldn't a union official ring him?

CHARLES: On a Saturday?

MARGIE: Farmers tell us they work on Saturdays, maybe trade union officials do too. Who taught you to think, Charles, or is that the problem, no-one did?

CHARLES: I'm to dine, am I, talk, am I, sleep, with a red under my roof!

CHARLES *stands there, eyes following the exit of the* KOREAN *'ghost' as it vanishes.*

MARGIE: This may sound finicky, Charles, but allow me to point out that under your roof is not the operative phrase. He is not under your roof. Under the terms of Father's will he is under my roof. You may own and run Xanadu the farm—I own, and run Xanadu the homestead.

CHARLES: That's all you can say?

MARGIE: Not all at all. A red...

The KOREAN GUARD, *glimpsed elsewhere, shouts a command.* CHARLES *stiffens.* MARGIE, *at last satisfied with her make-up, adds some jewellery.*

In my experience when you use the term, a red is someone whose opinions are other than your own. This too may strike you as odd, Charles, but after a long marriage, largely a blip on my radar somewhere between tedium and torturously dull, dinner with a person whose opinions are other than yours, I'm quite looking forward to!

CHARLES: We'll talk unionism at table will we, the wretched of the earth?

MARGIE: Perhaps we've become the wretched of the earth, but let's not discuss us, a far too tiresome topic. [*She takes her glass, swivels on her chair, stands.*] In this house, in my parents' and grandparents' time, talented people from all walks of life, of many points of view, gathered, and I grew up knowing the three things that mattered to them. Good food, good wine, good conversation, which for them meant lively debate on all that could be known. On all that could be known.

CHARLES: Bravo.

MARGIE: Gone with the wind, you may think. I'm fighting for the possibility of those days coming again—it may just keep Xanadu from our creditors.

CHARLES: Jolly good show—Mouse.

MARGIE: Suggestion, Charles. Dip into the Xanadu guest book, Charles. Turn to a 1919 entry. You'll find the names Pritchard and Throssell.

CHARLES: I'll look out for them.

MARGIE: Throssell VC, a much-decorated First World War hero. Pritchard, his wife, Katharine Susannah, even then a novelist of repute—also a founding member of the Australian Communist Party. Our guest a red? Not the first to visit Xanadu!

CHARLES: Pardon me for having a brother who died in Korea!

She has gone. The KOREAN GUARD *is framed in the doorway, behind* CHARLES. *Lights down.*

SCENE SIXTEEN

A hallway. ZELDA, *at one end, inspecting a painting,* ERIC *walking towards her, penguin-fashion.*

ERIC: The Xanadu hall of fame. What do we do?

ZELDA: We look at the paintings and read the captions, if we feel so inclined—I do.

He reaches her and reads a caption.

ERIC: 'Note how even after the introduction of photography the family insisted on having family portraits painted in oils. They did this because so many eminent painters were friends of the Risdon family.'

ZELDA: A George Lambeth.

ERIC: 'Painted at Xanadu during a stay.' [*He claps his hands flipper-fashion.*] If I clap will someone throw me a fish?

ZELDA: Yes. Me. A week-old flounder aimed at your head. Will you stop acting the penguin!

ERIC: I kid you not, I intend to eat a horse.

ZELDA: A Xanadu sheep's more likely.

Together, they inspect more paintings.

ERIC: Have you sighted the menu?

ZELDA: Seasonally dependent but lamb a permanent feature, so sayeth the brochure.

A bell sounds.

Do you hear music?

ERIC: Ar, the long-awaited dinner bell!

ZELDA: What are you doing?

ERIC: Waving to the Japanese tourists as I struggle ashore at Phillip Island under powerful floodlights.

They freeze. Countless candles and a chandelier suddenly illuminate the space. The piano, with MARGIE *playing, rolls in. Ditto a table setting at which* THERESE *is adding certain final touches. A transformation to the main dining room is underway.*

THERESE: … Like that film *My Brilliant Career*?

MARGIE: That's how Xanadu was in its heyday.

THERESE: The young Judy Davis?

MARGIE: Yes.

THERESE: When she stayed with her grandmother? You felt like that?

MARGIE: That sense of wonder and enjoyment, yes.

THERESE: Very grand, her grandmother, and very, very grand, her grandparents' house. They could have shot it here.

MARGIE: I wish they had!

THERESE: But that's my point: grand.

THERESE *spots* ZELDA *and* ERIC. *They gesture for silence, not wanting to disrupt* MARGIE'*s playing.*

MARGIE: Those were grand days. Balls, marriages, soirées, salons, musical events, parties after race meetings.

THERESE: The grand angle, I get my head around. Two midgets playing tin whistles and a line-up of freaks thumping drums I have difficulty with.

MARGIE: It's true.

THERESE: And from Sarawak: the India Rubber Man?

MARGIE: A contortionist. In 1921 when Wirth's Circus was en route to Horsham, my grandfather bailed them up and threw a party for the circus people.

THERESE: Laid on a few bales of hay for the elephants?

MARGIE: Indeed, in this room we had lion tamers, jugglers, aerial artists, head balancers, the India Rubber Man, all in the guest book.

THERESE: Do you two think she's having me on or what?

MARGIE stops playing.

ZELDA: Don't stop because of us.

MARGIE: If I'd known you were there I'd have stopped sooner.

ERIC: Isn't you playing part of it?

MARGIE: Plainly, it is now. Sherries for our guests, Therese.

ZELDA: Keep playing, please, makes me think of Melba singing here.

MARGIE: There's a photograph of her doing so top of this piano.

She resumes playing and ZELDA *begins to examine the album* MARGIE *has opened.* ERIC *falls in with* THERESE *who is at a sideboard pouring sherries.*

ERIC: They got you done up too, have they?

THERESE: Don't you like me outfit?

ERIC: Wanta swap? I feel wrapped in barbed wire. Bring the boltcutters—I've got nothing to lose but my chains.

THERESE: A change is as good as a holiday is my philosophy.

ERIC: If you don't eat you starve is mine. What are we gnawing on? I could eat the leg off a piano stool.

THERESE: Indian. Have you eaten Indian before?

ERIC: There you go. I knew I wouldn't be expecting it. I once spent a week in Madras at a trade union conference. Yeah, I've eaten Indian. What's the drum, north or south, Bombay or Calcutta?

THERESE: Mrs Risdon-Allyn has mastered many kinds of cooking from other countries but Indian cuisine she excels at, everyone says so.

ERIC: I'll take your word for it.

She takes ERIC *through the menu.*

THERESE: I'll start at the wrong end. Those little shortbreads on the sideboard, that's nan khatai, and next to them, 'cause you don't chill it, you serve it at room temperature, that's ras gulas. Sort of the dessert. For entrée, when I bring it, there'll be samosas, singaras, and pakhoras, they're served with chutney, podina chatni and dhania chatni. For mains, I recommend everything, but the dishes I especially recommend are the sukhe alu and the cauliflower bhaji, one's potato and the cauliflower bhaji's made from—

ERIC: Cauliflower?

THERESE: Your arm may be out of action but your brain's still following the bouncing ball.

ERIC: No cheek, girl. I can get you sacked. Go on.

THERESE: The centrepiece today will be the mogul biriani. In India it's the main dish on festive occasions.

ERIC: Which this looks like becoming, I can tell.

THERESE: Many an eastern cook is judged by how good their mogul biriani is. I'm sure you'll find in the mogul biriani department the Xanadu chef has excelled herself.

As MARGIE *is finishing the piece she'd begun,* THERESE *moves towards the piano with the tray of sherries and offers* ERIC, ZELDA *and* MARGIE *a drink.*

MARGIE: I'm a little rusty I'm afraid. To us.

ZELDA: The weekend.

ERIC: Menu's Indian, Zel.

MARGIE: You eat Indian?

ZELDA: At least once a week.

MARGIE: You may leave the decanter here with us, Therese, and go check the mains then bring the entrée trolley.

THERESE *places the tray on the piano top and exits to the kitchen.*

ERIC: So this pile/building dates from 1841, Mrs Risdon-Allyn?

MARGIE: Margaret, please.

ERIC: Margaret.

MARGIE: No.

ERIC: Aw. Where did I get 1841 from?

ZELDA: Eric's read the brochure.

ERIC: I never go to a meeting without being briefed.

ZELDA: Even if badly.

MARGIE: He's right in that the original homestead was begun in 1841.

ERIC: That must be it.

MARGIE: Burned to the ground in 1848. Lightning strike. That's when they started this building, on the same site, completing it in 1851.

ERIC: Theory being, lightning doesn't strike the same place twice.

MARGIE: Extended several times since. At one point an extra storey was proposed.

CHARLES: Abandoned as far too fanciful.

They realise CHARLES *has entered.*

ERIC: I thought I had it hard fronting the do like this.

ZELDA: Is this part of it too?

MARGIE: Is it, Charles?

CHARLES: Yes. Xanadu on Saturday night, as though in her father's or grandfather's or even her great-grandfather's time, any time but now, that's how we're selling the place these days, memorabilia and all that.

MARGIE: In full regimental regalia, are we?

CHARLES: Not formal enough for you?

MARGIE: Your dinner suit suits you better, but as long as we won't be reliving one of our unforgettable nights at Butterworth—

CHARLES: Should I put that in writing?

MARGIE: Provided we understand one another.

CHARLES: Margaret's great-grandfather was a military man.

MARGIE: As was Charles, they have that in common.

CHARLES: The resemblance ends there.

MARGIE: Great-grandfather was a Member of the Legislative Council.

CHARLES: I'm a mere Justice of the Peace. [*To* MARGIE] How am I doing, sociable enough? The wife's been playing piano. Full points for kicking the evening off with a recital, my dear. Could we hear something else?

MARGIE: I think our guests should be consulted on that.

CHARLES: 'Course they want to hear something else—see!

ZELDA: We'd like it.

CHARLES: Silly idea, Mouse, but why not, to get us in the mood?

MARGIE: Schubert's 'The Trout'?

ERIC: 'The Trout'? [*Clapping his hands*] Perfect.

CHARLES: Heavens no. A quickstep. And I'll ask Mrs Engleman for a dance.

ZELDA: What do you think, Eric, is that permissible?

ERIC: Life be in it, I say.

CHARLES: I'm a very adept dancer.

MARGIE: Would 'Call Me Irresponsible' fit the bill?

> CHARLES *and* ZELDA *dance.* ERIC *is by the piano.*

I've looked forward to this all day.

ERIC: This?

MARGIE: Chat. My chance to find out what someone like yourself thinks.

ERIC: About?

MARGIE: Wages, prices, foreign policy. Charles tells me you're a unionist.

ERIC: Way back, did a stint as an organiser. Found I missed following my trade, but shop steward at various times, health and safety officer, you could say I've paid my dues. Mind you, my own health is what I'm on about. That and...

> *He looks towards* ZELDA.

MARGIE: Zelda? Love then, let's talk about that. You're a lucky man.

ERIC: And don't I know it? Seven months ago down for the count, a vegetable. In she bowls acting like mountains are molehills. What I only later find out is all that time—

MARGIE: Her husband?

ERIC: She told you?

MARGIE: A little.

ERIC: An animal. He's taken her house, her children. Nights, crying herself to sleep. Days, not a word about it. Florence Nightingale putting me through my paces. Floored me when she spilt the beans. She'd been bringing me back from the dead, all I'd been doing was whinge about the physio.

MARGIE: You feel bad about that?

ERIC: About being blind to what she was caught up in, yes.

MARGIE: Wouldn't she have told you if she wanted you to know?

ERIC: I wish she had.

MARGIE: Sounds to me in all that madness you and her work were the sane part of her life and she didn't want the two confused.

CHARLES: A sherry stop, Mouse.

ZELDA: What the heck!

CHARLES: What the heck. This brass ding-a-ling, Zelda, was once upon a time used to summon the servants.

He rings the bell that's on the sherry tray. THERESE *happens to return with the entrée trolley.*

Wonder of wonders: it still works!

MARGIE: Entrée, people. I'll help Therese and leave you on sherry duty, Charles.

CHARLES: Of course, my dear.

MARGIE: [*to* THERESE] We'll set this out, then you can fetch the mains.

While MARGIE *and* THERESE *set entrées on the table, a standard lamp favours* CHARLES *as he fixes more sherries.*

CHARLES: Top idea, eh, wog food? The story attached is that Margaret's family has a connection with the sub-continent. Her great-great-grandfather, he who founded Xanadu and speaks to us from every brick, was a military man. In one of the regiments during the Raj. Sold his commission at the ripe old age of twenty-seven and that gave him the wherewithal. Used his influence to secure a land grant. Became a Port Phillip gentleman. Deserved to, of course. Services rendered. More here than in India. Led a few punitive expeditions against the locals, that sort of thing, exploiting his so-called military know-how. Piss and wind from toecap to topknot, the whole family as far as I can make out. Like a drink, do we?

CHARLES *serves sherries to* ERIC *and* ZELDA.

ZELDA: Eric lived on the land.

CHARLES: But left it.

ERIC: It left me. Cold.

CHARLES: Have I got this right? Father a sharefarmer.

ZELDA: In Gippsland.

CHARLES: Good dirt.

ERIC: But try keeping it where you want it.

ZELDA: The yabbie was public enemy number one. Burrowed holes through their dam walls.

CHARLES: Dairy, wasn't it?

ERIC: With vealers and pigs for a sideline.

CHARLES: Pigs. Who mucked the sties?

ERIC: Guess.

ZELDA: The pigs?

ERIC: The sisters were spared that task. It fell to me.

ZELDA: How many cows did you have to milk?

ERIC: The old man, the girls and me, per day, twice—

ZELDA: And did you know all their names?

ERIC: —a hundred and sixty, top—but never less than a hundred and forty—and if I were to tell you their names we'd be here till tomorrow.

CHARLES: Was it enough?

ERIC: At the age of five through to fourteen more than, but no, never enough, if you're talking keeping our heads above water. We were always a tin-pot operation.

MARGIE: I think we can start.

Entrées set, THERESE *has wheeled the trolley away.* MARGIE *bids them to join her at the table.*

CHARLES: Eric's got a tractor story I'd like you to hear, Margaret.

ERIC: How I broke the old man's heart?

CHARLES: Heard it in the workshop this morning.

MARGIE: You don't have to repeat it just for me.

ZELDA: It won't be just for you. I've only heard the kookaburra and the tennis ball.

CHARLES: This is a top tractor story, Margaret, you'll be riveted to your seat.

They're taking their seats.

Care for some naan, old man?

Focus on ERIC *as he does his spiel.*

ERIC: The old man called the string of farms we worked 'prospects'. Don't ask me why, they never were. We were getting kicked off the prospect we were on, on account of the old man had jumped off the tractor to shut a gate, left the thing in gear, it took off down the hill, he couldn't catch it, it ended up in the dam. As luck would have it—

ZELDA: The yabbies hadn't eaten through the dam wall?

ERIC: It was still holding water.

MARGIE: The tractor sank?

ERIC: In twelve foot of H_2O, and the same again of mud. Dam swallows Massey Ferguson. Owner is not pleased.

CHARLES: An accidently liquidated asset, Eric called it. Enough like the old days for you, Margaret, country people telling yarns, one to another?

ERIC: Owner gives us our marching orders. Nothing new there—we were always being shown the farm gate. What was new, and he'd never done this before, the old man asked me to come along to meet the new prospect. So I'm there this day, boots held together with baling twine, the behind hanging out of my trousers 'cause we wore rags, and we're checking out this, that and the other, and the new prospective owner's showing us the God-awful acres and the run-down machinery and the old man says:

THERESE: What do you think, Eric?

> THERESE, *as she brings food and tends table, will take part in what follows as 'the owner':*

ERIC: This is new—for the first time in his life the old man asking me my opinion.

ZELDA: Was it unusual to be asked your opinion?

ERIC: Unusual? Unheard of. I shoot him a what's-the-strength-of-this look.

THERESE: So this is your eldest?

ERIC: The old man introduces me.

THERESE: And how many children are there?

ERIC: Suddenly I'm putting two and two together.

THERESE: Four?

ERIC: The prospect's checking out how many hands he can count on in the field.

THERESE: One boy, but the girls work, you say?

ERIC: Suddenly the way of the world became very apparent. The old man was asking me what I thought because I was part of the deal. Ditto my sisters.

THERESE: And your wife's good, you say, with pigs?

ERIC: He wasn't just selling himself as a farmer, he was selling the whole family into rural bondage. None of us would get a wage, he'd be lucky to scratch a living himself.

THERESE: Any thoughts, son?

ERIC: Prospect's checking up how hard I'll work.

THERESE: Gonna take it on, follow in your father's footsteps?

ERIC: I tell him 'Nuh, I'm not in this', and watch the old man's face go white. 'I'm gonna head for the big smoke—a sane job.'

THERESE: I'll be in touch.

ERIC: You could tell he never would be. The prospect winds up negotiations.

The storytelling light favouring ERIC *starts to fade.* THERESE *becomes 'the father'.*

THERESE: You could have lied!

ERIC: First and only time I ever lied you took to me with a turnbuckle!… Sharefarming!

THERESE: You're no son of mine!

ERIC: It was feudalism.

CHARLES: This is the good bit, Margaret.

ERIC: The owner owned the land, the stock, the machinery. We did the work, who got the lion's share?

CHARLES: Eric makes 1950's Gippsland sound like pre-revolutionary China.

ERIC: Why not?

CHARLES: Landless peasants preyed on by wicked landlords.

ERIC: The old man was a peasant and we were the dirt on his boots. What's going on when a man's reduced to selling his wife and children?

CHARLES: Eric sounds almost—

MARGIE: Speaking of work—

CHARLES: Communist, Margaret.

MARGIE: Zelda's recently resumed her career.

CHARLES: Oh?

MARGIE: A bit like me. Opening Xanadu to guests, Eric, is the first job I've had, well, since marriage really, and I'm relishing the challenge.

CHARLES: And doing it to a tee! Tells everyone the homestead's history, the many famous people who've sat where we're sitting. Pritchard.

MARGIE: Not the only famous Australian who's stayed at Xanadu.

CHARLES: No. We've had all sorts, freaks from a travelling circus. Farrer, the wheat man. Did she mention Fletcher Jones—she often does. Mostly before my time, of course, before her time too a lot of these famous people, but Margaret tends not to live in today's world.

MARGIE: Charles, you will have noticed, does.

CHARLES: Helped found the Communist Party of Australia. Pritchard, Katharine Susannah.

ZELDA: I've read one of her novels, but that I didn't know.

CHARLES: [*to* ERIC] You did?

ERIC: No.

CHARLES: I thought you would have—

MARGIE: Charles.

CHARLES: Fact is, the only famous Australian I have met is Wilfred Burchett—and I didn't meet him at Xanadu. Eric'd be a friend of Wilfred Burchett's.

ERIC: Why?

CHARLES: But you have heard of him?

MARGIE: Where are you going?

CHARLES: Entrée served and still our girl hasn't sorted the wine.

MARGIE: Charles doesn't have a very high regard for Mr Burchett.

CHARLES: He was a traitor.

MARGIE: Charles fought in Korea.

CHARLES: Brother Alec and I went to that one.

MARGIE: Charles was a prisoner of war in Korea.

CHARLES: Brother Alec didn't return.

ERIC: [*aside to* ZELDA] How smart was Alec.

> CHARLES, *exiting for wine, launches into his anti-Burchett rave in a spotlight, with music under.* THERESE *will become Burchett.*

CHARLES: … And Burchett went into his damned spew. How the Americans had sabotaged the peace talks but through the tireless efforts of the Chinese People's Volunteers the negotiations had been revived. We booed him down. Fourteen hundred of us ringing the soccer field. Burchett addressing us from a table they'd set up. We took off our belts. Put a noose in them. You will hang, you bastard, you will hang. Burchett gets rather pissed off by all this.

THERESE: You people think when the peace talks break down and the Americans come this way you'll be liberated. I've got news for you. You are going that-a-way.

CHARLES: He's pointing towards China and we all know what he means. I'm in the front row. We say: 'We know what side you're on, the Chinese and North Korean side. Well, you can tell your side to get some proper dental equipment in here because men are having their teeth extracted with regular pliers.'

THERESE: Have you told the authorities?

CHARLES: Complained to the Chinese in triplicate.

THERESE: And?

CHARLES: Was tied up for seventy-two hours and told to reflect. I reflected. And maybe you should too, reflect on this: you know how many went to Boot Hill one day last week? Thirty-nine men. We saw wild dogs dragging bodies out of there that night. And wanta know something: we tried to catch those dogs, and those we caught—we ate.

THERESE: I could have you shot.

CHARLES: Six hundred have died from malnutrition and atrocities. You can tell them that at Panmunjon where those peace talks are s'posed to be happening.

THERESE: And how many have died because of you?

CHARLES: Everybody started to get at him.

CHARLES is at the sideboard. The light widens.

MARGIE: What's that, Charles?

CHARLES: I said no Grange Hermitage on the sideboard.

MARGIE: Does it matter?

CHARLES: It's in the brochure. It would be a sin to advertise something and not serve it. How can she forget something like that? The head of a pin's got more brains than you, girl.

THERESE: If you've any complaints about the way I do things I'd be glad to hear them.

MARGIE: None—and if there are, they'll come through me.

An arrested moment. The light fades down.

CHARLES: Then I remembered the main reason I was there. And I pushed forward again. 'My brother was killed and he's buried in North Korea. Could you help me to see his grave?' Burchett crosses his arms. 'If you want to see his grave, you beg.' I say: 'You bastard. I'll see you in hell before I beg.'

MARGIE: Some of the stories Charles tells aren't his. He mixes his own with those of the American servicemen he's met, or read about.

CHARLES: Does it matter? What has happened has happened!

The light widens.

ERIC: If I remember rightly the Korean War was a bonanza for the Australian farmer—wool a pound a pound and all that.

CHARLES: Only I was soldiering, not growing wool. [*To* THERESE] I'll show you where the Grange Hermitage is kept, girl, and maybe next time you'll remember.

MARGIE: Therese is busy here.

THERESE: I'm not going down the cellar with him, that's for sure.

CHARLES: As MacArthur said: 'I shall return'.

> CHARLES *exits.*

MARGIE: Look on the deeds of men with the eye of forgiveness, the Good Book says.

> *The phone has begun to ring and, at* MARGIE*'s bidding,* THERESE *moves to answer it.*

MARGIE: My husband is not always a pretty drunk, especially when—

ERIC: Pretty drunk?

MARGIE: As you've probably guessed, his Cold War experiences have not left him unaffected. His brother dying sometimes preys on his mind.

ERIC: That's the picture I'm getting.

MARGIE: He's got more than enough troubles, one way and another.

ERIC: I'd be right to suppose he's not cut out to be a farmer?

MARGIE: That too's part of it. I suppose what I'm saying is Charles is sometimes more brusque—

ERIC: Than he means to be?

MARGIE: Sometimes says things—

ERIC: He doesn't mean?

THERESE: It's for Eric.

ZELDA: Really? [*Getting up*] I'll take it. Eric didn't know he was coming here, so how someone knew where to reach him has me intrigued.

ERIC: Zelda's surprise. She takes me to all the best places.

> ZELDA *accepts the phone from* THERESE.

MARGIE: Has not had a happy life.

ERIC: I'll take him with a grain of salt.

MARGIE: Good. That said, you've paid for a bash in the Xanadu style. A bash in the Xanadu style you both shall have.

ZELDA: [*from the phone, to* ERIC] Mystery solved. Red Ted Ward.

ERIC: Also known as 'Labour'. As in 'labour ward'. What's he want?

ZELDA: I'm finding out.

ERIC: Can't be my health. He knows more about it than I do. Visits me religiously Monday and Wednesday.

ZELDA: The only one of that mob who does.

ERIC: Young, learning the ropes.

ZELDA *puts the phone down and rejoins them.*

He on fire and want me to put him out?

ZELDA: The main course looks sensational.

MARGIE: Thank you.

THERESE: Doesn't it?

ZELDA: Seems he rang earlier today.

THERESE *has been bringing mains to the table.*

ERIC: Why wasn't I told?

MARGIE: You mean you weren't?

ERIC: You kept it from me?

ZELDA: I didn't know.

MARGIE: Is Mr Ward a union official?

ZELDA: Is he? Does he think about anything else?

MARGIE: My husband took the call. It must have slipped his mind.

ZELDA: What a klutz.

ERIC: Who?

ZELDA: Me. I told him where—keep it under your hat—we'd be.

ERIC: What aren't you telling me?

ZELDA: Friday, as the day shift clocked off, GM management told six hundred employees not to bother turning up on Monday.

ERIC: Six hundred!

ZELDA: I knew this would be his response!

ERIC: Know another one?

ZELDA: You're a sick man, damn you. You're off the union and GM's payroll. The last thing you need do is buy into something like this. [*To* MARGIE] I'm sorry but this sort of thing makes me so angry.

ERIC: I'm calm, look at me, I'm calm.

ZELDA: Like hell you are.

ERIC: Across what gives, Margaret? Bosses wait till the end of the week. Spring something like this on the men as they're knocking off. There goes the chance to organise a meeting inside the plant. Come Monday those six hundred blokes'll be locked out, standing on the pavement rattling the gates.

ZELDA: Listen to yourself.

ERIC: We are talking six hundred jobs!

ZELDA: And is your job one of them?! Your job's getting your health back! This is ruining a beautiful meal.

MARGIE: No, no.

THERESE: Will I see to a few things in the kitchen?

MARGIE: If you would.

THERESE: *Bon appétit.*

> *She exits.*

ERIC: So what's the union doing?

ZELDA: He's just come from a meeting with the State Branch and they're about to go into a telephone hook-up with the National Executive.

ERIC: And?

ZELDA: Wants you on standby. He'll ring back if he has to pick your brains. I took the liberty of saying it would be alright to use this number.

ERIC: [*to* MARGIE] Is it?

MARGIE: Of course.

CHARLES: What my wife means is, of course—not!

> CHARLES *has returned. He carries wine and strapped to his back is a double-barrel shotgun.*

Drop of Grange, anyone?

MARGIE: Have you taken leave—

CHARLES: Leave?

MARGIE: —of your senses?

CHARLES: The taking of. We were married while I was on leave. Not the most sensible thing I ever did, but she joined me in Malaya. After our first child Margaret suggested I leave the army. Again, not the most sensible thing I ever did.

MARGIE: You know well enough why you left the army.

CHARLES: Sit down.

MARGIE: Charles—

CHARLES: I said: Sit down.

MARGIE: I think perhaps we should do as Charles bids.

ERIC: If you think I'm gonna put up with this sort of crap—

ZELDA: Eric.

They have stood, but now resume their seats.

CHARLES: That's more like it. Wants to use the telephone, Margaret. For union business. What would great-grandfather have said about that?

MARGIE: Great-grandfather died before telephones reached the district.

CHARLES: Wherever there are tables my wife's table talk has made her a legend. Well, you know well enough what your own father thought of the 1956 shearers' strike, we lived through it, remember? Would he countenance such goings-on? I don't think so. I warn you all to stay seated, I'll be watching your every move.

CHARLES *exits.*

ERIC: Come to Xanadu. Spend a night with the lunatic right. We're going.

As ERIC *gets up* CHARLES *returns.*

CHARLES: I told you I'd be watching.

ERIC *sits.* CHARLES *exits.*

ZELDA: Is he…?

MARGIE: It's most probably not loaded.

ERIC: All part of it, Zel. A dinner party with the New Guard. Note the Eva Braun-style lampshades—daintily made from the foreskins of forelock-tugging agricultural labourers.

THERESE *enters with* CHARLES *behind.*

THERESE: Fancy dress I can handle, pop guns is out of line.

MARGIE *steps towards them.* CHARLES *is aiming at* THERESE *hostage-fashion.*

CHARLES: I've asked Therese to join us. Any objections to dining with the servants? I feel I've been dining with them all night.

THERESE: Is he off his head or what, 'cause if he's off his head I'm for going home.

CHARLES: Home is seventeen kilometres away—you propose getting there how?

THERESE: I thought I'd walk along the tops of the barbed-wire fences!

CHARLES: Take a seat, my dear.

THERESE: What are you?

ERIC: A rural neo-Nazi.

ZELDA: Eric—

CHARLES: Quiet!

MARGIE: I hope this meets with everyone's approval, but I think we should get on with our meal.

> THERESE *sits.* CHARLES *sits, shotgun slung on the back of his chair.* MARGIE *starts talking him down gently.*

Charles is beside himself, aren't you, Charles? He's been through things no-one should have to go through and there's much that troubles him.

CHARLES: What would they know of that?!

MARGIE: Conditions were harsh and Charles found being a prisoner of war in Korea a distressing and disorienting experience.

CHARLES: I did what I did for the comfort of my men.

MARGIE: Not for his own comfort, for the comfort of his men. We should spare a thought for Charles. He was one of those unfortunate Australians who signed a confession.

CHARLES: Against my will.

MARGIE: Against his will. Saying he'd committed crimes against the Korean people.

CHARLES: I did it for my brother. I did it so I could see his grave.

MARGIE: Then came the truce. Prisoners were exchanged. But the army didn't really know what to do with Charles. Poor fellow had been taken prisoner, had seemingly gone over to the other side.

CHARLES: And didn't I pay for it.

MARGIE: They could hardly be expected to trust a person like Charles after that, could they? We met in Singapore. He was on extended leave. Got married. I became an army wife.

CHARLES: Never put me in the field again.

MARGIE: Charles' military career stagnated. We stagnated quite some time in Malaya.

CHARLES: We have fond memories, however, of that period.

MARGIE: A series of Chinese housegirls were so nice to us, weren't they?

> *The phone starts to ring. As* MARGIE *talks, the phone keeps ringing.*

Eventually Father and I persuaded Charles to retire.

CHARLES: Not my idea.

MARGIE: Not your idea, but in the circumstances the best possible solution. We came to live here. Father was alive then. And Charles set about learning a new trade, as it were, how to run Xanadu. Which, since Father's death, he's manfully done. Charles!

CHARLES: Ask not for whom the bell tolls, it tolls for thee!

> CHARLES *stands, aims, blasts the phone. The sound of a gunshot as part of the phone shatters.*

Care to answer it, old man?

THERESE: Out of his bloody tree.

> CHARLES *seems dazed.* MARGIE *moves to him.*

MARGIE: It's an interesting debate we're having in Victoria vis-à-vis our gun laws. As though they need changing. We country people are used to handling arms. We've been brought up with them.

> MARGIE *takes the gun from an unprotesting* CHARLES.

We object to city people telling us how to run our lives. Our guests are going, Charles. Tess, I'll ask you to gather our visitors' luggage for them, and ask our guests to wait for you by their car.

> THERESE *exits.*

If you could give Therese a lift back into town I'd be much obliged. I'd run her in myself, except under the circumstances I think it best for me to stay here.

ZELDA: With him?

MARGIE: Yes.

ZELDA: Can we call someone?

ERIC: The cops for starters.

MARGIE: Please. He seems impossible. In fact, he's no great danger, except perhaps to himself. There's a motel. Tess will explain I'll be meeting your accommodation costs.

ERIC: He's a madman.

> ZELDA *silences* ERIC *and they exit. A pause.* MARGIE, *realising the gun's with her, aims it at* CHARLES. *He senses what she's doing.*

CHARLES: Why don't you, Mouse?

MARGIE: Why don't I what?

CHARLES: Put me out of my misery. There's one live cartridge left.

MARGIE: Like I put out of their misery one hundred and twenty of our best breeding stock because you couldn't face it, because you let the dipping program fall behind schedule, because they were, due to neglect, diseased and rendered infertile?

CHARLES: You only have to pull the trigger.

MARGIE: Damn you, Charles. I am trying to run a business here!

> CHARLES *takes a draught of wine. Pause.* MARGIE *lowers the shotgun, breaks it, withdraws the unspent cartridge.*

But it wouldn't be that. Really, I'd be putting you out of my misery and that would be a selfish thing and not at all an act of mercy. How could I contemplate such an ungenerous deed?

CHARLES: I'll retire early if you're agreeable.

MARGIE: Thank you, I would appreciate being alone.

> CHARLES *exits. Alone,* MARGIE *goes to the piano. Sets the gun on the piano top. She starts to play a series of discords. Savage, angry sounds build and continue under. We hear the sound of a car driving off.*

SCENE EIGHTEEN

ERIC, *at an almost horizontal angle, is slumped, head out the window of a stationary car. Through the window,* ZELDA *is forcing pills into his mouth.* THERESE *sets down a car wheel.*

ZELDA: Found the spare?

THERESE: Got it.

ZELDA: The jack?

THERESE: It's coming. What are the pills?

ZELDA: They'll help, I hope. Thank Christ there was a torch.

THERESE: I'll go back, get Margie to ring ahead so the ambulance can meet you coming in.

ZELDA: Yes—they'll know which road we'll be on?

THERESE: There's only one.

ZELDA: Explain it's most likely a second stroke.

THERESE: Why's he talking like that?

ZELDA: He thinks he's making perfect sense. We hear gibberish. It's a symptom. Wiring in the brain's awry.

> THERESE *runs off. Stops.*

THERESE: Shit—you'll need this.

> *She hands* ZELDA *the wheel brace she's holding and goes.* ZELDA *has a tyre to change. A shadow puppetry scene results.*
>
> *The shadow of a wheel turning, turning, turning, as* ZELDA *works the jack, the wheel brace, removes a shredded tyre, fits the spare.*

ERIC: I lied. I did go back to the bush. Once. Union sent me. Tactic was get signatures from country people supporting our 'Made in Australia' stand to show how the rural community was divided, that some of 'em were with us. Part of the state the union sends me to I know nobody. I pull up in this one-horse town. Go for a drink. I don't have a clue how to set about getting one name, let alone the fifteen I'm supposed to gather. Two blokes in the bar, rednecks, right-wing hollow heads, fencers, drinking with the local squatter, bit like Charles, sort of a rural fascist, moleskins, R. M. Williams boots, League of Rights hairdo. New to town? Just got in, I say. Whatcha do? I decide why pussyfoot around? An organiser—Metal Workers Union. They stare into their beers. Looking for a friend, I say, which is true and getting truer by the minute. Unionist, eh? They can't resist. Looking for a friend round here? I sense 'em rising to the bait. He'd be after that red-ragger Jim Newhart, says Mr Own It All. The know-nothing who lives on Brick Kiln Road, says a fencer. That's him. I finish my beer.

ZELDA: Don't even try to speak 'cause I can't understand a word you're saying!

ERIC: They've no idea what a help they've been. Find Brick Kiln Road, find Newhart, turns out to be a retired fitter and turner who left the city to set up a vineyard. He signs my petition. And tells me three more who probably will, who put me onto another ten and pretty soon, twenty-five signatures to the good, I'm headed back to Trades Hall. Haven't got it up top. Flat-footed, simple-minded. Right-wingers. You can rely on 'em to shoot 'emselves in the kneecap every time. Not just arseholes—fucking fools!

ZELDA: Damn you.

ERIC: I'm alright.

ZELDA: What's that? Did I hear the word 'alright'!?

ERIC: Aaa-ri.

ZELDA: Sure, you're tiptop, one hundred per cent, following the bouncing ball.

ERIC: Ha ha ha.

ZELDA: Have you any idea how far this has set your recovery back?! Why'd you let him get under your skin?

The shadow play ends. Blackout.

SCENE NINETEEN

MARGIE *is at the piano, still lit by the standard lamp. Her discords cease as* THERESE *enters, in a state of shock, and goes straight to the phone.*

THERESE: He wants to drive. He insists on driving. She can't stop him. We get four hundred yards down your driveway, he's into a ditch and slumped over the wheel—rear tyre blown!

MARGIE: Who?

THERESE: Cool customers, physios. Goes straight into action.

She starts dialling again.

MARGIE: Who?

THERESE: Eric! Bloke's cactus. She shoots him his medication. Checks him out. Sends me back to ring ahead, forewarn the hospital, all this while I'm still in a state of shock. Think I still am. What's keeping 'em?

MARGIE: The phone's shot.

THERESE: That's something she didn't think of. She's probably as panicked as I am. Right. Christ. What now?

MARGIE: I'll try the phone in my room. You leg it to the Neisches and ring through from there—if we double up, we double up.

THERESE: Good idea.

MARGIE: Use my car.

She starts to go off, but comes back.

THERESE: Keys.

MARGIE: In it.

THERESE: Right. The car. I can't drive.

MARGIE: You can.

THERESE: I've lost my licence!

MARGIE: This is an emergency.

She starts out. Stops yet again.

THERESE: There won't be anybody at the Neisches, they'll be at the hall for the reception.

MARGIE: Then at the first farm you see a light on at.

A shot rings out from offstage.

MARGIE: Don't go just yet.

THERESE: It'll be in the papers, right? Page three. Page one. 'Mad week-end at country seat'. I need a job, do I need one this bad?

> CHARLES *steps forward, holding his service revolver.* THERESE, *to one side, awaits further instructions.*

CHARLES: I'm still here.
MARGIE: What are you shooting?
CHARLES: Myself. In the mirror.
MARGIE: Yourself?
CHARLES: Practising.
MARGIE: In the mirror.
CHARLES: A rehearsal.
MARGIE: For the real thing?
CHARLES: It may come to that.

> MARGIE, *mouthing 'go, go', bids* THERESE *depart.* THERESE *does.*

I don't deserve you, do I, Mouse?
MARGIE: It's said we each get what we deserve.
CHARLES: You deserve better.
MARGIE: Could be we all do.
CHARLES: It's the old war wounds.
MARGIE: Cold War wounds?
CHARLES: Old—old war wounds.
MARGIE: I misheard.
CHARLES: Catching up with me.
MARGIE: The way we were warned might happen? Yours is a damaged soul.
CHARLES: Hmm. You bitter?
MARGIE: Yes. Bitter.
CHARLES: Not twisted, though, the way I am?
MARGIE: No. Must be the one prayer of mine God's seen fit to answer.

> *The lights fade to refocus on* THERESE.

THERESE: [*sung*]
>> A lost weekend
>> A lost weekend
>> A case of not your place
>> Not mine, we take time in the country
>> We seek peace of mind in the birdsong and wine

It's summer, come autumn
The season it sours and lovers discover
Reason's a castaway cast down the mine
Years later we turn to
The family album
Is the shot we return to the shot we expect?
It's so long ago now
We barely know how
We got there or got back without getting wrecked
That lost weekend
One lost weekend.

THE END